DIALOGUES
On
A COURSE IN MIRACLES

DIALOGUES

on

A
COURSE
IN
MIRACLES

TARA SINGH

LIFE ACTION PRESS
Los Angeles

Library of Congress Catalog Card Number: 86-82912

ISBN 1-55531-130-X Limited Edition, Hardbound
ISBN 1-55531-131-8 Softcover

The material from *A Course In Miracles* and *The Gifts Of God* is used by permission of the copyright owner, the Foundation for Inner Peace, P.O. Box 635, Tiburon, California 94920.

Dedicated to Lucille Frappier and Jim Cheatham for their long hours of devoted work. Without their assistance, this book would not have been possible.

ACKNOWLEDGMENTS

I am grateful to the following friends for their help in the preparation of this book: Frank Nader, Aliana Scurlock, Clio Dixon, Norah Ryan, Sandra Lewis, Ted Ward, John Williams, Johanna Macdonald, Charles Johnson, Rachel Logel, and Connie Willcuts. And for those whose support has made it possible, my appreciation is also extended: Richleigh and Kris Heagh, Richard Michael, Acacia Williams, Joann Nieto, Nancy Marsh, and Selina Scheer.

CONTENTS

OUR COMMON GOAL

Ours is a common task. Each one is called,
And he will answer as he makes the choice
To give up madness, and to choose instead
To recognize and to accept God's Voice.
Each one will waken at the time and place
That he has chosen, and will take his part
In the Atonement's purpose. For he came
With resurrection's calling in his heart.
He must attain a glorious rebirth,
And scatter stars across the sleeping earth.*

*This poem is from *The Gifts Of God* (Foundation for Inner Peace, 1982, page 35) by the scribe of *A Course In Miracles.* It is an incomparable book of poetry containing some of the most important words ever spoken.

INTRODUCTION

MAN IS ENERGIZED
BY THE ACTION OF GIVING

Blessed is the man who yearns
to be consistent with the Will of God
in all that he does.
Having corrected the illusion of insecurity
and the fallacy of relative knowledge,
he lives by the pure energy of Gratefulness.

The man who lives by Eternal Laws
is protected by Rightness.
The energy of having something of his own to give
makes all things possible.

In proportion to his stability,
he exemplifies the art of living and is productive,
with something of eternal value to give.

The integrity of selfless work has no limitations.
It has its own purity and sanity.
To the degree man's work is meaningless,
he is dependent on being a body
and being a mercenary.
Thus he denies the spirit that he is.

It is the first thought that has the energy. Once
the student of *A Course In Miracles*[1] is dedicated to
bringing the Course into application in his life, he
has invoked the Presence Which makes transformation possible.

> *All the help you can accept*
> *will be provided,*
> *and not one need you have*
> *will not be met.* [2]

Unless a student gives his life to bringing the Course into application and becomes part of the energy of creation, undoing of misperception is not possible. *A Course In Miracles* is not theoretical. I was told directly by the scribe of the Course:

> "The Course is to be lived."

The mind that trusts gives no space to insecurity,
nor escapes into concepts of relative knowledge.
Compassion can never be nationalistic
nor separate into fragments.
Where unity is intact,
the Law of Completion energizes itself
by sharing the creative vitality of Love.

A Course In Miracles introduces us to the Law of Completion:

> *A major learning goal this course has set is to reverse your view of giving, so you can receive. For giving has become a source of fear, and so you would avoid the only means by which you can receive. Accept God's peace and joy, and you will learn a different way of looking at a gift. God's gifts will never lessen when they are given away. They but increase thereby.*
>
> *As Heaven's peace and joy intensify when you accept them as God's gift to you, so does the joy of your Creator grow when you accept His joy and peace as yours. True giving is creation.*

It extends the limitless to the unlimited, eternity to timelessness, and love unto itself. It adds to all that is complete already, not in simple terms of adding more, for that implies that it was less before. It adds by letting what cannot contain itself fulfill its aim of giving everything it has away, securing it forever for itself.

Today accept God's peace and joy as yours. Let Him complete Himself as He defines completion. You will understand that what completes Him must complete His Son as well. He cannot give through loss. No more can you. Receive His gift of joy and peace today, and He will thank you for your gift to Him.[3]

A Course In Miracles is a serious undertaking.
No one can read the Course
without inviting the Presence.
Instantly, interpretations cease,
and all that is abstract is undone.

Inherent in every Lesson is the energy
to bring one to the truth of it.
Each Lesson has to be approached
with the space within the mind
that endows it with the capacity to receive.

There is a space in man that is not contaminated
or subject to pressure,
nor is it affected by right and wrong.
It is an impersonal state
of eternal Gratefulness — ever present.

*   *   *

Throughout the ages, man has seldom known
the vitality of questioning his own conditioning.
How rare the one who has cleansed himself
of all answers and stands alone.

Questioning has tremendous vitality.
It stills the human brain
and highly energizes the senses.
The Silent Mind realizes
what lies beyond time and distance.

With the advent of *A Course In Miracles*
upon the planet,
direct knowing and liberation are possible.
Most scriptures are records
of what the Incarnations
and Prophets of God did upon the earth.
But with the dawn of *A Course In Miracles*
comes the step-by-step Divine curriculum
to liberate man from the limitations
he has imposed upon himself,
the bondage of his little knowings.

There is no greater energy known to man
than the power to question.
The Course starts with questioning
and endows the student with the clarity to undo.
It is the question that awakens
and not the learning.

The very first Lesson:

> *Nothing I see. . .means anything.*[4]

has in it the blessing to transform the student.
Having received it, one sees the truth of:

> *I have given everything I see. . .*
> *all the meaning that it has for me.*[5]

To realize:

> *I see only the past.*[6]

is to be liberated from it.

The Course does not teach,
it removes *the blocks*
to the awareness of love's presence.[7]
In the first twenty-eight Lessons,
one grows in wisdom and insight.
Nothing of the world has power over you
and you begin to realize the fact:

> *I am as God created me.*[8]

Fact has the vitality to end doubt and limitation
and to free the brain from collective memory.
But to stay with the fact
requires tremendous attention
and the capacity to receive.
Very few people are able to stay with a fact
and not escape into idea.
How few have ever seen the fallacy of idea
and stayed with the truth of the fact
that liberates.

The Course is True Knowledge —
the Thoughts of God.
It is timeless,
free of conflict and interpretations.

How futile is a life without virtue.
The awakening of intelligence
is different from training the mind
with skills for survival.

> ''A simple thing such as knowing
> one's own function in life

has become obscure and difficult.
Yet in each human being
there is an inner calling
and the abilities one is born with
to implement it.
The extension of his inner calling
would naturally introduce man to his function
and relate him
with the universal Laws of creation
of which he is a vital part.

''What a wonder to discover
that inherent in the function is the freedom
from the limitation of body senses!
To be related to Life Itself
rather than to thoughts *about* Life
would transform the very foundation
of our present educational system.''*

That which does not change is the only law.
Where is the man who lives
by the laws of love, truth, and timelessness?
Society may not value these.
But surely the individual
can discover his own eternal Identity:

> *I am blessed as a Son of God.*[9]

> *I am under no laws but God's.*[10]

This would have to be a decision
not made of choice,
for it is unlimited.
It is independent
but it affects the personal life of the senses.

---

*Excerpt from *The Voice That Precedes Thought* by Tara Singh (Foundation for Life Action, 1987), page xi. (Editor)

The vibration of the New World
is to come to new consciousness.
If it does not do this, it externalizes itself
and becomes self-destructive.

Out of this chaotic environment
and the insanity of the age,
with its tremendous scientific capacity
to abuse human energy
as well as the energy of nature,
emerges the Non-Commercialized,
Self-Reliant Action
for those who have heard in *A Course In Miracles*
the call to sanity.

> *The teachers of God have trust in the world,*
> *because they have learned it is not governed by*
> *the laws the world made up. It is governed by a*
> *Power That is in them but not of them. It is*
> *this Power That keeps all things safe. It is*
> *through this Power That the teachers of God*
> *look on a forgiven world.*[11]

Religion is a state of being that knows:

> *There is no peace except the peace of God.*

> *Seek you no further. You will not find peace*
> *except the peace of God. Accept this fact, and*
> *save yourself the agony of yet more bitter disap-*
> *pointments, bleak despair, and sense of icy*
> *hopelessness and doubt. Seek you no further.*
> *There is nothing else for you to find except the*
> *peace of God, unless you seek for misery and*
> *pain.*[12]

OUR PREPARATION
IS THE PARALLEL ACTION

The purpose of the Foundation for Life Action
is to be with Eternal Laws
so that it does not become an organization.
Being of one mind provides the unpressured space
that makes productive and selfless work possible.
We are not religious.
We are men and women who endeavor
to lead a life of ethics and virtue.

The Foundation for Life Action,
a federally approved, nonprofit,
educational foundation,
is dedicated to non-commercial life.
It does not accept charity, nor seek donations,
nor does it own property or a community.
It has evolved its own integrity of intrinsic work
so that we need not work for another.

Society, as it is, demands skills for survival.
We, at the Foundation, are attempting
to deal with this issue by being self-reliant
so that we have something of our own to give.

We have discovered
that Gratefulness is everlasting.
It transcends time
and makes self-transformation possible.

The Foundation for Life Action began in 1980.
We conducted weekend workshops
and ten day retreats throughout the country
in order to establish relationships
and introduce a new way of life

related to Universal Laws.
A correspondence program was established
with each person who attended a workshop
and genuine interest was taken in his life.

I discovered, however,
that the workshops were limited.
There was not enough time
to bring about real change within the participants.
It encouraged the illusion of "becoming."

Our educational system is based on the theory
of becoming something other than what we are.
Educated ignorance leaves the human being limited
and, as a citizen, merely trains him to get a job.
But the human being is boundless
and free of conflict.

In 1981, in order to have an extended period
with a serious group of students, the Forty Days in
the Wilderness Retreat was held in Colorado with
over one hundred participants who had previously
attended workshops and ten day retreats. At the
close of the Forty Days, the one-to-one relationship
was offered to each participant.

Following the Forty Days, I spent a year in
quietude to determine if the Course could be
brought into application. On the ninety-ninth day
the Lesson was: *Salvation is my only function here,*
and I realized how God's Plan for Salvation
originated. On the hundredth Lesson, *My part is
essential to God's plan for salvation,* the function
became clear.

> *Just as God's Son completes his
> Father, so your part in it completes*

> *your Father's plan. Salvation must reverse the mad belief in separate thoughts and separate bodies, which lead separate lives and go their separate ways. One function shared by separate minds unites them in one purpose, for each one of them is equally essential to them all.*[13]

"By the time you, the student, arrive at the hundredth Lesson, it is possible to blossom with the joy of your discovery and for your will to unite with the Will of God. Confusion over, you behold the support of the Universe behind you and discover how each day's Lesson keeps unfolding within you, in spite of yourself, because you let it be. God wills the Course to succeed.

"It is a reality and you abound in your gladness, eager to share.

> *You cannot fail in your efforts to achieve the goal of the course. You will see because it is the Will of God. It is His strength, not your own, that gives you power. And it is His gift, rather than your own, that offers vision to you.*[14]

"By the hundredth Lesson, you can glimpse the fulfillment of your life, the joy of creative productivity rather than meaningless existence.

"It is possible for anyone who takes *A*

Course In Miracles seriously to have the
love to share, laughters to laugh, the
strength of certainty, and a productive life
untouched by insecurity.''*

THE NON-COMMERCIAL ACTION BEGINS

In ancient times, teachers never charged fees
or lived off their students.
True Knowledge has never been sold.

Only when the Word of God is given you to speak,
does your life become Non-Commercial.

For the first time in the history of the New World,
the Non-Commercial Action began on Easter, 1983,
with the One Year Non-Commercialized Retreat:
A Serious Study of *A Course In Miracles.*

The Action of the One Year Retreat
has continued for four years,
at no tuition charge.

The New World has the potential and the vibration
to come to new consciousness.
The Forefathers knew that is its destiny.

Man has searched for lifetimes for the keys
which are inherent in the Course.
Saints and prophets tried to give us a glimpse

---

*Excerpt from Tara Singh's Gratefulness Journal, 1982, originally
published in March, 1982, in the pamphlet, *Holding Hands With You:
Non-Commercialized Life/The Path Of Virtue.* It was reprinted in *The
Voice That Precedes Thought* by Tara Singh (Foundation for Life
Action, 1987), pages 326-327. (Editor)

of the glory and splendor
of the thought-free state.

Now *A Course In Miracles*,
the first scripture in English
and the first to emerge from the New World,
has come with its step-by-step curriculum.
The Gift of God to His Son is upon the earth,
and with it, the Light to awaken us to awareness.

God, Himself, has initiated the action
through His One Son.
That One Son is you who read *A Course In Miracles*.
Its pure light cleanses one
of misperceptions and self-imposed limitations.
Never has the planet, or the Son of God,
received such a direct call to awaken.
The Course meets the need of man
for lifetimes — for eons.

The Name of God cannot be commercialized.
The wise, whose life is non-commercial,
is ever accessible, never too busy.
To him, life is sacred
and the one-to-one, individual relationship
is important.
Such a being attracts the earnest
and they come,

> "not to learn, but to Be."*

Once the student realizes
Being is complete unto itself,
non-commercial life begins.

---

*Refers to the song, "The Seventy," first sung at the Forty Days in
the Wilderness Retreat. See *The Voice That Precedes Thought* by Tara
Singh, page 282. (Editor)

Having outgrown nearly a thousand dollars a day income from workshops and retreats, the Foundation for Life Action sponsored the One Year Non-Commercialized Retreat: A Serious Study of *A Course In Miracles* in Los Angeles, on Easter, April 3, 1983, with forty-nine participants from all over the country. During the entire year, we held a twenty-four hour Prayer Vigil for peace on earth and goodwill amongst men. The Retreat began with sessions held at 7 A.M. and 7 P.M. daily, and continued with countless individual meetings and small group sharings. From the world's point of view, it was attended by an interesting and varied group of people. Among the participants were health care professionals, social workers, secretaries, writers, teachers, computer experts, accountants, an artist, an assistant film director, a librarian, an engineer, a machinist, and an electronics technician.

Since the end of the One Year Retreat on Easter, April 22, 1984, twenty people have remained with the Foundation, at no tuition charge, and have dedicated themselves to bringing *A Course In Miracles* into application in their lives and coming to Self-Reliance.

It is our decision
to live a life free of consequences.

Self-giving will not exchange its Gratefulness
for an easy life.

Non-Commercialized Action
is more than prosperity.

The wise does not live
by personal convenience.

The Foundation for Life Action is a School for awakening, for training those who are to be amongst the Ministers of God. The purpose of those at the Foundation and the School is to make internal correction and overcome illusions.

Man staunchly believes in freedom although it is only a concept and, therefore, meaningless. Who is free of fear, loneliness, ambition, or conflict? What would it take to realize the fact of "being free"? To see the fact as the fact has its own action.

The Course does not teach but shares the Thoughts of God:

I am not a body. I am free.

and also gives the clue:

For I am still as God created me. [15]

Therefore, there is nothing to seek, but only to realize one's own, God-given perfection. To realize the truth of this was our undertaking at the Retreat.

> "Know that your judgment, whether good or bad, has no place. So, if you have heard the truth of this, then forever you have the key to liberation.
>
> "You are as perfect as God created you, and you have the protection that has never been contaminated, nor ever will be."*

*   *   *

---

*Excerpt from *Commentaries On A Course In Miracles* by Tara Singh (Foundation for Life Action, 1986), page 148. (Editor)

People are conditioned to want to learn. They are programmed to believe that "I am this" and "I want to be that." The fact is that it is "becoming" and not "being" that controls the human race. Invariably each person wants to be the opposite of what he is. "Becoming" is the most difficult urge to undo.

This book consists of dialogues.

Objective thinking has very little meaning for us today, but what we call dialogue must be objective and impersonal. Feelings and beliefs have no place in it.

There are many questions to be asked. Nothing delights a teacher more than seeing a thought through to the end and, thus, be free to be part of the impersonal intelligence of Love. Dialogue is the best form of undoing. It is not a learning but an awakening. One discovers that the attention one gives is what intensifies itself, and liberates man from bondage and dependence.

Inherent in man is an unwillingness to be awakened. Even the preoccupation with learning becomes a distraction, an evasion. During the four years we discovered that resistance to undoing prevents the student from bringing the Course into application. We even deceive ourselves with a willingness which exists at the periphery of unwillingness. Even in an ideal atmosphere, the inherent unwillingness finds a way to remain intact.

We read the Course, and daily, on the hour or the half hour, try to recall the Lesson to remembrance. But everything at the physical and conscious level becomes habit. The function of the

Course, however, with its frequent practice periods, is to break through the ritual of habit to which we are subject and by which we live. The Course questions and awakens one from the delirium of a habit-bound, routine life by offering the Holy Instant.

It has been our experience that dialogue is the best means to arouse interest and attention. To see the fallacy of abstract thought and come to objective thinking, the student must participate. It is insight that breaks through conventional thought. And it is the attention that one gives which invokes insight, or the Holy Instant.

But to bring the student to dialogue, where he acts on his own energy, is arduous. In the classes, when dialogues took place, we did not accept answers as truth, or opinions as valid. Discrimination heightened. Exactness and precision were insisted upon. We had to confront the intrigue of passive listening, for the classes were not to be lectures.

The belief in learning, with which we are so heavily conditioned, makes dialogue difficult. Serious dialogue has the vitality to see that knowledge, as we know it, is only the definition of thought and ideas; that as long as results are sought, one is limited by conclusions; and that truth and love are intrinsic and independent.

Dialogue is a miraculous event upon the planet. For where two or more meet in His Name, there He will be in the midst.[16] It can only be between two people, or a small group, who have dedicated their lives to be consistent with the Will of God. Dialogue is self-inquiry. It is not analysis, for analysis rests on conclusions and is limited to the isolation of personality. Analysis is words, not truth; its phraseology evades the light. We hide behind our feelings and reactions and limit ourselves to cause and effect, while each Lesson of the Course sets us free of duality.

The Holy Spirit is our Teacher. He is free of words and extends the stillness of the Peace of God. He will not let us escape into memory.

The Holy Instant empties the human brain of insecurity, pain, loneliness, and its isolation. In dialogue, the boundlessness of love and gratitude transpires through each cell. Its peace is blessed and we are eternally healed, no longer detached from the Universal Mind. It is Rightness that makes life meaningful.

A Course In Miracles is Absolute Knowledge. It takes away the need of having a guru, for you can establish a direct relationship with it. An authentic encounter is most blessed. Its action does not end, irrespective of how and what one feels. Each Lesson of *A Course In Miracles* provides the space, letting the stillness within the student work.

*I will be healed
as I let Him teach me to heal.*[17]

God is the Strength in which I trust.

*What would give you the ability to be aware of
all the facets of any problem, and to resolve
them in such a way that only good can come of it?*

*Of yourself
you can do none of these things.*

God is your safety in every circumstance.

It is not by trusting yourself that you will gain confidence. But the strength of God in you is successful in all things. The recognition of your own frailty is a necessary step in the correction of your errors.[18]

In the Bible, Jesus had said, "I CAN OF MINE OWN SELF DO NOTHING."[19] Do you see the spaciousness of humility, the detachment of an impeccable mind that has outgrown all misperceptions, the glory of a man who stands alone free of thought?

"FORGIVE THEM;
FOR THEY KNOW NOT WHAT THEY DO."[20]

The light of these last words of Jesus is part of the One Mind we all share. It is this Universal Mind that formed the Divine Thought of Forgiveness.

Forgiveness offers everything I want.[21]

It is the power of forgiveness that awakens man from the sleep of forgetfulness to his God-created Identity.

A Course In Miracles states:

> *Forgive us our illusions, Father,*
> *and help us to accept*
> *our true relationship with You,*
> *in which there are no illusions,*
> *and where none can ever enter.*[22]

The Foundation for Life Action is a School. It is non-commercial and does not charge fees. It will not accept those who want to be students, but only those who are students. People at the relative level are preoccupied with either a person, place, or activity. Unfulfillment and alternatives prevent one from being consistent at all levels of one's being. Only the true student has the energy of first thought dedicated to realizing:

I will not value what is valueless.[23]

The student is the one who has the capacity to formulate the right question and, in dialogue, to see a thought through to the end. This requires an energetic mind, having "the ears to hear."[24] Such a student is provided by Life. Rightness takes care of all needs.

Tara Singh

CHAPTER ONE

1

"FORGIVE US OUR ILLUSIONS"[1]

Forgiveness recognizes
what you thought your brother did to you
has not occurred.
It does not pardon sins
and make them real.
It sees there was no sin.
And in that view
are all your sins forgiven.
What is sin,
except a false idea about God's Son?
Forgiveness merely sees its falsity,
and therefore lets it go.
What then is free to take its place
is now the Will of God.[2]

There are two things which have become very detrimental. First, we do not hear a truth, and second, we think we can apply it *later*. Then later, the truth gets repeated again, and again we cannot quite hear it. This goes on year after year, lifetime after lifetime probably. Even when the Son of God comes, we cannot hear Him. We cannot hear it right now either.

Why have we not looked into this? We are not dealing with the Hebrews of the era before Christ. We are talking about our lives now, present-day individuals. What have we done to ourselves that we can't hear, that we can't bring things into application? We have become casual, defeated somehow, and mediocre. Why doesn't mediocrity bother us? Our own. What have we really done about it? When are we going to put away our resistance, our postponement, our mediocrity — meaning, our half-heartedness?

Do you know how difficult it is to speak of things that are holy, that are real, that are of truth, knowing they will be turned into ideas? You are responsible for making of this Holy Instant a lie by bringing it down to time. When it is of time, it is meaningless and therefore, no longer a Holy Instant. It has no reality. What is of time is just illusion. Its understanding is an illusion and its misunderstanding is an illusion. Nothing that is external is real because everything that is external is of time. That's a truth. Would you hear it now?

If you hear what we are saying, you will know the true meaning of forgiveness. Forgiveness means you have understood that nothing that is external is real; what is external is of time and therefore it's not real.

Student: * If it doesn't exist, then why forgive?

Listen again to what *A Course In Miracles* says:

> *Forgiveness recognizes*
> *what you thought your brother did to you*
> *has not occurred.*
> *It does not pardon sins*
> *and make them real.*
> *It sees there was no sin.*

If you could really know that, that whatever is external is unreal — as a truth — then for the rest of your life, could the external ever upset you? And if it upsets you, have you really understood forgiveness?

Could we agree on this, that nothing we know through our physical senses is real because it is external and therefore of time? We can understand this, at least as an idea. If this is understood, then we can say that whatever *is* real — that which is not external and not of time — would have to be internal. Can we be grateful for this, that the issue has been brought into focus, to its essence? And now, because we understand the issue we can be responsible. As students of *A Course In Miracles*, we have taken on to live by forgiveness, to live by internal values — that we will no longer be regulated from the outside. This is a giant step.

Dialogues On A Course In Miracles is taken from class sessions given by Tara Singh with a small group of students who study the Course under the sponsorship of the Foundation for Life Action. During the sessions, which are recorded on audiotape, a microphone is sometimes passed from one student to the next and therefore, when reading the questions asked or comments made, more than one person is represented. (Editor)

> *Student:* Mentally — intellectually — it makes sense to me. But I know that the pressure of time and the external things is going to try to demolish this little light you are kindling within me.

All the more reason why we must be responsible. Otherwise we will fall back to our old value system of like and dislike, the world of unforgiveness.

So then, what is external is of time, and therefore an illusion, an unreality. That is the only world we know. But the Lord said:

"FORGIVE THEM;
FOR THEY KNOW NOT WHAT THEY DO."[3]

We have become His students and therefore, we are to live by internal values.

Whenever we are confused, whenever we get angry, whenever we get threatened, we can say: "That is of the senses. I know the power it has but I will live by internal values that are not of time." And then He would help for we deserve the help. Our call for help — which is not necessarily calling with thought but our wanting to remain honest, our wanting to turn to the internal — is already a blessing given to us. He is leading us by the hand[4] whether we know it or we don't know it. We could not possibly come to that peace otherwise. All we have to do is to drop one and the other is already there. Can we see that we don't have to seek it, there is no "becoming" in it?

> *Student:* When you say that everything that

is external is unreal, the difficulty I
have is that I can intellectually understand how something, like this
wall, would be of time. And I can
say it's not real in an eternal sense.
But this minute, this instant, what is
this? Is this wall real? Is it here?
How is it unreal, right now?

To the physical senses, it will never be unreal.
But the wall being real or unreal is not complex.
Would it not be a better question to ask: "I work all
day at such and such. I am doing these things. Is
that all unreal?" Don't you see? It brings us to
question how we live? That would be a valid question for it applies directly to you, to your life. And
we can go into that.

We began by saying that everything external is
of time, and time is unreal. What is real is not of
time; it is eternal because it is timeless. And it's
internal. Is that the premise?

Student: Yes.

Don't move away from that. We are going to
come back to that barometer on and on. We have
taken on that we will forgive. We will forgive because at the time level, it is needed. Whenever we
hold grievances towards another, it is more real to
us than the wall. We know all the wrong things
about the other person. We are hurt; we have been
abused, insulted, mistreated — whatever we may
want to call it. We keep those grievances alive within us. And every new cell that is built in the body is
also being contaminated with those grievances.

> *Student:* Are you saying that the grievances actually become a part of *me*, of my body?

We have to understand there is a renewing process of Life. And *it* is constantly changing cells, just like it is constantly keeping the blood in circulation. But the poison of our hate, our fear, insecurity, and anger, is also continually being renewed. We keep them alive. So every new cell that is born becomes just like the one it replaces — contaminated by our grievances. We are going counter to the renewing process of Life.*

If we have understood this, responsibility comes. And one is grateful for that. Can you please see this? By understanding something, I become responsible. And also I am grateful. But we, for the most part, have dulled ourselves. We have made ourselves incapable of responsibility and therefore, incapable of being grateful. We try to discipline ourselves, force ourselves, deny ourselves — all the while keeping grievances alive. But we are fighting against nature, the function of which is to cleanse and renew us.

Each minute the body cells are being renewed and we contaminate them again, just as fast. We are responsible not to contaminate the cells, either with hate or with fear. So then, new cells would come into being that have ended the yesterdays, the past. That's the purpose of this renewing process. Why are we going contrary to it? It's just a

---

*For further discussion on how the individual perpetuates grievances, see *"Love Holds No Grievances"* — *The Ending Of Attack* by Tara Singh (Foundation for Life Action, 1986). (Editor)

fact — you're irresponsible. Are you now going to *be* responsible, having understood this? This unwillingness to be responsible is the problem, isn't it?

> *Student:* It makes sense but I don't know if I can live up to this.

Supposing someone brought you a glass of water and I told you, "Look, there is poison in that water." You wouldn't drink it, would you? So why do you make that understanding effective and not this one? Why are you contaminating your mind?

Are we beginning to have some glimpse of the insanity of it? Life created a body and keeps on renewing the cells so that it gives us the potential of outgrowing the past, the heredity, the programming, the conditioning, all of that.

Would you now take the responsibility to know that everything that is external is of time and therefore unreal, and be free of it? "I have to live by internal values so that I'm not affected by what is unreal. If I'm affected, then I am still protecting myself. I still hold on to the opinion that I'm separated. I still want to correct the other. I'm great." And all the energy goes into that. What are we going to do about it?

We have taken on to live by forgiveness because we have understood that what is external is not real anyway. *We* give it reality. And now, we stop giving it reality. Then you have awakened something within you that is real, that undoes the unreal automatically. It's almost effortless.

> *Student:* Is this what *A Course In Miracles*
> means when it speaks of God's Plan
> for Salvation?[5]

Let us see. What would the attributes of God's
Plan for Salvation be? God's Plan would be timeless and it would be internal.

> *Student:* What does that mean?

It means that anyone who is part of God's Plan
would not be afraid of failure. Please follow this.
He would not be afraid of failure. He would be self-
reliant, therefore not survival-oriented. Survival is
still the issue for us as long as our values are of time
and of the externals. Being survival-oriented means
that we think there is a future, thus validate time
and the external.

So, if I have undertaken to forgive a brother,
then somehow he can't do anything to me — no
matter what he does, he can't affect me. I have
taken that stand. Then have I not proven that the
external is unreal? What makes you think survival
is real?

This is self-reliance! Why? Because we have
realized for ourselves that self-reliance is possible,
and dependence and the fear of survival are only
projections. Unless we come to this state I am
talking about, unless we come to self-reliance, we
are not being true to God's Plan. Either we are part
of God's Plan or we are part of our own plan of
survival, which is unreal.

Nothing external can affect God's Plan. And
therefore, if survival is still going to affect us, we
will get busy trying to *achieve* it. But achievement

has no meaning in God's Plan because the motivation for achievement is from a false premise. It is not an internal action; it is brain action. The world is dominated — ruled — by achievement. "I've got to do something. I've got to accomplish this, that, or else I can't survive." Isn't it?

Can we see that achievement goes towards the external which does not exist? We must not forget the fundamental basis, that what is external, what is of time, is unreal. Please don't deviate from that. Achievement then is survival-oriented, time-oriented, and unreality-oriented. But God's Plan for Salvation has its own self-reliance. It can only be God's Plan to those who have understood the laws and have seen the wisdom of self-reliance. God's Plan could not possibly be based on any other foundation than self-reliance. It is an internal issue.

> *Student:* I see that there are two forces at hand. One is the fear of survival, and the other, the need to do something about it.

Yes. But "doing something" is not necessarily to move toward achievement and accomplishment, but rather to move towards correcting misperceptions. Our main emphasis, then, is correcting misperceptions, correcting the impurities, correcting the programmed brain — that we would not live under its authority of educated ignorance.

And one man in this world has to challenge the authority of ignorance over himself, the authority of fear that is born out of time. Fear is never right now; it is always tomorrow. It does not enter the present. If we could stay with the present, there would be no consequences, no fear, nothing to accomplish because then we become co-creators.

Without the Will of God, everything is unreal. The Will of God is not afraid of survival and consequences. The Will of God is in the present; it has no past; it has no future. No one can come to forgiveness in its true sense, nor to self-reliance in its true sense, nor to God's Plan for Salvation in its true sense unless he sees the perfection of creation that exists right before his eyes. How the leaves grow, the flowers bloom, the sap rises in the tree, the wonder of the circulation of blood in the body! Everything, for that is creative. It has no opposite to it; there is nothing opposite to God's Will. What is there to fear then when all is provided? Would this not bring a revolutionary transformation in us?

So, *we* have to change. We have to love correction. You may say, ''I don't know what to do.'' Well, I know that is what you are going to say because man has said it for a million years. Why do we shy away from that correction?

> *Student:* I shy away from it because it makes demands of me, that *I* have to do something.

You have to make corrections. Not only will you forgive the other person, but you now have to forgive yourself every time you want to go towards achievement. You must turn it around and make the correction within yourself so that you come to your own self-reliance.

Student: I would like to go into that movement towards the external, that moment in which a choice is made to move towards the external, that first little spark of movement. That seems to be where correction is necessary because after you have gone two or three steps in that direction, it seems like it has to play itself out. Correction then is something that has to be very swift. I would like to explore that, to know the real essence of what correction is.

So, what is the question?

Student: Either the question is of application, or the question is of prolonging, continuing.

Why make it continual? You are contradicting yourself. It is either continual or it is in application. This is a very interesting point. I say, don't continue, and you have it in application. Nobody needs to write a thesis about correction unless they want to "continue." And there are many so-called teachers who "continue" because they are still achievement-oriented. This is the error that we want to correct now.

By continuing, you can explain to me and I can explain to you. To me, it is still an evasion. If I do not get into relative thought, does it continue? If you can see the fallacy of continuing, *it is in application.*

Student: How do I do that?

There is no activity at all, no "how" to it. Just drop what is of time and you are in the timeless.

It's so beautiful! There is nothing to do. And no one else can do it for you. It's that simple.

It has been made clear that what is external is of time and therefore, an illusion; it is not real. Can it be any simpler? You may not want to hear it and say, "Explain it to me again." You know, doze off a bit and come back. I say, it's already explained. It is said; it is stated; it is a fact; it is a truth; you have heard it. The searchlight is given to you. You have been given something complete that time and casualness cannot take away. Nothing can take it away because it is not of time. If you have heard it, it is completed. Why go on with the old? Why get into your relative thought?

> *Student:* I understand it, but it is not my truth, my own direct experience.

Let's try again. What is external is of time and the body sees only that. So, I now question that. That's all. Will you question with me?

> *Student:* Yes.

That's fair enough. Now we are both looking in the same direction. But the premise need not be explained over and over again. What is external is of the senses, is of time and therefore, not real. It is real to the body but it is not real in actuality. And now we want to live independent of that. Something else has to happen. I say that if you have understood this — just this — that what is external is of time and unreal, then a change has taken place in your life.

This must become your conviction. Right now.

This is not the seeking of achievement but a correction. And therefore, the external can no longer totally take you over because now you can question it. Is that clear?

> *Student:* Yes.

What is clear?

> *Student:* That what is external is of time and it is not real.

Precisely. It's not real, just as fear is not real. Fear makes it seem real.

A Course In Miracles says:

> *Every illusion is one of fear,*
> *whatever form it takes.*[6]

It is so basic. Isn't survival based on fear? Isn't achievement based on fear? And then everything we do is to achieve rather than to correct. Once this is established we can see what the basic thing is that activates everything else.

> *Student:* It seems abstract for me to say that because it is based on fear, it is not real. For instance, my neighbor is external to me. I see his body but that doesn't mean he is unreal.

He may not be unreal, but if he is your enemy, then the fear becomes real to you and *fear* is unreal. Either you have love for him or you are afraid of him. To one person, he is beautiful; to another, he is a monster. But it's still the same person. And I want to deal with those issues, the fact that we project.

> *Student:* It's becoming clearer. So then it is
> my love or my hate that deter-
> mines. . .

You can love your neighbor today and hate him
tomorrow. So, how we project those illusions is
what we want to deal with now that this premise is
established — that what is external is non-depend-
able and has no certainty in it. We can begin to
question what we are doing with our lives. Are we
survival-oriented? Are we fear-oriented? Or is
there some other certainty, something else that
takes place independent of the brain?

Give it a little space and it will make sense. We
know projections and projections can shift from
minute to minute, from day to day. What we have
to deal with is the thought system that projects.
Thought is insecure; thought wants to achieve;
thought resists correction; thought wants to learn;
thought wants to continue; thought wants to explain; thought resists truth. Would you then give
thought authority over you? These things we must
confront because in God's Plan for Salvation those
thoughts have no meaning.

I am not saying that you will accept all this now,
but you can discover for yourself that thought has
no meaning. It has no meaning because it is of
time, and it is projected. See the potential of this!

We must get this clear. Insist on it. I am sharing
this with you because we all have the same brain.
Have you ever thought about what happened to
Jesus? They whipped Him, spit on His face in front
of the high priest, and flogged Him. Hands tied.
These are our laws — the laws of thought by which

we live. They were using the same thought that we are using. There is no high priest, there is you and me. Don't you want to do something about it? If you don't, alright, you've made the decision. But being wishy-washy, things never change.

I'm sorry to say this but I don't see another way to explain it. Just look at what this country did to the Indians. We never kept a treaty — just murdered them right and left. We gave them blankets infected with tuberculosis; took their land. And as soon as we became a world leader we declared it by dropping the atomic bomb on a civilian population. Any consideration for the human being would have first demonstrated to the Japanese the power of the atom bomb — as a warning ahead of time — by dropping it over the ocean rather than on people.

I am not saying that one set of people is better or worse than another. Cruelty and fear have no nationality. I have also seen the massacre in India between the Moslem and the Hindus. Violence has increased and not lessened.

The violence in man continues. We are using the same thought system as did those who crucified Jesus. Is there greater self-honesty now than before? Or is the populace any less self-centered?

When have we ever looked into where thought originates, what it is? Everything can be justified. But what a thing is, is what it extends. And now we are attempting to end the extension of misperception, to end the fear of survival, to end the illusions. Then we will not be regulated by the externals in the name of accomplishment or in the name of survival.

> *Student:* I see the wisdom of what you are saying. It is a different outlook that makes me independent because with this approach I can question everything myself.

Yes. It is another outlook with which to see things. We want to find out what motivations are there, and we see that underneath it all, is fear.

> *Student:* Anything I perceive with my senses is unreal because it is only my thought that perceives it?

It is also only your thought that gets you upset or makes you attached. And as long as there is attachment, you don't have relationship. You see, we can bring it down to fundamental levels. Relationship, as we know it, is external because it is based on the senses. Therefore it is not real.

Either we get attached to what is external or we get repulsed by it. Either we like it or we are threatened by it. And neither of them is real. That world is not real; it is a world of deception. You may not yet know what *is* real, but you do know what is *not* real. And this you can question. To that degree it no longer totally takes you over.

> *Student:* It becomes evident that anything that brings about a judgment in me, or anger or fear, is not external to me. I am responsible for my reactions. The issue is internal.

But are you also beginning to see that as long as there are wantings, there are going to be reactions? Are you seeing how interlinked these things are? As long as you live by the externals which are not real, by time which is not real, then wanting and liking also become unreal. If you choose to stay with wanting, then you are preferring illusions. Question these things deeply so that they don't deceive you anymore. In the end we will have to confront the unwillingness that is in each of us.

> *Student:* I am aware that these things have a hold on me but I'm beginning to see that they are unreal. And I am willing to do something about that.

Can we take this a step further and see there is no "that," there is only "you"? You have images and there is nothing external to those images. The images are based on survival and what is pleasurable. At the pleasure level, you like this, you dislike that. At the survival level, you want security. And when you are without it, you get affected. Can you see that *you* are the one who is changing, that there is nothing outside of you that changes?

A Course In Miracles states:

> *You will escape from both together,*
> *for the inner is the cause of the outer.*[7]

and

> *Your inner and outer worlds*
> *. . .are actually the same.*[8]

> *Student:* I will watch the changes in me.

Watching is not good enough. We have been doing that for twenty years, a hundred years. If the external is not real to you, then you need not be concerned with change or non-change. It is finished.

Please listen carefully because that is the illusion. We think that the external can change, that it can be improved, that it can get worse and so forth. But I said, *you* are the one who is doing it. The minute you see this, you come to the peace of God that is within you. Immediately the illusions are replaced with love and truth.

I want to take the learning out of it because as long as we are interested in learning, there is no Holy Instant, no awakening, no miracle. We have to end the learning. The minute learning ends, we are with the Holy Instant and it has its own action. If you are still relying on the brain, then you remain part of the changeable. There is no other. You are the one who is changing.

> *Student:* What are those forces that make you change?

Survival. Fear. All of those things. The changes you make are illusions because they are in time. There was a time when there were no skyscrapers. There was a time when there were no planes. What is external is of time and, therefore, not real because it always changes. These illusions have great power. We want to get out of that world — of unreality and illusion. And now we are getting another basis for looking at things.

> *Student:* How does one look at things independent of thought?

You have to first stop the thought by seeing that it is unreal. There is no other way. Seeing it as unreal awakens one. And that awakened state then unfolds other things. It is one's own direct experience. Do you see that?

> *Student:* Yes. It makes sense.

To the degree it makes sense, you would be less regulated by thought. It can't tempt you, it can't annoy you.

> *Student:* Because of this clarity it has less hold. But can thought ever know the eternal?

Wanting to know the eternal is to get into another deception of thought which says that you have to "become." It is moving further away from your reality as God created you. Rather than seek the eternal, come to forgiveness that sees the external as unreal. Forgiveness is a cleansing. It is a liberating factor.

Come to forgiveness about those people who preoccupy your mind. Why let the past intrude upon your serenity? Or deprive you of it?

If you feel deprived, you need outlets. What would it be if you weren't preoccupied with things? We don't know what that state would be, do we? Obviously it would not have the same needs. It would be something very different. We are trying to discover that. But we can start with what we *do* know — what has a hold over us and regulates us.

So then, we have started with undoing. That is consistent with *A Course In Miracles*; it is consistent with what Jesus was doing; and it consistent with what Mr. J. Krishnamurti[9] was doing. The only danger is if we make of it a learning. We want to come to the Holy Instant, where it becomes your conviction. You have a responsibility, don't you see? It is a decision that you make. Then it's not casual.

Forgiveness is the first step because it is not of time. How it awakens! It shows us that the internal is real and it is each one's responsibility to keep it unaffected by the external illusions. Every time the correction is made, a miracle has taken place. You have become a co-creator. Self-reliance has become a fact. Once you have something to give, insecurity is not your concern.

We have something to give that is not of personality, that is an extension of what creation is, what God's Will is, what love is, that is not subject to time — the eternal.

I would like to share with you the Lesson I read today from *A Course In Miracles.*

> *I came for the salvation of the world.*[10]
>
> > *Here is a thought from which*
> > *all arrogance has been removed,*
> > *and only truth remains.*
> > *For arrogance opposes truth.*

Can you imagine, we have been arrogant all along, opposing that which is timeless? The arrogance is: "*I* can do it. *I* can manage. *I* have the skills." We have all kinds of techniques — all kinds of "means" — which are but defenses against the truth. The truth is Love. The truth is God's Will. And we say, "I don't need it. I can take care of myself." Then, when we get into crisis, it is: "Can you come and do it for me?"

> *But when there is no arrogance*
> *the truth will come immediately,*
> *and fill up the space*
> *the ego left unoccupied by lies.*

So, our thought system is based on lies. If the external is unreal, our thoughts are lies. Are we seeing the connection? That the external is unreal and thought makes it real? That thoughts are lies?

> *Only the ego can be limited,*
> *and therefore it must seek for aims*
> *which are curtailed and limiting.*
> *The ego thinks that what one gains,*
> *totality must lose.*

The ego's giving is a loss and its taking is a loss. It lives in total illusion. How can we become self-reliant if we are living by the laws of loss and gain?

> *And yet it is the Will of God*
> *I learn that what one gains*
> *is given unto all.*

What we gain is eternal, of Heaven. If I come to clarity, I share it — it is for all. And what has come from Heaven no time can stop. It continues until time comes to an end.

Now the prayer:

> *Father, Your Will is total.*
> *And the goal which stems from it*
> *shares its totality.*
> *What aim but the salvation of the world*
> *could You have given me?*

There is no other plan He could give the Son of God but the salvation of the world.

*And what but this could be the Will
my Self has shared with You?*

What I share with Him is what I share with everyone else. And in this sharing there is no learning — there is no time — because it is continually being shared but I am absent from it. Time takes me away from it. The purpose of *A Course In Miracles* is to end time with miracles.

I came for the salvation of the world.

That is our function.

If that becomes totally clear, we can see that as part of God's Plan for Salvation, we live by forgiveness and "In God We Trust."[11] Otherwise, it is all just ideas.

We are here to receive the gifts of eternity for all mankind. Each one of us. Nothing that is yours is limited to you because it is limitless. Whatever is yours is of God and therefore, everyone's. "LOVE YE ONE ANOTHER"[12] is made possible.

CHAPTER TWO

2

APPLICATION
HAS NO EFFORT

Forgive us our illusions, Father,
and help us to accept
our true relationship with You,
in which there are no illusions,
and where none can ever enter.
Our holiness is Yours.
What can there be in us that needs forgiveness
when Yours is perfect?
The sleep of forgetfulness is only
the unwillingness to remember
Your forgiveness and Your Love.
Let us not wander into temptation,
for the temptation of the Son of God
is not Your Will.
And let us receive only what You have given,
and accept but this into the minds
which You created and which You love. Amen.[1]

This prayer is very auspicious and meaningful for it gives one a real strength — a strength that comes from rightness. It is an encounter with something that is not subject to past, present, or future — not of time. It brings a joy and a blessing and a rightness that is not of mere words.

The prayer completes something. Completing means bringing illusions and deceptions to an end. It is not a ''doing.'' And in the instant in which something is completed, there is also a beginning.

I can only express it in relative words but what happens is independent of both. It is a completing and that is true; it is a beginning and that is true; and, it is a freedom from both and that, too, is true. It is not of personality nor of time, for it is not a ''doing.'' It brings one to a new beginning which has no doubt in it, no wanting in it, no lack, no dependence. You can't even say what it is but you know that what is of time will no longer be the same. And you feel blessed.

We are here to bring *A Course In Miracles* into application, and that means that we are no longer into learning. The world wants to *learn* about things but we are concerned with bringing the Course into application — right here, right now. The learning phase is over.

We can agree with this but we don't really know what is meant by application. Application is not an effort. Where there is effort, there is desire: you *want* to accomplish it. Then you are still interested in learning and self-improvement. And it is all an evasion of application.

Application is not difficult. It is our habit patterns and psychological make-up that prevent it. Therefore, we can't seem to really learn, in its true sense, because when there is a truth or a fact given, we interpret it.

Please don't just agree or disagree with me. You must insist upon knowing it. The Course deals with fact. We ignore the fact and interpret it in the way we *want* it, or the way *we* think it should be: easy, difficult, pleasurable, and so forth. I am saying, *your interpretation is what you have to deal with.*

Interpretations are not of God and we don't as yet know anything else. If we could really see this, we would stop and think, "Is this my interpretation?" And many times, in the beginning, we would get confused because we won't know if something is interpretation or if it is a fact. And that is alright. At least you have come to the point of seeing that you don't know which is fact and which is interpretation.

And so, what is application? Application is to be with the Absolute. Either you go toward the body — gratifying its desires, its wants, and its habits out of your own selfishness, insecurity, and unfulfillment — or you relate with that which brings you to who you are as God created you. Application is never possible unless we outgrow what is of the earth. And there is so much need in the world for what is of Heaven. You become His entrusted child as you overcome your needs and your wantings and find where what is of Heaven is needed. As you become aware of your brother's needs, then it is given you to give.

There is no end to what we can receive if we have the capacity to give it. It is as simple as that.

Application, then, brings something of the Kingdom to earth. Wanting and knowing this and that does not; it is of the world because thought is of the world. Are you willing to make that change? You may say yes, but then you have to bring it into application. And as long as we interpret things and just want to learn, then application is evaded.

> *Student:* I don't understand.

If we could come to the fact, there would be the vitality. You would have the conviction, the integrity, to say: "I agree with this and I am going to bring it into application." Then you are subduing the earth forces,* your own temperament.

> *Student:* Yes, but this is still subject to my interpretation of what even this means.

Until you have come to the fact you have every right to make a demand, that you want to know it. So don't get confused or think, "Oh, I don't know how to apply it!" I said I will bring you to the fact. But once we have come to the fact, then *you* are responsible. It is in application right then. Is that fair enough? But you don't come back tomorrow to learn the same thing all over again. The minute time comes in, postponement comes in and the vitality is gone. Time is no longer a reality when the fact is seen and application is in effect.

---

*For a detailed discussion on "earth forces," see *The Future Of Mankind — The Branching Of The Road* by Tara Singh (Foundation for Life Action, 1986). (Editor)

> *Student:* Once a fact is made clear, then it is my responsibility to bring it to application. Is it also my responsibility not to be satisfied until I see it as a fact?

Your responsibility is to the application of the fact. Once a fact is shared and it is yours, it is your responsibility from that point forward to subdue those forces that oppose the application of it.

Now, in Part II of *A Course In Miracles,* there are different themes which are covered, followed by a series of Lessons. The first of these themes is, *What Is Forgiveness?*[2] Then comes the Lesson:

> *Peace to my mind*
> *Let all my thoughts be still.*[3]

This is the key. Please see it in a very simple way and rejoice that we can bring something that is not of time into application. This is something mankind has struggled to do over millions of years. And now it is possible.

> *Peace to my mind.*
> *Let all my thoughts be still.*

Peace to my mind can only be when all my thoughts are still. And this is the issue: we don't want to still *all* the thoughts. We have to see why this is so. Why do we not want to still all of our thoughts? That would be the issue, wouldn't it?

Now, we could take up that fact — that we are not willing to listen to what the Course says: that unless we still all our thoughts, we are not at peace. If we don't want to still all our thoughts, then what is it that we do want? We want to first judge and then forgive. Remember this Lesson is under the theme of *Forgiveness*. And because we judge, we are not at peace. This action of judgment is of thought. This is the way we have lived, isn't it?

But *A Course In Miracles* is saying that you have to first let all your thoughts be still. Forgiveness, then, is not possible as long as you first judge and then forgive. Could we see the truth of this? To judge first and then forgive is the way of the world: "She did this, that, so forth, but I am going to forgive her." This approach is still based on thought with its judgments and it can only lead you to being more and more tense within yourself. But if you have silenced all your thoughts, can there be judgment? Without judgment, there is no need of forgiveness.

You see, once the judgment has taken place it is no longer forgiveness. We have never understood forgiveness. If I do not judge, is there the need to forgive? Forgiveness comes first. It is: *Peace to my mind. Peace to my mind* brings all my thoughts to stillness.

Judgment is of thought and the forgiveness we have known is of thought. There is no peace in it; there is no stillness in it. And now we want to know: what is the stillness and what is the peace?

We are beginning to understand, fundamentally, what application is versus learning. There is no need of learning because if I go by learning, first I judge you, then I forgive you. We are attempting to step out of this set pattern: judgment first and forgiveness later. So, our first response is always of thought and there is no peace in it, no stillness in it. Are we beginning to see the fact that this is how it works and this is its set pattern?

> *Student:* I don't know forgiveness as you speak of it. So the forgiveness I know is false?

Yes, the forgiveness we have known is not real because it is not of peace or of a still mind.

So, what am I going to teach you? I am going to teach you that, "I don't know what forgiveness is but I *do* know what it isn't." Once you have seen the false, it effortlessly goes away.

> *Student:* Unless I have a vested interest in keeping it?

Of course. If you have a vested interest, then you would go on with the false. Then I say you are not a student of the Course. But I would help you come to the fact that what is of the earth is unreal. And as we begin to see the unreality of thought, we will be willing to drop it.

So, the unwillingness is what? The unwillingness is to drop the unreality of thought. The only thing a teacher can do is to show you the unreality of thought.

> *Student:* If thought is not real and I drop it, what takes its place?

The Course gives us the answer. It says:

> *What then is free to take its place*
> *is now the Will of God.*[4]

It is saying that *only* the Will of God is true.

Since there is only the Will of God, then whatever that Will wants to extend or to be, it must also be mine. Please listen to this. Only the Will of God is true. And there is only the one Will of God because what is true is not limited.

Please see the fact of this. Once a fact is seen, then it is *yours*, not *mine*.

So, only the Will of God is true and the Will of God is One. What, then, is the Will of God? What does it extend? I would say that the Will of God is the only thing there is because it has no opposition. Therefore, how can we have separate or personal plans? Inherent in thought is this contradiction that gets us confused, and finally the thought wins and we deviate from the Will of God into personal will. This is where the deception comes in.

Please follow this. There is only One Will. The Will of God being One, we are then automatically part of that One Will. And what it wants we must also want even though we have lost sight of it. So, our will and God's Will are one and we are in accord. But where deception has taken place, unreality has come in, and we are beguiled.

> *Student:* If there is only the Will of God and I can't be separate from that, how is it that I can be beguiled?

We are obviously beguiled.

> *Student:* Yes. I am trying to see the consistency of these two statements. From the thought point of view, it would only seem possible if my deceptions can be condoned in some way as an

extension of the Will of God; otherwise, how could I be deluded?

You see, we have to establish a fact. The fact is
that thought will never know peace and stillness.
Therefore it will never know the Will of God. But
we can know what we do that interferes. That is a
law. If we understand this law, it will be in application all through; we have established a meeting
ground. ''I will not know what the Will of God is; I
will not know what peace is; I will not know what
forgiveness is. As long as I pretend to know it, it is
of thought.'' The forgiveness we know is of
thought; the love we know is of thought, and so
on. So now, I want to show the falseness of all that.
And that which sees the falseness is something we
have not yet known. That which sees the falseness
is not of thought. Thought cannot see falseness. So
then, in seeing the falseness of thought, another
awakening takes place. Once you are awake, the
illusions can't take you over.

We want to *learn* about these things without
ever coming to that point. We still remain with the
false. Application demands that you dissolve the
false. Just being clear about it is not enough, even
though it makes you feel better; but it is still partial
knowledge. Truth, then, can only be shared with
those who are responsible, who are truly grateful.

So, we can agree the only thing we need to do is
to see the deceptions. That which undoes the
deceptions is without a name because it is not of
fear. This is an action that takes place within you,
some awakening. Only then will we see the fact of
it. Put energy into it and insist upon it so that it
becomes *your* truth.

> *Student:* May I recapitulate these steps so that I am clear about this? There is only one will, the Will of God. There is no opposition to it and therefore, I must have the same will.

Yes. And if it doesn't have an opposite, it must be whole and holy. And also, it extends — it extends Love because nothing could exist without it. We can call it by another name — creation, if you like. It is always perfect. We have used the example that a child is perfect at every stage. He is never touched by imperfection — from the day he is born to when he dies. In creation, everything is always perfect.

So then we could say that our will, if it is God's Will, must also move towards perfection. And if I start seeing the false as the false, automatically I become one with it.

> *Student:* How can the will move towards perfection if it is already part of perfection?

It was and is, and it extends what it is. God's Will extends what it is. We are part of God's Will but we are not extending what the Will is, which is perfection or Love. But as we recognize God's Will we will come to the same Love and whatever else the Will is.

So far we have been deceived, that we are not what we are. And now, we meet to see that this is not God's Will. Then are we not moving towards perfection? And that which is moving us towards perfection, by undoing the deceptions, must be God's Will too because that is its function.

Both of us then start moving toward that perfection. This inherent movement cannot have effort. We need effort to go away from it. That is why we invented time and personality and struggle. But to go towards it is ending time — ending misperception and coming upon it. And in that there is no effort.

For millennia we have believed in effort. Some people have sat on a board of nails; others have meditated nine hours a day, and so forth. We thought we needed to work to get something. And this has become a pattern for eons upon eons in mankind. Every cell in the body is conditioned with that. But it keeps us away from God's Will! We have to reverse the process. The minute we reverse the process, healing takes place and we come upon that which we are.

God's Will and my will are only one if I am not projecting something else. If I were with God's Will, I would be at peace and all my thoughts would be still. That would be the truth. That would be God's Will.

Peace to my mind.
Let all my thoughts be still.[5]

And He teaches us what that is in *A Course In Miracles* — if we can heed it, not give validity to that which is unreal, and undo the deceptions.

He is the Teacher in charge of the process of Atonement.[6] He will do it for each one of us. What will He do? He is going to dissolve the deceptions, the illusions, the wantings that we have gotten caught in. He helps us see they are unreal; they are based on fear, insecurity, divisions, and separation — things we give reality to. So then we see that *He* is extending the Will of God.

Perhaps now, with this background, we can start reading the Introduction to Part II and be able to hear a little better.

> *Words will mean little now.*
> *We use them but as guides*
> *on which we do not now depend.*[7]

So, even though words are used to communicate, when we come to the fact they are no longer necessary. Therefore, we cannot hold on to words anymore. Whenever we are confused, it will be because we are holding on to words. These principles must be established. So then observe how the words are also going to dissolve it.

The wise uses words to bring another to the fact, and when they both have come to the fact, then there are no more words. We want to hold on to words and activate the computer brain which can never be still. It can never let go all its thoughts.

> *For now we seek*
> *direct experience of truth alone.*
> *The lessons that remain*
> *are merely introductions to the times*
> *in which we leave the world of pain,*
> *and go to enter peace.* [8]

This is the purpose of our meeting. The purpose is application of the fact, to see the false as the false, and to know the Will.

> *Now we begin to reach the goal*
> *this course has set,*
> *and find the end toward which*
> *our practicing was always geared.*
> *Now we attempt to let the exercise*
> *be merely a beginning.*
> *For we wait in quiet expectation*
> *for our God and Father.*[9]

And now *we wait in quiet.* We have come to a point where the learning and seeking have come to an end. We come to quiet rather than to a conclusion of thought. All conclusions of thought are still false and need to be undone.

Forgiveness must be that we can come to quiet. In that quiet, what another person does or does not do cannot enter. We have to find that actual space within ourselves because as long as the brain is active, we cannot know the Mind of God or our own mind.

In order to forgive and not judge, we must come to the quiet of the brain. Then we are part of that mind in which there is no separation and no thought, no judgment and no forgiveness.

> *We wait in quiet expectation*
> *for our God and Father.*

What is expectation? When you are in expectation of something, you have ''the ears to hear.'' You are fully alert and anything that you are not expecting cannot intrude upon it. A truck could pass behind you and you wouldn't hear it. We seldom, if ever, come to that intensity of expectation.

Expectation is when you are totally, wholly attentive. Having seen that thought beguiles you, you are not going to be misled by thought. It is meaningless; it's just illusion. Come to expectation — that you not abide by anything but that which is of God.

When we come to that expectation, it brings about a certain consistency at all levels of our being. Learning does not. Learning is partial. What else could learning be if it still goes on with deceptions? It is still self-centered. Expectation is not self-centered because you are not projecting what *you* want — the desires, the images that you nurse. In expectation, there is no projection because you have already seen that thought is not real, although it has become a pattern and it takes you over. I hope that after this Lesson you begin to see that even though you are not yet free of thought, it has less power over you.

> *Student:* When the Course says, *we wait in quiet expectation,* it seems to imply there is a knowing of something. Is it a recognition of what thought is?

No, because the knowing of something is still of thought. And God's Will is not of thought. Expectation is the state of "nothing," when there is "no thing" in it. Expectation and "no thing" are one and the same. And thought always has a thing. Since we always project, we are satisfied with the "thing." When there is a thing, it is manufactured by the brain. You can develop a discrimination that knows when anything is interfering with the expectation, that that is not it.

Expectation is necessary to come to peace and to quiet. We can't just overlook this. If you can be appeased by a thing, then know whatever the thing is, it has sabotaged the expectation. If you accept anything, the expectation is no longer there. You have substituted something else.

You are responsible to not let anything intrude upon the expectation. In order to know peace, in order to know God's Will, in order to know anything, do not accept that which is of thought as real because it interferes with the expectation. You are responsible to keep the expectation impeccable.

Expectation holds "no thing" as real. It is so alert that "no thing" comes in. That is expectation! It doesn't know what God's Will is. It doesn't know what peace is. It doesn't know what forgiveness is. But it does know that what you put into it is not it. Is this your fact now?

> *Student:* Yes. I will undo any thought that intrudes upon the expectation.

Let us not get lost in the world of senses. Keep this jewel with you; it is like a candle within. Don't let anything blow it out. Say to yourself:

> *Peace to my mind.*
> *Let all my thoughts be still.*

because they are not His Thoughts. They are the ones we manufactured. To come to expectation, be wise and let all your thoughts be still. All during the day call upon that and you will see: He will be with you wherever you are. As you start to undo your thoughts, expectation will grow. It is a way of life. It is not a way of learning. It is a way of application.

His Will is perfect and creative. It is not dormant; it is alive. But the activity of thought is insane. It deviates from His Will and then struggles to find it. Trust in Him Who is in charge of the Process of Atonement, for He will awaken us. This will be your gift to yourself, to all humanity, and to God.

> Father, we had prayed and asked that illusions be removed. We are beginning to understand the healing we need is here when we are ready to bring *A Course In Miracles* into application.
>
> *I will be healed*
> *as I let Him teach me to heal.*[10]
>
> We feel Your Presence. Our hearts are glad and we thank You. We thank You for Your blessing. Amen.

CHAPTER THREE

3

THE ILLUSION
OF THE OPPOSITE

Forgive us our illusions, Father,
and help us to accept
our true relationship with You,
in which there are no illusions,
and where none can ever enter.
Our holiness is Yours.
What can there be in us that needs forgiveness
when Yours is perfect?
The sleep of forgetfulness is only
the unwillingness to remember
Your forgiveness and Your Love.
Let us not wander into temptation,
for the temptation of the Son of God
is not Your Will.
And let us receive only what You have given,
and accept but this into the minds
which You created and which You love. Amen.[1]

I would like to make it very clear
that the prayer we have just read is to be brought

into application. It is demanded. You cannot justify that you are going to do it "tomorrow." There is no time. That is the method we have tried all of our life — postponing, compromising, evading. We do not meet here to *learn*, but to bring *A Course In Miracles* into application. Therefore, please listen to the prayer carefully.

Forgive us our illusions, Father.

Everything that is of personality — projected and pursued — is an illusion. Is this clear? And we meet together to come to clarity. We have said that once it is clear and it is your fact, then it is in application. Until then, insist on getting it clear so that you do not accept someone else's authority over you. I have no authority over another, nor do I want to have.

*And help us to accept
our true relationship with You.*

Is that the reason you are reading *A Course In Miracles?* To have a true relationship with the Creator, with the Father? That being so, we cannot bring illusions into that relationship. Otherwise, this prayer will mean very little.

*Help us to accept
our true relationship with You,
in which there are no illusions,
and where none can ever enter.*

That is what the prayer is.

There is another prayer I would like to include:

*Father, this is Your day.
It is a day in which*

I would do nothing by myself,
but hear Your Voice in everything I do;
requesting only what You offer me. [2]

That means you have no wants. When you say, *requesting only what You offer me,* you don't have the terms to dictate "I want this and I want that." The prayer cannot be true if you have a wanting and a wish for which you are going to plead. Then you don't have a true relationship with God because you are not acknowledging that His Will is perfect. If His Will is perfect, then you need to know the Will — what the Will has to offer you, not what you want.

I hope this is clear. If you have any attachment, any disorder in your life, these things are not going to be possible because illusion will enter into it.

> *Student:* This is still unclear to me because there are things that continue to deceive me.

The Will of God exists, as your will exists, to come to clarity. But if you are violating your will, you will never know the Will of God because they are both one. You cannot have any attachments, any fear that regulates your life, because that is not part of the Will of God.

> *Student :* I am not without attachments. I would *like* to be without attachments but I can't say in truth that I am.

What is attachment? Is it not always in relationship with some person or some thing?

> *Student:* Sir, I have been ignorant for so many years and during that ignorance, I have gotten committed to things. I have obligations, responsibilities. How can I be free of it?

To be "free of it" doesn't mean that you throw the other person out of the window. There must be a freedom that we don't yet know.

> *Student:* I would like to be free but I don't know what to do. I am entangled.

When we say the prayer, *Forgive us our illusions, Father,* we are also invoking the Presence of the One in charge of the process of Atonement. Is there the willingness to heed what He has to say? Because only what He has to say would liberate us. How we would be liberated, we don't know. If we knew, we would have done so by now.

But His Presence is there. Therefore, we can open up and say, "This is the issue and I don't know how to resolve it." Then there would be the undoing of certain assumptions and illusions. Alright? Either we have a relationship with God or what we have needs to be undone. And we meet together to undo that.

May we continue with the prayer and we will come back to your issue?

How remarkable that it says,

> *requesting* only *what You offer me.*

Not wanting. One has to first come to that recognition within — as an integrity, as a conviction — that God's Will is perfect. Therefore, we can always question when we are not at ease.

Peace to my mind.
Let all my thoughts be still.[3]

That is still our Lesson. In order to live according to this, we have to resolve all the other deceptions and illusions, don't we? So we meet to do that. Not to impose. Each person can then say, "I have this issue. . .that issue." But we start from the premise that whatever our issue is, it needs undoing. And *A Course In Miracles* says:

requesting only what You offer me.

From this day forth, you will no longer be in wanting because there is no lack in God's Plan for Salvation. The wanting could only be there if you start from the premise that God's Plan has a lack; then you will want. Isn't that what all "good" Christians do: "Give me this. Do that for me"? But the Course says:

requesting only what You offer me.

A Course In Miracles is teaching us how to pray. You will never, then, be ruled by wanting because you can undo the wanting — the illusion of wanting that still takes you over.

We have said the One Who is in charge of the process of Atonement is in charge of bringing the separation to wholeness, of bringing illusions to truth so they get undone. Therefore, you cooperate in bringing the illusions to truth. But if you are attached, you are going to defend the illusions. Then there is no meeting ground. No one is demanding of you that you do it. It must come from your own yearning, your own longing to be one with the Will of God. It *must* be *your* need!

Requesting only what You offer me is the most wonderful attitude of a person who wants to bring it to application. In one stroke, all wishing and wanting ceases.

> *Student:* When the prayer says, *requesting only what You offer me,* is it referring to things that happen or is it in the sense of "no thing"?

It would have to be "no thing." To be true to the Father, we have to put all illusions away. Our dedication to that one relationship would not allow any illusions in it because we want to make our relationship with God true. That is what the prayer is saying: *true relationship.* Since we have never had a true relationship, we start with having one with our Creator.

We come back now to your particular issue of attachment and entanglement. At this level of the "you" and the "me," you have a separate will and I have a separate will, and we clash. It is difficult to bring clarity where there is war. Please try to appreciate this.

For instance, a husband has a will and his wife has a will. When a man has a wife who is the boss in the house, his words are meaningless because he lacks inner strength. Then he is not the husband. He is irresponsible. And eventually, both have suspicions of each other. Is that a husband-wife relationship? Or is it a relationship with something else: gratification, dependence, exploitation, and abuse. It is a relationship between two images. And that is *not* relationship.

Then just have a look at yourself and what you

do. Become aware of what kind of husband you are, what kind of friend you are, what kind of true relationship you have or don't have. How long would your marriage last?

You see, we can't have one true relationship while other relationships are wrong. Or rather, you can't have a true relationship while there are the dependencies and attachments.

> *Student:* I am shocked to realize that I don't have my own voice, that my words are not factual. And I am equally shocked to admit that I am ruled by another, even by my wife.

I would like to introduce another approach — that you not say "by my wife." For us, there is no "other." Let us make this clear for all times. For us there is no "other." So, if you have any illusions about what is in your head and in your heart, then that is where you must come to some purity, some undoing. If you bring in a third factor, another person, it will never end because you are making the issue external to yourself. The issue is *always* internal.

I hope you see the wisdom of this. And that for the rest of your life you will never make a problem with another. You undo it in yourself. You make the correction within yourself and you blame no one else. Otherwise, you will fall back into the deception of "judge and forgive."

> *Student:* I don't know how I can do this because I have difficulties with other people.

We do not acknowledge the "other"; we only

see the problem is in *you*. And the problems are the illusions. You are to be set free of illusion in order to come to a true relationship with your Creator. It is independent of another. It is each person's direct relationship with his Creator. If the other person doesn't want it, do you think it can prevent you from being liberated? It would be a tremendous injustice. That would mean you are controlled by another, not by God or God's Will. Can you see the beauty of this?

Student: It takes away the excuses.

Yes. And it takes away the opposite — the illusion of the opposite. Under no circumstances can we justify deviating into ''another'' or into an ''opposite.'' Because there is no ''other,'' therefore there is no ''opposite'' either, and you stand by that.

So, there is the answer. The answer is for *you* to find out that *you* are the one who is attached. Are we not always using the ''other'' to justify our own weakness? And then we want to be the hero or the martyr. And if a wise person corners you, you will find out that you cannot drop either the attachment or the weakness. You need them. They are your means of escape. You'll shiver in your aloneness, talking big, that you are going to bring it into application.

Could you live without your attachments and illusions? When you can't give them up, you use them for blaming others, for excusing yourself. If you live in your illusions, how can you be truthful and responsible? Can there be responsibility and honesty outside of the Will of God? Outside of the Will of God there is nothing but illusion. Let us get that clear too.

Student: I sense the attachments are the source of my weakness and that, I have to face.

As an idea?

Student: I don't want it to be.

Of course, but wanting has no meaning. And the more you pressure yourself, the more you will get confused; and then, probably sick, too.

You see, we live in deception. Take it away, we fall apart. But can you see that it is just your misperception that needs to be corrected? This is the correction of the illusions that stand in the way of application. Application can take place but it requires having order in your life. Otherwise, we read what *A Course In Miracles* has to impart but we rejoice in the disorder and wallow in "I am *going* to do something." And all the while, we love the disorder which we use — the wife, the children, and so forth — for postponement.

Now we are saying: there is no "other." There is confusion in *you* and we will see if that can be undone. You cannot project "another." The minute you project another, you are back in the same thought system, the relative thought system of man.

A Course In Miracles deals with Thoughts of God and the Absolute. If you go for things of time,

Peace to my mind.
Let all my thoughts be still.

may not be possible. If you can't do it now, what makes you think you will do it later?

Student: What exactly do you mean by ''go for things of time''?

Things that have names; things and feelings that have names. It is the opposite of ''no thing.'' No thing, no other, no problem. The misperception is what gets corrected so that we can bring the Thoughts of God into application.

You will soon find out that mere wanting won't work. This has to be actual. And so we come back to the prayer:

Forgive us our illusions, Father,
and help us to accept
our true relationship with You,
in which there are no illusions,
and where none can ever enter.
Our holiness is Yours.
What can there be in us that needs forgiveness
when Yours is perfect?
The sleep of forgetfulness is only
the unwillingness to remember
Your forgiveness and Your Love.
Let us not wander into temptation,
for the temptation of the Son of God
is not Your Will.
And let us receive only what You have given,
and accept but this into the minds
which You created and which You love. Amen.

Find out, what is the truth of this? Can we be sensitive enough to capture not only the verbal, but also what lies beyond the word? The content of it? Not only the meaning but also the quality, the beauty, and the strength of the words *A Course In Miracles* uses?

Most of us are caught in a network of words. Our whole thinking process is a verbalization — making pictures of images — and in that we are caught. We are seldom, if ever, actually free from words and ready to go beyond explanations or descriptions of the words.

Can we heed the words of *A Course In Miracles*, the Thoughts of God? Can we have ''the ears to hear''? If you have doubts about the Thoughts of God, then know you do not have a true relationship with Him. And if it is true, you would rejoice. To be a stranger to doubt and despair! What a state that must be! There is no problem it could not solve. All problems are but illusions and misperceptions. The externals are forgotten.

> *Student:* This is most meaningful. At least it brings it back to the point where I would most likely see that I have made the problem. And seeing that I made the problem would release me from the problem.

At least from the externals. Let's put it that way, from the externals. And then, if it releases you from the externals, you are not going to have much of a problem left. You can go on dealing with those illusions, but you will no longer be distracted by them. Where there is no distraction, there has to be the words of strength. The Thought of God can undo the relative thought system of man. That is why *A Course In Miracles* is meant for application.

> *Student:* I am seeing that, all through the day, I have tried to pinpoint different things and there are some illusions

more obvious than others. They seem to be everywhere.

Let me say this. To begin with, don't deal so much with the situations outside of you. They are there, but don't get too picky with the externals. Otherwise, you are making that valid. Don't make the external valid or there will be no end to your misperceptions.

The relationship is between you and God. That happens to be true. And the prayer doesn't talk about anybody else but you and God — *your* relationship with the Father. And so, focus on what is in *you*, the impurities, the illusions and so forth that prevent you from bringing the prayer into application.

> *Student:* There is something in me that makes me think I don't have the strength, and makes doubt valid.

The strength of the words of *A Course In Miracles* will deal with that. It is only at another level that the illusions exist. In actuality, they do not.

> *Student:* So we are talking about something that will deal with the externals?

Yes, because the external is something I project either out of pleasure or out of fear.

> *Student:* What we are coming to now will dissolve the externals?

Yes, because order comes into your life. You and I can only bring order into our life when we have become responsible. The man who lives a responsible life, his words have strength. The strength of the Word of God has seldom been realized in the world. His words have been bought and sold, but seldom has anyone realized the strength of them. Application is to realize the strength of the Word of God. It is very different.

> *Student:* What I am hearing is that I can no longer look for order outside of me.

When you have order inside of you, can there be disorder outside? So, start correcting there.

> *Student:* To have order in my life is not necessarily an external order. It is more a perspective or an approach to life, is it not?

Yes, but *you* are responsible for the order in your life. So, start correcting disorder.

> *Student:* And the disorder in my life is that which I can take to a friend from whom I can get the strength to bring it to order? Is that correct?

You can't take it to a friend and still be victim of the disorder outside. Once it is clear, it is clear for all times. Time will not touch that. This is the difference. You and I understand everything today and on Tuesday we forget it. The strength of the words cannot be interpreted if you have "the ears to hear." That order cannot be violated because otherwise you bring it to disorder again.

Whatever becomes clear is for always because it is not of time. If you try to bring it down to the relative level, then you are the one who is in disorder. Clarity is not of time. Then when you meet problems of time, you have order and strength.

You are responsible for the way you read the Course now. As you start bringing one Lesson into application, you will begin to see your outer disorder has no meaning because the Course is the Thought of God. It is the Absolute Thought, not the relative. But we hear it and make it relative. Therefore, it does not come into application.

> *Student:* I have a lot of difficulty dealing with the externals. And I can say it is because of my interpretation of it, but my frustration is real. Somewhere I know I create the frustration but it's still there.

Alright, but you do understand that the external is of certain illusions that we project and we produce? The external is also that we are attached to someone, or we have a relationship we don't know what to do with. Then we say that the world has tried to correct it externally, but there is problem after problem after problem. And the correction does not take place, as a rule. Even if the first got resolved, it is not really corrected because there will be another problem and another.

Our responsibility is to deal with the illusions within ourselves that depend on the external. A life without these illusions may have a totally different relationship than we know. But do we see that as long as there is the opposite, there is the relative knowledge with which we try to solve things?

So then, where does the illusion take place? Where does the misperception take place in you and me? This is what we have to dissolve, to undo. See the wisdom of it, that that is where it has to be undone. When there is order in your life, then everything else has to be different. You would relate differently because the correction takes place within you and you bring illusion to an end. When you are clear, then you are out of it too.

You simply do not deviate into relative knowledge. Can we rejoice that in this lifetime this is possible? Gladness is having the right premise of dealing with the self — *Know thyself* — rather than with the outside things.

As a matter of fact, at one point you would not even be able to say you are a body. I assure you. Even the body thoughts will seem external to you. To the Spirit, it is external. And we have not known that thought system that has no conflict, no duality. It is the Absolute. It knows the truth. It knows the Will of God and lives by Divine Grace. It knows no wishing and wanting for the external has become secondary.

> *Student:* I see the need to become responsible within myself.

Can you be responsible for your words? If you are, then they have the strength. If you are responsible for your words, they will have the strength.

> *Student:* As you were speaking, I saw there has been a movement in my own life. It seems to be taking care of the externals. Years ago, I had many more involvements. I have simplified so that I don't even have things outside of myself that I can use as an excuse. And I see the joy of really coming to self-

reliance and being responsible for my own life, my internal life. I don't think there is anything that can stand in the way of application anymore.

We will see. You have committed yourself never to project another, to resolve the issue internally so that there is no ''other''; there is no opposite, therefore, no problem. It is going to take everything one has got. Relative thought must live by problems. But at any rate, it is possible. When we are willing to see what the illusions are, we can deal with them.

> *Student:* I have understood from what has been shared that as long as there is an ''other,'' there is disorder in my life and any attempt to correct something with an ''other'' is a lie.

As an idea we understand. But this demands application, the removal of all illusions. Has it become your single purpose to remove all illusions and bring them to truth — yourself? That is the responsibility.

> *Student:* I appreciate that the application will demand everything of me and that it is uncompromising.

Application is only possible when your words have the strength behind them. Then you can honor your words.

> *Student:* How does one deal with self-doubt?

Well, how does doubt come into being? If you let time come in, then you are going to create the doubt, don't you see? So you can say, "I have seen it now. The doubt may still come but I am not the weak person I was before." All of this is involved in the application, but at least you are starting from the premise that you are determined not to hide behind these issues.

That is why we spoke of the importance of going beyond the word to the actual strength of the word. The words of *A Course In Miracles* are the Thoughts of God and we never seem to get the strength of them because we remain at the relative level. But now we are to bring to application the vertical words of the Course and deal with those illusions. You will find out: What does it take to bring illusions to truth? Miracles would also become part of your life — some confidence that you can do that, some reverence for the Presence that accompanies the words of the Course.

You can't just believe that you are weak. We must see that there are other factors that brought us to the Course. Now we can read it differently because the Lesson is to be brought to application. That becomes the focus. But it is not a learning.

The other thing is not to tire yourself too much and do the Course as the last thing in the evening. Then one gets too sleepy. We have to be wise. If we are going to give our lives to the Course, we can't do it as a ritual.

There is a responsibility we have not to be so worn out, nor to put other things first. Is *A Course In Miracles* your first love? These are some of the responsibilities you and I have to take.

I would like to read again from the Introduction to Part II of the *Workbook For Students.*

> *Words will mean little now.*
> *We use them but as guides*
> *on which we do not now depend.*[4]

When you get into problems, call to your remembrance, *Words will mean little now.* And you will see they will have very little meaning. In fact, they don't really mean anything; *you* are the one giving them the energy.

So, begin to do the exercises that way. That is why the Course insists every hour, every half-hour, do this remembrance. Why? Because it says we are in the sleep of forgetfulness.

During the day, then, when you see the problems getting too big, you can say to yourself, "They mean nothing." As the problems begin to mean little to you, you will have less illusions. These are things we *have* to bring to application. They are simple, and yet we don't do it.

> *For now we seek*
> *direct experience of truth alone.*[5]

The remembrance of this brings you to the direct experience of seeing the problems have little meaning. That remembrance is your direct experience. And that remembrance, then, is the miracle. It becomes alive in you.

> *The lessons that remain*
> *are merely introductions to the times*
> *in which we leave the world of pain,*
> *and go to enter peace.*[6]

Now, we have to also see, since we are reading this, that it is a world of pain we are caught in. As an idea we have seen it, that there are the illusions and we want peace. But if we are not moving in the direction of peace, we are going to give a lot of importance to pain, loss, and gain. Then I will remind you, ''What about the peace you gave your life to?'' And you will have to admit that you gave your life to the world of pain, loss, and gain — not to peace.

You see, there are going to be many such contradictions at the relative level. These are things to be corrected. There is so much to bring to application.

> *Now we begin to reach the goal*
> *this course has set,*
> *and find the end toward which*
> *our practicing was always geared.*[7]

This you have to see. If it is just an idea that you want to come to application, it would have no meaning. The Course is geared toward a certain goal; this is what it says. If you live by the principle of,

> *Nothing real can be threatened.*
> *Nothing unreal exists.*[8]

or,

> *Forgiveness is my function*
> *as the light of the world.*[9]

you are consistent with *A Course In Miracles*. Are you deep down? Or is it very weak in you? That is what we have to strengthen then, isn't it?

We want to, but then twenty-three hours out of the day we don't. Are we fooling ourselves? We have to find out: do we really want to live the Course? What the Course says is Absolute; it is already done and it is possible. You say, "I want that." But your actions speak differently. We have to see how they contradict. Whatever the illusions are, we can correct them — *if* you *really* want to bring the Course into application. If not, you will merely agree and remain caught in the illusions.

> *Now we attempt to let the exercise*
> *be merely a beginning.*
> *For we wait in quiet expectation*
> *for our God and Father.*
> *He has promised*
> *He will take the final step Himself.*[10]

Do you believe that He will take the final step Himself? Without trust, you cannot wait in quiet expectation. You see, if you don't deeply trust, then you trust only your weak thoughts. You do the ritual of sitting quiet and reading, but your trust is not in God. Find out what trust is. If there is not the trust, there is no expectation either.

If you *know* and firmly believe that nothing else can do it, then you have the trust. You wait and you are answered. If you are waiting for a ritual — and whether you get answered or not, it's still alright with you — then you won't hear the answer. It is important that we come to a point where we have no alternative but to hear the answer. The answer is Absolute; the alternative is something that we have to dissolve.

Because we have the alternative, we trust the alternative; we don't trust God. Which one do *you* trust: the alternative or God?

> *Student:* I have been trusting alternatives, that I see. And where I thought I was not, I see I was making demands. And that wasn't expectation either.

Without the trust, you can't be with the expectation.

> *Student:* I also see that as long as the alternative exists, my trust is in the alternative. And that is the first thing I need to correct.

We need to undo the alternative in order to have the trust. And to bring it to application, the help is given by the Will of God. When there is not the alternative, who could deny you the action of rising to the height of your own being? Everyone talks about taking the next step, but who does? Deep down we have so many other plans, desires, and unfulfillment.

> *Student:* To this point, I have trusted my own thinking. And surely this would have to begin with something other than my own thought?

Yes. So then we are never expecting. There is no expectation because there is no space for expectation. "I know what I want." And then thought splits itself. Thought's other name is "conflict." What is thought? Conflict. That is its proper name. It can say, "I want God's Plan. I want application." But there is conflict, isn't there? Even our expectation is a promotion of conflict. And that is what we have to end. There is no other problem!

> *Student:* I see that my expectation was never really expectation because it had the alternative that I valued more than trust.

And in that we trust. Therefore we live in conflict. Conflict with the brother, conflict with God. And we can't say,

> *Peace to my mind.*
> *Let all my thoughts be still.*[11]

You cannot say that as long as you are in conflict. If you do, it is a lie. There is no way of bringing that Lesson into application as long as there is conflict.

> *Student:* I see how I have let my alternatives strengthen my weaknesses. I would have never known it was all from conflict or that conflict itself is an alternative.

To end the conflict is to end thought. Everything else is forgotten: the external, people, wives, problems, everything. The issue is within.

We can be grateful then for *A Course In Miracles*, the Thoughts of God that have no opposite, no conflict, no alternative, no problems. We can be grateful too for His holding us by the hand and leading us[12] to think with Him[13] — with His Thoughts, free of illusions. And in that there is no conflict. I pray that gratefulness accompany every breath you take.

Please don't forget not to make any problems. A

problem is a clear indication that you are promoting conflict. It is not consistent with the Will of God. There is conflict at very subtle levels which we may not understand at times. But there is also another conflict which we deliberately make by acknowledging a problem.

So, start there. Don't ever acknowledge a problem, for if you do, you are deliberately promoting conflict. It's not that problems will not come, but you can discover the illusion of the problem, right then, and the mischief of the conflict that you keep alive. Therefore, *you* are responsible for the conflict and the projection of problems.

You have undertaken to step out of illusions and of conflict. Give your life to that.

CHAPTER FOUR

4

"HELP US TO ACCEPT OUR TRUE RELATIONSHIP WITH YOU"

Forgive us our illusions, Father,
and help us to accept
our true relationship with You,
in which there are no illusions,
and where none can ever enter.
Our holiness is Yours.
What can there be in us that needs forgiveness
when Yours is perfect?
The sleep of forgetfulness is only
the unwillingness to remember
Your forgiveness and Your Love.
Let us not wander into temptation,
for the temptation of the Son of God
is not Your Will.
And let us receive only what You have given,
and accept but this into the minds
which You created and which You love. Amen.[1]

How would you read this prayer?
What does it mean to you? And what part of it is in

application in your life? It has to be Absolute Truth. We have spent a great deal of time on it. What is in effect in your life *now*?

> *Student:* What is in application is that I am no longer *attempting* to forgive.

What does that mean?

> *Student:* What I mean by that is, I am no longer finding fault first and then trying to do something about it.

What else? What help have you asked of the Father, that was not as a ritual? What have you done to have a true relationship with the Father today? What did you do in which there were no illusions today?

> *Student:* Many times I recognized a judgment about myself and about others. In the morning, there were encounters at work, questions about certain procedures, miscommunication that took place with my assistant that would cause me to judge her. I asked that that judgment be suspended or removed rather than my focusing on what it was she had done or not done in the work.

Do you mean to say that you made contact with God or Higher Forces?

> *Student:* I think that the closest I came was in trying not to focus on what it was that took place and not focusing on my judgment of the situation, which I have not done in the past.

Was that just a thought?

> *Student:* It released the situation. I don't know if it began with a thought. I assume it did.

Did you see that no illusion would then enter?

> *Student:* I saw that my judgment was an illusion and that it began with me.

Yes, but those could just be words, don't you see? It is your honesty that is required. Lack of honesty inevitably turns against a person. It forfeits knowing the truth of, *Our holiness is Yours.* If it violates the holiness that is yours and you resort to right words, it won't work. Every person is responsible for what he says. And that doesn't mean that you can just say the right words. Cleverness is irresponsibility. The inconsistency would show up right away. Be responsible for the words you use.

Let's move on to the next person. What part of this prayer have you lived by?

> *Student:* The nearest I may have come to application is with the section, *help us to accept our true relationship with You.* To me, that was like the Lesson, *Peace to my mind. Let all my thoughts be still.*[2] I am becoming more and more aware that when I try to be still, or quiet, or let my mind be at peace, I can recognize the motivation that comes in even if I don't immediately see that it is a thought, or see its movement. And to me, when that movement is not there would be the true relationship the prayer speaks of. I am trying to see when the movement is there.

More so than when these sessions began?

> *Student:* Yes. For the first time in my life I have some sense that I am not alone. I feel that the true relationship exists. I don't realize it yet, but it is possible.

Alright. Who is next?

> *Student:* When I start the day I am more aware of watching what my thoughts are doing. And then, as I get more and more active, I get caught up in them and forget to be watchful. To me, that is the sleep of forgetfulness — that I get caught up in most of the day.

You see, everyone can say they have done something with the prayer. And that "something" we have been doing for the last twenty years. I want to see if there is a change that has *already* taken place. That is what I want to know.

The change that has taken place is what I want to deal with. "How would I know if a change has taken place?" could be your question. When a change has taken place, everything you do is from another space, another state. It is not that once the incident has happened, you try to rearrange it.

So now, if someone says to me, "My state has changed," it is probably a lie; you would be using those words because you heard me saying them. You can imagine your state has changed. But it cannot be manufactured. I think it was Thoreau who said we are always sliding below our aspirations and that the most disastrous things that have ever happened to mankind are his ideals.

Having ideals has destroyed man. Anyone who talks to me about ideals has not understood what we are saying; there is no communication. Ideals have destroyed man because they are not actual. I am talking about the actual. The actual is not an incident. You can tell me you ran into someone's car and you didn't get upset. But you are describing an incident. I want to know what your state of being is irrespective of the incident. Has your state changed?

You cannot give me ideals because ideals are irresponsible. They are not actual. I just want to know the actual. Isn't that simple? So, what has been actual in your day?

> *Student:* Not making a problem out of something. I have a tendency to worry about things and then the thoughts go wild. I'm trying to put an end to it.

Perhaps you could put an end to the friction with your mother?

> *Student:* If I don't understand the friction. . .

No, no, wait. We are saying that if you had already come to this other state, then you would have less friction, wouldn't you?

> *Student:* Yes.

Alright. Friction should have shown you that there is something *you* still need to do, or you are not on top of the situation.

> *Student:* Something that I would need to do within myself?

Obviously. You have to see that the friction took place and therefore you are still the same as you were. So now, what can you say that is not an ideal?

> *Student:* Are you saying that talking about a problem and a solution is an ideal?

The ideal is the imaginary. It is what one *tries* to be, when in actuality that is not what one is. And that's irresponsible. *You* are responsible for the actuality of your state. So, you have observed your state but it still came to friction, did it not?

> *Student:* Yes.

Then you can't give me the ideal that you are changing or you are *going* to change.

> *Student:* I see. I have to state the actual, that there is friction.

Exactly. Otherwise, you are depriving yourself of the real taking place. And unless we insist upon it, you wouldn't know what I am talking about. May that be of more value to you than justifying an incident.

So then, we have to be honest and reliable and responsible for what we say. If we are not, we will never get the actual. And this meeting takes place to bring you to the actual. Change can only take place when you deal with the actual, not when you pursue the ideal. With ideals, we fool ourselves; and with ideals, we remain what we are.

Is not the actual, for us, the deception of lack, the illusions of insecurity and unfulfillment? That is our actuality. It is something *we* made. And therefore, we can do something about it. Because it is something *you* create, only *you* can do something about it.

> *Student:* I see the rightness of it, but I must admit that I actually enjoy deviating at times.

Let us first change the language we use. You say that you "enjoy" deviating. Perhaps the right way would be to say, "I like the stimulation of pleasure." We must be careful to use the right words because joy is independent of thought. You like the stimulation of pleasure and therefore, it limits you to the body and makes you self-centered. Self-centeredness is always going to result in consequences. Could you say that is understood? And you will watch out for that?

> *Student:* I see the need for it now.

The prayer says:

> *Forgive us our illusions, Father,*
> *and help us to accept*
> *our true relationship with You.*

In what manner is it possible for the son who is separated to have a true relationship with his Creator? It is something *you* have to find out. Your values have to change to Timelessness, don't they? This shift of values can only take place when you insist upon the actual and not the ideal.

The actual means that there is a relationship with that which is eternal, that which is of God. How can you have a relationship with God if you are with earth-bound thought and earthy things? If you are still preoccupied with things of the earth, then can your interest be in having a true relationship with the Father?

If this shift of values has *already* taken place in you, then your whole perspective changes. It is like the poet who says, "I walk through the bazaar, but I am not a customer." Then no matter what you do, you are attuned to something else.

> Student: I hear what you are saying, that I have to make that distinction of whether I am with things of the earth — of personality, of self — or whether I am with another state that is related to this prayer.

Yes, but has that already taken place in you? It should have by now. Our relationship with Eternal Laws is already in effect because we have undertaken to bring the prayer to application.

> Student: Unfulfillment would have to be ended, then, in order to be with the state you are speaking of?

Yes, that is a good way of phrasing it. Whenever you are touched with unfulfillment, you know your relationship with God is not yet a true one. The unfulfillment, then, is the actual. Unfulfillment is still of time. That which comes and goes, that which subsides, is of thought and of time. And these are not real — although they regulate our life.

Could we never depart from a sense of holiness because the minute we deviate from that, our relationship is no longer true with the Father.

> *Student:* The sense of holiness then would be stability?

If you are in tune with it, yes. Holiness is when you come upon that which is not of thought. You feel blessed to be liberated from things of the body, from things of time. If you rejoice in holiness, then you keep it alive. But if you get caught in unfulfillment, then your values are of the earth and of thought. So then, our whole value system can undergo a change today — right now.

> *Student:* If I value lack, then I have not changed?

Yes.

> *Student:* And the unfulfillment will keep me from true relationship?

Yes. Therefore you feel a sense of holiness when you no longer live by the laws of lack. Unfulfillment and lack are of our own making and thus, they are illusions. Your relationship with everyone, then, must be from fulfillment. How do you now feel about this?

> *Student:* It takes all my concentration and my body is having resistance to it and saying, "No!"

You are making the body an actuality, and so the body would rule you. And the body gets old, is subject to sorrow, and finally dies. These are the consequences.

> *Student:* I see that these are the consequences. My pattern has been to make it a goal to deny the body, to overcome the body. But today, the body rules me.

If holiness is present in one as an actuality, that person is very joyous. He would have no sense of lack at all, would not feel deprived. One doesn't feel deprived when one is holy. Otherwise, one would put conditions in the way of God. Holiness is vast. It doesn't condemn oneself or another. It knows no lack and it doesn't waste.

So, what were you saying? That you are attached to the body?

> *Student:* My thoughts show me limitations everywhere.

What else do you expect from thought? What do you expect from insanity? Either we are insane or we are holy. If you are holy, then you have some richness within yourself. If you are insane, you are with lack and unfulfillment. Which do you want: insanity with its lack and unfulfillment, or holiness?

> *Student:* I don't want to be preoccupied with my body.

The body has its own needs and they are not all bad. But if they intrude upon holiness then that is a different matter. Have you understood what I am saying?

> *Student:* That I cannot use the body as an excuse not to be with holiness. And that I project a goal which denies my holiness as well.

And all the while we want a true relationship with God. It doesn't mean much, does it?

> *Student:* Today I discovered that my goals were more important than holiness

> itself. I don't know what my holiness is.

Holiness is right relationship with God, to be able to say, "My first love is God." And then in order to have true relationship with God, you live by holiness rather than unfulfillment and lack.

> *Student:* I can see that it's necessary to make God my first love, but I can't say that it is in effect. I still deviate and I don't really understand *why* I deviate.

We deviate out of lack and unfulfillment.

> *Student:* That makes sense to me, but when I sit quiet and I want to be clear, I don't feel clear. And I want to have that clarity. I want this to be in application in my life.

Yes, but the point is that when one sits quiet, so to speak, and *wants* to become clear, the clarity may still not be there. The brain may be less active, and many people mistake a good relaxation for meditation. They think they are hitting nirvana. But we are talking about your state of being in relation to everything that you do. Your very premise is based on insecurity, is it not?

> *Student:* Yes.

Alright. And no one takes that away — the insecurity. Insecurity is consistent. And now we are changing it to the consistency of holiness rather than insecurity. You come to some impeccability, some sense of responsibility, some stability in which nothing else really has much meaning. And therefore, it is the need of your purity, your determination, your integrity, that Life recognizes and then meets. Life helps.

"God is my first love." Can this be the most important thing in life for us — a dedication not merely from the mind but from the heart? If it is not actual but only an ideal, you'll deceive yourself and the deceptions would continue.

You have something of eternal value within you — something joyous inside of you. When you have stepped out of lack and unfulfillment, you are grateful for what is there. It is possible to take the next step of having a true relationship with God. The very reading of the prayer already makes the application of it in your life possible.

> *Help us to accept*
> *our true relationship with You,*
> *in which there are no illusions,*
> *and where none can ever enter.*

All illusions are born out of insecurity, lack, and ingratitude. You may not know what holiness is, but you certainly do know what illusions are, what insecurity is, what lack is. When you have stepped out of insecurity and lack, you are grateful. Gratefulness and lack do not go together.

Why? Because as long as we feel lack and are unfulfilled we are not grateful. And it is impossible then to have a relationship with God. As long as there is lack and unfulfillment, we deviate into illusions. In order to deviate, we use time. If we were not going to deviate, there would be no time. Time exists for us *to deviate*. But we can cut time the minute we see the deviation, that it is not real. This way we would not be using time for the wrong means — as a deviation — but to cut down the deceptions, the illusions.

Time is used for deviation. Time is also used in order to become something other than what you are. And our premise is that what you are is holy, what you are is of God. And therefore, we can't deviate from it. See the illusion of ''becoming'' that uses time and starts the conflict of having to be something other. Therefore it gets caught in the illusion of ideals.

That is how we have lived. That is how you have lived. And now we undertake not to live by deceptive ideals since it has been made clear and it is our conviction. Once having understood it and come to clarity, it will be easier for us to come to the remembrance of it.

> *Student:* I would like to restate this for my own clarification.

Very well.

> *Student:* When I have an image that I need to do something differently or I must never do this again, then I am projecting a different state that I want to be in?

Yes.

> *Student:* And that movement is the creation of time, the delay — I *think* I can improve?

Yes. That approach has invented and projected time which, in reality, does not exist. When I *want* to change, I need time and pursue the ideal. And it can only end in illusion.

> *Student:* Yes, it is basically a deception, a lie to myself any time I accept that pursuing the ideal will bring about a change. My mind will produce those things. . .

When it is insane. Insanity is based on unfulfillment, lack, and "becoming." And it manufactures time and is regulated by thought. It projects time and uses it to be other than what God created you. And therefore, you can't have Holy Relationship with God when you have deviated. Can you, then, no longer be part of insanity?

> *Student:* Yes, but I do have a question. When I get caught up in the confusion and I want to come back to clarity, I find that it becomes an idea.

Can you see that the deviation into thought is an idea? Trying to "find that state" is the idea. The minute you are led by thought or live at the time level of perceptions, *that* I call being insane. It is part of insanity because it is not real. Have you now undertaken not to live that lifestyle of illusion?

> *Student:* Yes. I see that "becoming" is a deviation in itself.

Time is used for "becoming" and this we see is an evasion of *what is*. We don't know *what is* because we are always evading it. Now we can correct the evasion. How simple it is! You may refuse to correct it and say it is arduous, it is difficult, but you can't say it is complex. If it is simple and it is not complex, then know it is something that *you* do to project time and illusions. And because you do it, you can end it also.

You are responsible for what is projected by you or created by you. And whatever you project is insane. When you are irresponsible, you project lack. When you project lack, you are part of insanity. To be responsible, then, means you will have no ambition, no lack, no unfulfillment. Otherwise we cannot possibly have a true relationship with God.

And the Course says very clearly,

Our holiness is Yours.

God is holy and when I no longer deviate into illusions, into insanity, then it is "our holiness" — yours, mine. Everyone is part of the holiness of God. Holiness is the opposite of insanity.

Knowing you are holy as a conviction, you'll be less subject to getting upset. Therefore you use time to bring correction rather than deviation. This does not mean you will not fall back into insanity, but you can correct it. Instead of pursuing ideals, you cut time and make the correction. You no longer use insanity to deviate. The minute you step out of insanity, holiness is there.

Insanity is projection, lack, ideals, unfulfill-ment. Those projections are real to the human brain but they are not real to the Mind of God that He shares with us. The Mind of God we share is holy. The prayer points out:

> *help us to accept*
> *our true relationship with You,*
> *in which there are no illusions,*
> *and where none can ever enter.*
> *Our holiness is Yours.*

What have you understood?

> *Student:* If I have illusions, I am not with the state of holiness.

You may not know what holiness is, but you do know lack, ingratitude, thought, and the use of time — that these are insane. Recognize it as being insane and immediately undo it. Make those corrections in yourself and you will come to that which is a miracle.

The miracle lets you see that the ego is the maker of illusion — the illusion of unfulfillment, the illusion of ingratitude, the illusion of helplessness. They are not real but we give them reality. And now you can refuse to do so because you have understood that we project them and give them reality, but they don't exist. You must observe that what you are doing is what is maintaining them. That is the key. You have received the key: what you project you — *and only you* — can undo. Nobody else can.

> *Student:* Does undoing involve doing something or just observing what is taking place?

The minute you start "doing" you are with insanity again. Any kind of "doing" is part of insanity; it is part of thought that starts from the premise that you have a lack. That is why we said we use time to become different or something other than what we are. For millennia man has been caught in "becoming" and the illusion of self-improvement. The self is not to be improved; it is to be outgrown.

In reality, there is no unfulfillment, there is no insanity. But you and I live according to that. We give it authority. Because *we* give it authority, *we* have to end it!

> *Student:* It all seems clear but what I have found is that it is almost involuntary.

Then you have to catch yourself. When you give authority to insanity, you use thought, don't you? And without thought you couldn't do it. There is no illusion independent of thought.

> *Student:* I want to be free of thought. Perhaps I am making a problem of it.

I would say that your "wanting to be free" is "becoming." Your "wanting to be free" is desire; it has a goal and it has a knowing of what you would *like* to be. You don't know the actuality of that and therefore, it is an illusion.

When you read this prayer, *Forgive us our illusions, Father,* you can understand that thought projects illusions, and without time there is no thought, without thought there is no time. Without thought and without time, there are no illusions. The illusions are, "I am a sinner. I am guilty. I am insecure. I am afraid. I am helpless." Or, "I am a big-shot." And none of these are real. You just have to see unreality as unreality. You don't have to do anything else.

When we use time for becoming something other than what we are, we live by ideas, we live by time and by thought. And we condemn ourselves to a sense of lack, of unfulfillment, and ingratitude.

Again we repeat: SEE this as evasion. When we deviate into thought, into ''becoming,'' we are evading the present moment; we are evading *what is*. We don't know *what is*, but we do know we are evading it. So, see the falseness of that. That's all.

The Lesson of *A Course In Miracles* reads,

> *Peace to my mind.*
> *Let all my thoughts be still.*[3]

To come to *Peace to my mind,* we have to stop evading. If we don't stop evading, we can't say, *Let all my thoughts be still.* Our mind doesn't come to stillness because we want to keep some thoughts. We want to drop many of the thoughts but not *all* of them. And it is quite clearly put:

> *Let all my thoughts be still.*

Find out what impurities, what unfulfillment, what ingratitude, what lack, keeps the thoughts active. Do thoughts not always want something of time? They want to possess or they want to evade. Thought is of time!

Get to know yourself inside out, for without the discovery of ''know thyself,'' you will not know the Lesson, *Peace to my mind.* You can discover that *Peace to my mind* is only an ideal with you. But this is not what you *really* value.

To come to this is to outgrow the world of illusion, of thought, of projection. Then *our true relationship with You* and *our holiness is Yours* become important. You have to find out if God is your first love, or if thought and things of time are your first love.

In actuality, even lack and unfulfillment are ideas because they are only thoughts in time. They do not exist in actuality because thought doesn't have validity, time doesn't have validity. They interfere in the peace. And now you know exactly what to do. Ask yourself: "Why are the thoughts bothering me?" You have to find out and get to know yourself. And you'll get to know what?. . .If God is your first love.

If God is your first love, then you have the right premise. If God is your first love, the minute you catch yourself and see your thought projecting, you'll put an end to it. Either you are in love with insanity or you are in love with God. So then, are you deceiving yourself?

> *Student:* I will be less likely to do so now having been shown the insanity at work by which I live. I'm grateful for it's being so thoroughly presented. It will still come up probably, but I will correct it.

When you do, you will find out that miracles are real. We have always felt the need of time to correct, but that is the old way and leads to illusions. Now you can correct the insanity without the use of time. What do you use?. . .Miracles! Otherwise, you don't need miracles and this is a course in miracles. It offers miracles to the Son to end the insanity. What a blessing upon the Son!

Miracles take place when you start cutting time and undoing insanity — not when you are content and comfortable with your illusions. Application is for the very serious who cannot live in insanity!

Again, we come back to *Peace to my mind.* The word *peace* is essential. We have never given our mind to peace because we have never dropped *all* the thoughts. The flowering of *A Course In Miracles* is peace. We are attempting, in these sessions, to bring you to that peace. They have no other function but that. And if things of the world and of thought — which are of your own making — are still important to you, then know that you love your insanity and not your holiness and peace.

Once having seen this, what would you call change? ''I want to change my life''? ''I want to change my values''? Every ideal we hold merely promotes a change from what we are to what we *should be*. We think we have to ''become,'' to ''do'' in order to make a change. And we have used time to do so. I said, the doing is what continues to prevent us from changing.

So the question still remains: ''What is change?'' Or, ''How do I change?'' Change comes when we end deception and insanity. Then we *are* changed. We are changed because neither time nor thought can affect us. We *are* with the peace of God. And therefore, we drop all our thoughts.

Let all my thoughts be still.

We no longer use thought to become something else. Change that comes from thought is no change at all. ''I am a carpenter. I want to be a mechanic.'' There is no change; self-centeredness is still there. That deception has been seen. When we no longer deceive ourselves by using thought to ''become,'' then there is no thought by which we are regulated.

Change takes place, not by ''becoming,'' but by ending insanity. This is very revolutionary. By not supporting illusions, we end insanity. That is the only thing we can do. Everything else is an illusion that we pursue. Instead of ''pursuing'' the undoing, *Let all my thoughts be still.* There is nothing else for us to do but to undo that which is of time, that which is of thought. Once that is done, a change has taken place. Change occurs in the undoing and *that* is the only change.

> *Student:* I am happy that things are made clear and that I can be responsible. My responsibility is not to accept lack and unfulfillment as real. And if I do, knowing that it is insane, I'll undo it.

There is great joy in that. It is not going *towards* anything. It is stillness that brings about the change. And therefore, your life is no longer a struggle. Who knows what would be born of that stillness! That state could say:

> *God is my life.*
> *I have no life but His.*

> *I was mistaken when I thought I lived apart from God, a separate entity that moved in isolation, unattached, and housed within a body. Now I know my life is God's, I have no other home, and I do not exist apart from Him. He has no Thoughts that are not part of me, and I have none but those which are of Him.* [4]

This Lesson of *A Course In Miracles* describes the state of stillness and peace of: *Peace to my mind. Let all my thoughts be still.* Personality and insanity have come to an end.

The Lesson goes on to say:

> *Our Father, let us see the face of Christ*
> *instead of our mistakes.*

If you could see the Christ in your brother, then you would see the Christ in yourself, for there is only one Son. The brain divides and only sees what is divided and with different names, but the mind does not. The mind only sees that which is of God. It requires some transformation.

> *For we who are Your holy Son are sinless.*

We believe in the insanity of punishment, non-forgiveness, judgment, guilt, and all the rest of it. These are just beliefs. They are not real.

> *We would look upon our sinlessness,*
> *for guilt proclaims*
> *that we are not Your Son.*
> *And we would not forget You longer.*

You are the Son of God. That is your premise. When any lack touches you, you can undo it. When you start from guilt and ''I am a sinner,'' you are preoccupied with correcting that and forgetting God. When you forget God, you have a lack because that is the only thing the brain knows. When you deviate from the remembrance of God into thought, you make time and insanity real.

> *We are lonely here,*
> *and long for Heaven,*
> *where we are at home.*
> *Today we would return.*
> *Our Name is Yours,*
> *and we acknowledge that we are Your Son.*

CHAPTER FIVE

5

WHAT IS ILLUSION?

Forgive us our illusions, Father,
and help us to accept
our true relationship with You,
in which there are no illusions,
and where none can ever enter.
Our holiness is Yours.
What can there be in us that needs forgiveness
when Yours is perfect?
The sleep of forgetfulness is only
the unwillingness to remember
Your forgiveness and Your Love.
Let us not wander into temptation,
for the temptation of the Son of God
is not Your Will.
And let us receive only what you have given,
and accept but this into the minds
which You created and which You love. Amen.[1]

I would like to ask a simple question. What do you think illusion is?

> *Student:* Illusion would be what I think without wanting to include God, without wanting to include the Thought of God.

Yes, that is very nice. What else?

> *Student:* It is thoughts that occur in my mind as something that I want, values I have in life and by which I live.
>
> To me, it is what I make in opposition to God — the concept of myself and my brother and what the world is.

Could we say then that illusion is something opposite to what I am? Shall we start there? Are we in agreement that illusion is the opposite of what I am? So, we will leave God alone for the moment. If you are in agreement with this, then have you now put the opposite away?

If we still value the opposite, then we are deliberately living in illusions as a defiance of truth, of God. What are we going to do about that? It's that simple. But what good is the clarity if we still keep on wanting the opposite? Who is going to stop that?

Can we see that time only comes into existence when we project an opposite? We understand this as an idea, but what good is it if we can't bring it into application? And if this truth is not brought into application, then neither will we be able to apply any other truth. We can go on day after day, year after year, isn't it?

> *Student:* I agree that it is rational, it is direct — that illusions are the opposite of what I am. But I am caught in them.

Then what are you going to do about it? Whatever you do would reveal whether you are serious or not. You see, truth is not truth as long as we go for the opposite. How can we say this prayer, *Forgive us our illusions,* if we have never discovered the illusions and we still live by them? Would we not be hypocritical saying to God, *Forgive us our illusions,* when we don't mean it? *And help us to accept our true relationship with You.* We don't have a true relationship with Him, nor do we *really* want one.

So then, what do we do? We have defined what illusion is. It is wanting the opposite of what is, the opposite of what I am. And we go on that way, don't we?

Can we also see that learning more is another illusion. It doesn't matter whether Jesus were here or Lord Buddha were here or Mr. J. Krishnamurti were here. It is still something that you and I have to do — to stop the illusions. And why is it we are not truly interested in that? How would you answer this question?

> *Student:* When you say ''stop the illusions,'' is it something that I stop, or is it that I stop giving energy to the illusions?

Peace to my mind. Let all my thoughts be still.[2] This means, ''Peace to my mind. Let all my illusions be still.'' You and I have to do something and we can use whichever word we like: stop, drop, still, whatever.

> *Student:* It has to start with me, I see that.

We have learned to go *toward* something. We go

toward illusion, we go *toward* enlightenment, *toward* learning. And going *toward* anything is an illusion because it creates an opposite.

> Student: Would it be safe for me to say, then, that illusions only occur when I go *toward* something?

Yes. But now that you have an understanding of this, what difference does it make?

> Student: It seems clearer but I am not sure what difference it would make.

Of course it is clearer because someone has brought it to that point. Having been brought to your attention, can you do this, *Let all my thoughts be still?* What have you done about the illusions? If you are still in illusion, then what good does this do — the learning, the knowing of illusions? Knowing is an illusion too. What are we going to do? Obviously, we don't want to let go of illusions. And we may even know this and recognize it, but we still can't drop the illusions.

> Student: I may be mistaken but somehow I do feel that I have gained a great deal in having this brought to my attention. I can't say that the tide has totally changed in my life, but it is a more significant change than I recall making at any other point. I don't feel I am regressing. I think this gives me something solid internally that I can count on now; that I can check certain thoughts. I see though that I am probably not even aware of the degree to which I am controlled and blinded by my illusions.

> I obviously must not be aware of the
> larger part of myself that has not
> changed or taken a stand against
> illusions. Is it that another aware-
> ness has to come for me to see what
> you are saying? Or in order to let go
> of the belief that things have
> changed in me?

It is a change within no change. It is a change
within time, which is not change at all. That is the
real illusion.

> *Student:* I don't follow you yet, sir.

You see, there is no in-between. And one of the
illusions that mankind is caught in is that there is
the gradualness. That is like changing at the same
level, so to speak. And that is one of the big
illusions. How many people are meditating,
punishing themselves, seeking, reading, studying
— and probably very few, if any, are not caught in
the illusion that they are *improving,* that they are
getting closer. But that is an illusion.

What difference does it make to you now when
an illusion is made clear? This is a very different
kind of questioning. We have to deal with that
which evades. Anything one will say is going to be
an evasion. And we would justify the evasion by
saying, "This is necessary." But that is another
illusion. What you are really saying is that illusions
are necessary. That is how I hear it.

> *Student:* Are you saying that I believe time is
> necessary, "becoming" is necessary?

Yes. And that is an illusion. But are you going to
stop time or "becoming" or improving? Are we

beginning to see that some of the illusions are obvious, but others are a little more subtle and they are more dangerous, so to speak? They are all illusions nevertheless. But somehow, we do not want to let go. And the world says, ''Don't!'' If you had no illusion, the world would have nothing to give you, nothing that you would want from it.

> *Student:* Sir, in my situation, if I think that I have changed. . .

Is there a situation?

> *Student:* In my mind right now.

Yes, but then you deliberately want to assert illusion. At least you can catch yourself, that what you call ''situation'' is your own images, and therefore, you can cancel them out. When you start cancelling them out, you will have very little left to say. You would have little to say because before pronouncing it, saying it, you would already recognize that it is an illusion.

Our meeting, then, would be very energetic because the attentiveness would be there, your brain would be alert. It would have an intensity of attention. These things are laws.

So then, why are we reading *A Course In Miracles*? As long as we are asserting illusions, we are judgmental and that is not of forgiveness. Forgiveness is free of illusions. And the way things are presently, there is little likelihood of our being free of illusions.

> *Student:* When you speak of the illusions, I see that I don't want to make the same mistakes today that I made

yesterday. I don't want to repeat
that pattern.

That is beautiful. You don't want to repeat the
same mistakes, but how are you going to succeed?
How will you deal with the illusions?

> *Student:* I use thought to think my way out
> and I see that that isn't going to do it.

I don't think there is a mistake in the world that
is not an illusion. The prayer we have been studying in *A Course In Miracles* says something very
beautiful.

> *Our holiness is Yours.*
> *What can there be in us that needs forgiveness*
> *when Yours is perfect?*

How can there be mistakes or illusions where
there is perfection? When we are not part of that
perfection, then there are mistakes or illusions.

> *Student:* And all of the ''doing'' continues
> that?

Certainly. You see, knowing a truth as an idea is
probably necessary to begin with; otherwise one
would be totally lost. And so, one reads sacred
books, scriptures, or goes to see wise people. But
unless one puts the illusions away, that knowing of
truth is of little value. *Knowing* that it is a truth is
still an illusion. But the *reality* of truth has no illusion in it. So, what do we do? How are you going
to solve this issue? You see, a teacher can only
bring you to this point.

> *Student:* Knowing a truth at an idea level is
> beneficial to a certain extent because
> it focuses it and that is very helpful.

It shows you that there is truth but you still deviate. For an individual to come to even that is very difficult. Probably lifetime after lifetime goes by and we don't *hear* a truth. You see, we minimize everything. We don't see that for eons man has been on this plane going through sorrow, pain, suffering, illusions, attachment to this, vengeance for that, and so forth. The disorder continues on and on and on. And seldom have we known happiness. We have known pleasure, certain sensations and thrills, but we have seldom known anything that is not an illusion.

And yet, some part of us yearns for that opportunity. "I wish someone would tell me!" Well, we don't have discrimination and so we get deceived. We hear of Jesus healing the sick and giving sight to the blind and we say, "This is it. He is indeed the Son of God." But still we are not going to drop the illusions.

> *Student:* I see the irresponsibility of staying with illusion. No one can deny that. It is clear that there is no one who can do anything about this but myself — who can make that decision and be willing to drop the illusions. And obviously, I haven't done it. I am seemingly comfortable the way I am. And so the discontent, the passion, the willingness necessary to go toward God and drop the illusions — these things are not there in me.
>
> Just seeing the futility of the illusion, is this enough to generate the passion to know God?

One can suppose all kinds of things, isn't it? May I answer in this way. The teacher says, "I will bring you to the point of seeing truth exists, although it is seen by you as an idea." Therefore, speculation about truth ends. The teacher makes it clear. You know it is so — logically, rationally. He has brought you to that point. It is the only thing the teacher can do — if he is a teacher. No one can do more than that. And you can be grateful for that. Then, observe what *you* are going to do about it. What you do or don't do is the issue, isn't it?

What I am trying to communicate is, that a teacher brings you to the point from where you can't be deceived anymore because you *know*, you have seen it. Now *you* have to do something no matter where you are in the world: whether you are in prison, whether you are in the hospital, on the farm, in an office. It doesn't matter. *You* have to do something about it.

The teacher who would bring one to that point could only do so if the other person has some real interest. It is not possible to come to that point if there is not genuine interest. Also, Life would not make it possible for you to be brought to that point if the potential was not there.

Student: Whether I recognize it or not?

Yes. Rationally, we can see that. So then we have a responsibility. Responsibility and freedom are synonymous. The responsibility could set us free from illusion. Gratefulness could also set us free from illusion. The awareness of these things energizes one. So what is it you feel is lacking in you?

Student: I don't think that I really know gratefulness as you express it. I seem to lack the focus that stays with it. I see some of my tendencies and I experience being uncomfortable when they come into focus. I can get clearer about them but it's as though this meeting, this exchange is what becomes the high point. The rest of the time, the energy or the focus varies and it never comes back to this intensity. I don't know how to generate that energy in myself. I still don't quite bring it to something.

If you understand it in the right spirit, that Life afforded you the opportunities, you would also see the responsibility that goes with it. Would you not respect the Life Action that has brought this to your attention? That kind of awareness of certain facts may bring some vitality into one, some appreciation, and something else could take place. We can't just say, "I'm unwilling. I don't know what to do about my unwillingness." We *have* to do something.

Student: I can see that for me to meditate and try to come to it would not be it either.

Yes, but to say "to meditate" is another illusion. It may not require meditating. You see, we always think it requires this and that — something other. Gratefulness would be for *what is.* Responsibility would also be for something that's there. You are responsible to something that already exists.

Gratefulness does not require time. Strangely enough, neither does responsibility. Irresponsibility requires time. Responsibility does not because responsibility and freedom are synonymous. How then can we continue being irresponsible and not have consequences?

> *Student:* I understand you to say that the responsibility is to being attentive. I admit that the illusions are still there. I'm trying to come to know what you're saying. That's trying to *become* something. Is the solution just simply being attentive to what you're saying and rationally understanding it?

Understanding has some vitality in it, as do gratefulness and appreciation. It's like being lost in the woods and then you recognize something: ''Ah, that's the path!'' Something like that. It energizes one.

> *Student:* Perhaps I take for granted that so much is given. I'm aware that I do and that it's wrong. But it's like something else controls me.

Well, illusions are in control. Irresponsibility is in control. Lack of attention is in control. And then one feels, ''I am a body through and through.''

> *Student:* I feel happy that somehow something is changing internally. My Lesson in *A Course In Miracles* today reads, *I loose the world from all I thought it was.*[3] How appropriate that you would now be helping me to loose that hold that illusions have on me. I know I

> have wallowed in time. There has not been the real fire to step out of it. But I do feel something genuine has been transmitted that makes my life meaningful. It changes something fundamentally.

That's good. The purpose of Life is always to help.

> *Student:* There is a very basic irresponsibility in me that I see the need to change so that it not be there anymore. And that is that I always work things to my own advantage. Sometimes it is deliberate; sometimes it is unconscious, but I see that it rules me.

That's the function of the brain. Your brain is no different than anyone else's. If you could see that — and learn from it — then seeing the consequences of wrong action would awaken you to not doing that again. You would not move from the motive of juggling things to your own advantage. A real change would take place if you could see that. If one does not identify with the brain, then one can learn.

What is the source of our sorrow? What is the source of all sorrow? The source of man's sorrow is that he lives by expedience. Expedience means self-centeredness, what's good for "me." And that's the function of the brain. It works things in its own favor. And then we get better and better and better at it. But there are the inevitable consequences. The consequences are the sorrow. Consequences and sorrow are the same thing. And in this we are caught.

Seeing then that working things in one's own favor is the function of the brain, you won't defend it. Rather than to blame another, you will ask yourself: "What did *I* do that was inconsistent? What is the truth of it beyond the justifications? What did *I* do that brought this consequence about? Otherwise I would not be in this difficulty." Leave the other person alone. It would take care of our working things into our own favor.

If we could really see the way the brain functions, probably we would also hesitate to bring things to our own advantage. The brain doesn't know that the consequences are around the corner. But there is no way that we can avoid the law of consequences and sorrow if we follow the dictates of the brain. We must do something to merit consequences.

If you were not attached to anything, then you could say to the brother, "What would you like?" You would always be at the point of having something to give, isn't it? When you don't have your own vested interest, you are out of it. Could we always be in the position of knowing that whatever we work in our favor is going to be at a price? If we really understood the law of cause and effect, we would be responsible. It *is* possible to live a life free of consequences.

As we have said, we can bring a person to the idea of a truth, but then it has to be applied. Truth, when not applied, turns to poison. There are also consequences for hearing truth and not bringing it into application. A man who hears and lives the truth burns illusions. His life is outside of the realm of cause and effect. No power on the earth can affect him. He affects it. Something so simple and so beautiful and so necessary is what we want to impart — and would you choose to remain lost in yourself? Say to yourself with certainty: "It is gone forever." This has been made possible. Can consequences touch you then? How can unreality come and assume some kind of form before such a person? The strength of those words would dispel it.

> Student: Yes. It is I who keep insecurity alive in me, who keeps reinforcing it.

Alright. So now someone says to you, that is not necessary. *A Course In Miracles* says there is no lack. Then why do you keep it? Can you see how insane thoughts are?

> Student: They go contrary to what is.

Yes. It is an illusion that one gives validity to.

This afternoon an elderly lady came to see me. She has travelled the world and met many people, has spent years in India. Finally she came to her real question. She said, "I am eighty years old and I would like to know about *death*." I said, "I don't know and I don't want to know about it." She asked, "Why?" I said, "Death is a Law. Why do you want to have an opinion about it?" Thought could not touch it. There was nothing more to say.

From here, I would like to share with you Lesson 224 of the *Workbook For Students*. Please listen carefully.

God is my Father, and He loves His Son.[4]

This is a truth — and yet we cannot hear it.

God is my Father, and He loves His Son.

What does this truth do to you? . . . Probably nothing. In *A Course In Miracles,* we have the Thoughts of God given directly to the Son of God. And it speaks directly to *you.* "God is *my* Father." And we say, "I don't know who they are talking about. Surely not me!" Why?

The Lesson begins:

My true Identity is so secure. . .

Now if you think it is secure, do you need to worry about tomorrow? Would you worry about tomorrow unless you had projections and illusions about it? Why would you choose to have an illusion of tomorrow and live in fear today? Can you see the insanity of it?

Let me explain that when we talk about taking illusions away, we are not saying to get rid of your sweater, your car, your house — things you have. We are talking about the psychological illusion of "tomorrow."

My true Identity is so secure,
so lofty, sinless, glorious and great,
wholly beneficent and free from guilt.

Is it not guilt that projects illusions? Each person suffers from guilt because he is doing something that has no meaning in reality; it does not exist. How can you be strong inside if what you do is but an illusion? That is the *sleep of forgetfulness.* Why do you accept it?

. . . and free from guilt,
that Heaven looks to It to give it light.

Where there is light, there is no illusion. The

light is your being attentive. Being attentive has an affect on the brain. This attention is energized by the Mind of God the closer it gets; just as the nearer you are to a fire, the more you feel its heat.

As we become more attentive and interested in anything in a deep way, we are not projecting illusions. And for that one creative moment, an artist would starve. How beautiful it must be to be attentive that way!

It lights the world as well.

The light of Heaven is what you become because you see the illusions as unreal. And to do that, you have to come to attention. Attention in itself is more powerful than the illusions. As you come to light, you begin to light the world where almost everyone is caught in the illusion. And you say, "No, this is not so." In that way, you would start removing illusions. It is a joyous thing and it lights the world as well.

Now, if we are a light — and we must be because the Thought of God says so — then why do we want to evade the light and pursue the illusions? Somewhere *we* make a choice. The choice we make is usually insecurity or pleasure and the consequences for both is sorrow.

It is the gift my Father gave to me;
the one as well I give the world.

You have the gift. The gift must be something that makes you grateful and joyous in the receiving and in the giving. What a glorious life it is then! Something that increases as you give. And it has no limits.

> *There is no gift but This*
> *that can be either given or received.*

It is the gift of that which is Absolute, that which is of God. All that is of God — whether it be light, whether it be forgiveness, or whether it be giving — whatever it is, you receive it and you share it. That is real. Nothing can touch it. And the world needs it as much as you need it.

It is very beautiful if one begins to explore. There is only One Son although at the body level we are divided. And so, you receive the gift and you give it to someone else. But it is only *in your mind* that there is someone else. In reality, there is not ''the other.''

The gift could only be received by someone who is going to share it, who has the purity of wanting to give. And it will only be given to someone who is capable of not projecting ''another.''

For instance, we see this in the animals. When the young ones are born, there is no sense of separation between the mothers and the newborn. Therefore, they protect and they give. Similarly for you who would receive the gift of light and love, the separation has ended. As long as you think there is a ''you'' in one form or another, you have isolated yourself.

All you can do in isolation is to breed illusions, to protect yourself from isolation. Then you think you have a body to hide in. It is rather miserable, isn't it?

> *There is no gift but This*
> *that can be either given or received.*

> *This is reality, and only This.*
> *This is illusion's end.*
> *It is the truth.*

To know this is to know the reality of what forgiveness is, what love is, what loving your neighbor or your self is. Life is One. The brain separates ''you'' from ''me.'' Once we are separated, we think of ourself first; we commercialize life and exploit one another. And we remain caught in the consequences of that illusion.

Why can't we, today, see that Life is One? Why can't we say, ''Well, alright, I know it as an idea but I will try to weed out those instances in which I think the other person is different from me.'' Start from the idea level: ''It is an idea but it makes sense.'' At the physical level, it is an idea. But at the higher level, it is not. If you start living according to the higher level, even though you are at the idea level, are you not closer to that? So, start from the idea level of caring for your brother. Let that be your direction. What do you think the action is in this?

> *Student:* Is this not again moving *towards* something? Is going towards Heaven different than going towards any other direction?

There is a difference here. We have said that man moves *towards* something. And moving ''towards'' requires time, thought, a gap. Therefore, that is the illusion.

When I say to start from the idea that Life is One, that your brother is not separate from you, you will not try to take advantage of another. You

come to some kind of courage and strength in yourself.

> *Student:* But how is this not moving toward
> something?

That's a fundamental question you are asking.
And it's a beautiful question. And you could say:
"You're contradicting yourself." I say there's not
the contradiction at all because in order for you to
consider that your neighbor is not separate — even
as an idea — or in order for you to consider that you
cannot take advantage of your brother — even
though you don't see him as one with you — you
have to come to a moral principle.

The moral principle is that you won't take
advantage of another. I say, that's not moving
towards One Life. That is the elimination of
illusions. It's the illusions that prevent you from
considering your brother as one, isn't it? So, you
are not moving *towards*. You are just not heeding
those illusions. I hope you see this! How subtle and
beautiful it is!

We want to move *towards* goodness and forgiveness and love. But moving *towards* anything, we
have said, is an illusion. It is accepting separation.
Therefore, anything we do from the brain level is
an illusion.

> *Student:* I don't see how the idea of oneness
> doesn't become a belief that I use in
> the same way as moving towards
> forgiveness, or moving towards
> love.

We cannot move towards love without giving
up illusion. So, it's more a giving up of illusion.

Somewhere, then, we have to question that. Am I moving *towards* love? If I am, then it's an ideal. But if I am eliminating illusions that prevent me from giving, then I'm removing illusions.

> *Student:* So, in effect, you are actually moving towards love because you are removing the blocks?

Only in the sense that you are doing something. In reality you are not moving towards love at all. Either you start moving towards love or towards God — and then make of it an ideal — or you see what prevents it, the illusions. *You* make this correction. The correction removes the illusion of the separation, but it's not going anywhere. And this you discover in yourself. No one can give it to you. It is *you*, your own sensitivity, your own awakening that discovers it. Only revelation could discover it in the true sense. There would be the miracles cutting the illusion of time that projects the blocks.

And so, as I said, Life is One in reality. As an idea, it is separate. But make right use of the idea, and you are with the real not, the idea.

> *Student:* The difficulty I am having is in really giving recognition to myself, that I am doing something honest.

Every time you remove a block, you are doing something honest. And don't be afraid to take the credit. Alright? Because a miracle would happen.

> *Student:* That's what I'm seeing, that I don't give credit to that moment, that beauty. It happens and I don't stop to look at it or appreciate it fully. Yet

> I know the brain didn't manufacture it. It was given, and I don't give it the space.

It is possible to come to a sensitivity, to a slower pace. The action is not to pursue and seek, but rather to remove the blocks and know that there is no lack, that it's perfect, that we are blessed. And therefore, whatever we do becomes intrinsic.

> *Student:* I see that I either want to hold on to that moment or I'm too busy to pay much attention to it.

Alright. So then know that if you're preoccupied, you are absent. If you want to hold on to it, you're insecure. And miracles did not bring that about. Miracles would have to undo it.

> *Student:* It is a miracle then that is showing me I'm trying to hold on to it?

Of course. That would be the miracle's first function. But we are going to get busier and busier. We all do that. We get busier because we don't want miracles. We're constantly afraid that a miracle is going to come in. Insecurity would block it automatically. And man is more insecure now than ever in the history of mankind.

And that is why *A Course In Miracles* is given as a gift to all mankind. It doesn't require any belief on your part. It deals with facts. You can depend on it. It's solid; it's rational; it's logical; it's factual. Step-by-step. You can't deny it.

When you start with a fact, you have no illusions; you have no belief; and you don't project. One fact introduces you to another fact. You begin to share the energy of the Oneness. The fact has the vitality to bring you to wholeness. It's a very different way of thinking, so to speak, if we can call it thinking. And that is what one wants to share and impart.

And so, the prayer of this Lesson reads:

> *My Name, O Father, still is known to You. I have forgotten it, and do not know where I am going, who I am, or what it is I do. Remind me, Father, now, for I am weary of the world I see. Reveal what You would have me see instead.*

If you could say this prayer with all your heart, the One Who says, *I am in charge of the process of Atonement,*[5] would be with you. The prayer would have meaning. It is a true prayer. You have forgotten your name; He has not. It is known to Him.

And what is your name? You are not separate from God. How could you have a separate name? How we deny wholeness and holiness! If you are part of the wholeness, could you lack anything? And is the light of your wholeness not needed in a fragmented world that is groping and filled with hate and friction?

Life is One. We are an extension of God and we are to extend what God is.

CHAPTER SIX

6

UNWILLINGNESS
VERSUS
THE CAPACITY TO RECEIVE

*Forgive us our illusions, Father,
and help us to accept
our true relationship with You,
in which there are no illusions.*[1]

What is it in us that does not want
to accept? *And help us to* accept *our true relationship
with You.* We say this is what we want. And yet we
do not deal with that which does not accept.

> *Student:* I see that I am the one who does not
> accept, that this is something *I* must
> do. But it is not clear to me what
> prevents me.

What prevents me from accepting are the illusions that I produce, I project, I follow. We love the
illusions. Yet, *in which there are no illusions* means
that in true relationship there *are* no illusions.

Begin to see the contradictions in our life. We

don't really mean it when we say, *Forgive us our illusions* if we are going to remain with illusions. Can we see, then, that self-knowledge is taking place as we are reading? *A Course In Miracles* is the Thoughts of God and each time we read the lines it has newness to it because True Knowledge is so vast.

> *Student:* If each time I read the Course I get a different understanding, can this not be said to be but my own personal interpretation of it?

Yes, but only until you have gotten to know True Knowledge. Self-discovery will continue in you and you will soon realize that everything we know is but our own interpretations or other people's interpretations. Is there ever a moment in which interpretation is brought to a halt in you, one single moment in which you are free from illusion?

The prayer continues:

> *Our holiness is Yours.*

It is easy for us to accept that HE is holy, but have we ever stopped to think that we are holy too? What effect would that have on each one of us if for the first time in our lives we could identify with being holy? What would that do to us?

> *What can there be in us that needs forgiveness when Yours is perfect.*

Even forgiveness is outgrown because God is perfect. The Course makes it clear that we are already perfect but do not recognize or identify with that perfection. Holiness brings one to that perfection. There is great joy in that. There is completeness in every line of the Course, for True Knowledge is complete in itself. You do not need the next line to complete it. And anything that is of True Knowledge is not the least bit difficult.

> *Student:* True Knowledge remains an abstract term to me.

Let us see. What are the characteristics of True Knowledge? Sri Ramakrishna[2] said that seeing unity is True Knowledge; seeing diversity is ignorance. We only know diversity and ignorance for the most part. Start there. Begin to understand True Knowledge by seeing its different aspects.

For example, what is the difference between a door and a wall? The door has hinges. It can be closed and it becomes the wall. So then I develop discrimination: the wall does not move but there is a part of it now called a door that can move. It has the facility to move. Now I have understood this although I have not become the door nor the wall.

Similarly, we want to understand True Knowledge. The prayer points out, *help us to accept.* If it says "accept," then it is something that is being given. From that we get a clue that True Knowledge is something that is ever giving. Therefore, I do not have to *seek* it.

Do you see the miracle that takes place? In one split second you can become transformed, having understood it is something that's ever giving and you have only to accept it. If you have understood this, then you will never seek. This is a step you take with your own energy. Then have you not already accepted something that has led you to this understanding, that you do not need to seek? What is this energy? This energy has freed you from your illusion that you had to seek it. That I call true understanding. Then True Knowledge has become a part of you.

See the beauty of it. Where are the illusions then? Where are the illusions when somehow you have blundered upon True Knowledge? True Knowledge is, when the Course says, "accept." You do not have to seek. Then you have dissolved the illusions. You have accepted True Knowledge that dissolves illusions. In those lines of the Course is that gift, that boon.

And you say:

> Father, this is Your day.
> It is a day in which
> I would do nothing by myself,
> but hear Your Voice in everything I do;
> requesting only what You offer me,
> accepting only Thoughts You share with me.[3]

Again, it says "accepting." Not seeking. Therefore, anything I seek and want is not it. *Accepting only Thoughts You share with me.* Can we see that whatever I achieve and struggle to gain in some way becomes my bondage?

Requesting only what You offer me. So then, I put the illusions away. That is my only request: to receive what You offer me. *Accepting only Thoughts You share with me.* Whether I request or whether I accept, it would be True Knowledge. True Knowledge is complete, is absolute, is non-dependent. And you find that it is ever present and ever giving. You have to receive it because it is ever giving. Therefore, *we* must receive it. Request; receive. Why don't you want to receive that which removes illusions? You would say, ''We love the illusions. What are you bothering us for?'' Is that not so?

> *Student:* What is given is always there and I'm incapable of receiving it. I still want an activity, something that my brain can take a path of action on. So then, I don't know *how* to receive.

Could that really be true, that you don't know how to receive? You would not be raising that question if someone had not given you the idea that you need to receive. If you heard that, can you say you don't know to receive?

Therefore, receiving requires no effort. Could you see the beauty of it, that to receive requires no effort? Your struggles are over! Don't you feel liberated? Why can't we come to gladness? The minute True Knowledge comes, gratefulness comes.

In receiving, there is no struggle. In seeking, I virtually kill myself. We are like a parrot that has been locked up in a cage all its life and when you open the door it doesn't want to go out.

Why don't we make the discovery that in receiving there are no efforts, no struggles? Why doesn't one allow True Knowledge to touch one? In True Knowledge, there is no limitation, therefore no seeking, no wanting anymore. It is total. It is complete.

And you say, "I want to be free. Never mind True Knowledge." Don't you see? It is like looking for yourself in different rooms. Run upstairs, "Is he there? No? He's not in the bedroom either. Where did he go?" And someone says to you, "You are it. What are you running around for?"

What is the difficulty in seeing? We discovered "accepting" requires no seeking. It is ever there and I must learn to receive. And now we are discovering something else, that in receiving there are no efforts at all.

Student: What do you mean by "efforts"?

Effort comes into being when there is an opposite. And then you want to "get there," so you seek. Effort would never come into being if there was not the opposite. And now we probably think we have to make some efforts to be effortless.

In True Knowledge, there is no effort. True Knowledge always has it to give. Relative knowledge always wants. Why can't we understand that? Has it ever been put any simpler than this?

Student: Wouldn't we automatically receive if we had "the ears to hear"? Is having "the ears to hear" not a prerequisite?

Certainly. But somehow we evade the receiving. If you've heard it, you have it. There would be no effort at all.

Student: It happens right away?

It's right there, don't you see?

So, we come then to that which does not accept,

does not want to receive. I want to deal with that issue. What is the resistance in us that does not want to receive? We don't have "the ears to hear." We see that. But is it a fact that we do not want to receive? This would require self-knowing.

>*Student:* We conclude that we cannot receive.

Yes. And I say, can you prove that to me? I say that's not a fact. But you're not going to find out for yourself if it is a fact or not. You will say, "Well, tell us how it is." And I will. And you still will not discover it. When I tell you, it is still an idea for you. There is something you're refusing to do. Are we seeing that?

So we start once again, if you don't mind, because I have to bring it to that. We have said that True Knowledge is always there. And the Course says, "accept."

>*Requesting only what You offer me,*
>*accepting only Thoughts You share with me.*

>*Help us to accept*
>*our true relationship with You.*

Then we say, "Well, we can't receive it." I said, is that a fact? You are always receiving. Either you are receiving True Knowledge or you are receiving your choice of illusions which denies it. And you are responsible for that. There is never a time when you are not receiving. You are always choosing between having "the ears to hear" or having the illusion.

And it is the illusion that prevents one from receiving True Knowledge. You are receiving the illusion. That's what we have to see. Do you see how swift it is? You *choose* illusion. *You* choose illusion. You cannot convince me that you do not receive, that you don't know to receive. You but make the choice for the wrong thing that you want to receive.

That is a breakthrough if you see it. We make the choice constantly. And the choice is: "I don't know." It always gets down to ignorance — helplessness, helplessness — ignorance. And you believe that. Your trust is in that, that you don't know or you don't know how to receive.

But I say that every time you don't know to receive, you are making a decision. You are passing a verdict over yourself. And the Course says:

> *Be not content with littleness.*
> *. . .there is no form of littleness*
> *that can ever content you.*[4]

If you still want to remain in that dilemma, that's your choice. It is not helplessness. It is a choice, a *deliberate* choice that each person makes because we have free will.

You have to come to knowing the deceptions that take place — in you. Then you can receive True Knowledge. What would it do? It would undo the deceptions. And you could be liberated in a split second, for all life. The miracle turns to revelation. Revelation will turn to transformation. Or, you snuff the light instantly because you listen to the interpretations going on in you. So then one man's knowing has become his bondage.

> *Student:* It becomes very difficult to ask a question when faced with what you're saying, that my knowing is my bondage, because my question is from my knowing. And so I'm left without a question.

Why is it you don't want to receive? Why is it you're so self-convinced? Why do you keep this illusion alive? And you say you don't have a question? On the contrary, you are full of questions.

> *Student:* Yes, I see that.

As long as there is doubt, there is seeking. As long as there is doubt, there is brain activity because doubt does not know peace. So, don't behave so holy that now you don't know what to ask. Somehow we choose to become numb and then we withdraw, we shy away. And we find safety in withdrawal.

Let's use the Course phraseology. The Course says that the ego is afraid and it has its various techniques. And you think there is nothing you can do against it. But I say the ego is at your command. The ego can be undone by the ever-present grace of God or True Knowledge which is there for the asking. And it is effortless.

> *Student:* From what I understand, I hesitate to ask a question because it seems to dissolve itself right there. Yet I see that there is a point from which it becomes illusive, and that is the point where I'm making the decision to evade. Could we explore that point where the decision is made to evade?

Yes, I would love to. I think that is what we need to explore. So, what do you think prevents it?

> *Student:* I am aware that there is a part of me that evades. But I don't seem to be able to grab a hold of it. I always go off into a side track — it's never that point of evasion itself.

We see then that we do not have the capacity to be fully attentive. Without that capacity we cannot still the deception. Without that capacity we cannot receive. If the capacity to be fully attentive were there, that would mean we could take care of the deception. The capacity would only be there when deception is not. Once the capacity is there, the receiving is automatic.

Not having that capacity is the belief of the ego. We prefer to heed the ego's conclusion that ''I don't have the capacity and therefore I am not fully attentive.'' And in that state, we can always deviate.

This swift movement that deceives us and prevents us from coming to the capacity to receive, in this we believe. What vested interest do you have in believing in that? As we are getting closer to the issue, we see that it is not as illusive as we thought it was.

Somewhere there is this inherent unwillingness in man that he has to face. There is an inherent unwillingness in the very thought system of man. Would you agree with that?

> *Student:* Yes, I would.

If the unwillingness was not there, the capacity would be there. And one other thing has been made clear, that we do not have to seek it. We just have to see that we do not receive it.

We do not have to struggle or seek. Are you not glad for that, that you do not have to seek anything? One could have gone on for lifetimes in that deception! Do you think that this moment is the happiest moment of your life, the most blessed instant that has ever taken place since the day you were born, since the day you separated, maybe a billion years ago? Do you consider this moment so precious, that you have heard that you do not have to struggle to receive?

There has to be immense gratefulness. What a gift, that in a few minutes you have dissolved one thing — that you do not have to struggle to achieve anything, that seeking is false and unessential. Then something has happened in your life!

This very energy would then deal with the unwillingness. It is getting into focus. It is no longer vague. We're not by-passing anything. We are dealing with the fact. Can we take that kind of step? It's the gratefulness that will give you the vitality, the capacity. Can you see that?

> *Student:* I thought I had to struggle for every-thing in life — whether it's ambition, whether it's desire, whether it's what I call a need, or whatever I want to do. I'm beginning to see that I have to learn to accept, that it's always there. I have understood this, at least intellectually.

Understanding is only complete — is only True Knowledge — if we have discovered that it is the unwillingness we have to deal with. Self-knowledge is essential. We need know nothing else. We just need to know what the unwillingness is.

> *Student:* What is this unwillingness?

You tell *me* what it is. You want me to tell you and therefore preserve your unwillingness! No one can tell you what it is. You need to discover it. Did we not use the word "self-knowledge"? Each one of us must discover for ourselves what that unwillingness is. *You* have to understand it. That's self-knowledge.

Are you fully interested in the unwillingness? Are you fully interested in understanding, exploring unwillingness?

> *Student:* It seems that my unwillingness always comes back to me, that I want to maintain being "me." It's my identity. And that's one of the things that I feel very strong about not wanting to give up.

Why?

> *Student:* It's like I'd be gone. I'd have no identity. And the closer I get to "me," that is where the evasion seems to come from.

Would you say you have never known what unwillingness is? But now you have discovered that unwillingness is that which ever evades. So then you have a responsibility here, sir. You have a responsibility to not evade.

If you are responsible, there is no unwillingness. Unwillingness does not exist by itself. Unwillingness is a very alive thing that functions. And its function is to evade. If you have understood that it evades, then it is your responsibility *not* to. If you assume the responsibility, then there is no unwillingness. Unwillingness is irresponsibility. Shall we call it by that other name?

> *Student:* I can see that intellectually, but it seems more involuntary than that.

Because you're still evading. Unwillingness always evades. So, we've discovered another fact, that unwillingness is alive in us all the time. If the grace of God is ever-present, then unwillingness is ever-present too. And you have to be responsible.

> *Student:* The Course says that to call on that strength would be the only way that that could be resolved.

Why don't you call upon the strength? Do it right now. Why speculate? You see, it's again an evasion. So, call upon that strength.

> *Student:* I call upon the strength of the Holy Spirit that I may not evade and I may know the truth that there is no evasion in me, for I am God's Son. In Christ's Name.

(pause)

> *Student:* Somewhere I stop a little bit short.

How do you know?

> *Student:* I feel so different but I don't know just what it is.

What if you were not to conclude? Listen carefully. You are going to know that either you are receptive or you are unwilling. Is that simple?

Student: Yes.

The issue is clear?

Student: Yes.

Either you are receptive — and if you are receptive there is no unwillingness — or you are unwilling. One or the other. When you conclude, the unwillingness is there. But what if you did not? Why do you trust your conclusions?

Student: Because I make that voice my self.

Why? Why should one accept the conclusion that is of unwillingness? Conclusion would have to be of unwillingness, isn't it? The other we don't know. But it certainly would not be anything of thought or anything of unwillingness. We settle for the conclusion and maintain the unwillingness.

The minute we conclude, we are no longer attentive. We close up. You have to see that. You make the choice of being attentive or of being unwilling. One does play a part in concluding. Whenever one concludes, whenever one "knows," then it is unwillingness. It refuses to come to innocence.

Wouldn't a man be wise if he was innocent? What purity that must be! And you don't have to achieve it. You just have to stop concluding. Which would you rather have — as a fact, not as a wanting?

Student: The innocence.

Oh no, because then you would have it. What's preventing it? The unwillingness, isn't it? You say you want innocence, but can innocence be something wanted?

Student: I would give up my conclusion.

If you gave up your conclusion, then you would receive innocence. Would you accept it? Would unwillingness allow you to accept it?

I'd like to introduce you to something else. When you and I are this attentive, does anything external exist?

Student: Not really. It doesn't have the hold.

It would free man from the worldly things. That's obvious, isn't it? The more attentive we become, the less meaningful the outside things. And when we are not attentive, we get down to a sublevel. Then we want pleasure. We want domesticity and routine. And we live in a world of illusions.

So, can we start simplifying our life and bringing order in that world? Anything that controls you from the outside, bring order to that. Bring honesty to it.

There is unwillingness at a very subtle level but there is also unwillingness at a pleasure level. Regarding the subtle level, we say we can't handle that. It's too swift. We deviate. I say, ''OK my brother, we won't insist upon that.'' But the other is more tangible. Therefore bring order in your life. Begin to not be attached to this, not be distracted by that. Listen to the words: not attached to this, not distracted by that. Bring order in your life, simplicity, more space, less pressure therefore less worry. Start there — slowly, slowly — and find out what the unwillingnesses are at that level. Those one can deal with.

See that we give energy to insecurity, to pleasure, because we cannot receive what is of God. We have built a world in which we struggle. And in this other world we live in, there are attachments, there are distractions. Could you bring honesty to that world?

There are a number of ways of dealing with this basic issue of unwillingness. Unwillingness is only in relationship to not wanting to accept, not wanting to receive. That is its basic function. This non-acceptance is what unwillingness is. It is the ego's arrogance. What do you think the ego's arrogance is going to do but produce moods and sorrow? Is there suffering in the world independent of the ego?

When that becomes our own self-learning, we can take care of it and we would be less subject to the tyranny of unwillingness. Could we really see that unwillingness is only a stubbornness, an arrogance not to accept grace? If you do not accept grace, you are *unwilling* to accept it, and you will suffer. Nobody else is doing it to you.

Unwillingness prevents us from receiving that which is the grace of God, that which is eternal. Unwillingness thus confines us to the vested interests of the body senses. And whenever we accept that, we also accept the misery that goes with it, the pain. Can we understand, in a basic way, that unwillingness produces the misery? Therefore we have a barometer.

Student: I get so confused.

You get confused when you want to keep unwillingness alive.

Student: Sometimes I feel so miserable.

Well, you have made your unwillingness very strong. Can one really come to the clarity that sees misery, sorrow, and moods are all associated with unwillingness, that pain and unwillingness are inseparable? Don't accept insecurity as real. Don't accept pleasure as real. They are merely deceptions. They're real when we cannot receive that which is always there. We have to start growing that way. Outgrowing things. Then one day we will outgrow deceptions too.

So the wise man first brings order in his life. No attachments, no distractions. He sees, "This hinders me." Then the unwillingness is being undone, step-by-step.

Is that your interest?

Student: If I try to think of how I would do it, it does not seem to work.

You have seen how unwillingness projects insecurity; it projects pleasure that then puts one in a bind. And because one is in a bind, one struggles to achieve. It's all relative. It's all unreal. Seeing this you will end a whole circus of unreality. In the ending of it, you will find your energy and your capacity because you have begun to bring order. And Life would help you in the bringing of the order.

Then accepting has taken place. If you have accepted it, then you have received it. Have you accepted it?. . .

CHAPTER SEVEN

7

THE DECISION
FOR HOLY RELATIONSHIP

We have come to a decision, a commitment, to live by Holy Relationship. But there is no point in taking a vow or making a decision if we don't really know what Holy Relationship means. If it is only a goal and an idea for you, it may give you a sense of status — which is highly revered by most people — but it is more from self-centeredness than it is from inspiration and, therefore, part of special relationship. We are inspired when we see the truth of something, when we see the perfection, the holiness, the naturalness of it. If Holy Relationship is just an idea, then it remains at the idea level and we will have difficulties in bringing the decision to application.

You see, we can agree about things but ''agreeing''doesn't mean that that's what we really want. All through the ages we have made of things just goals and ideals, and therefore, the inner conflict has remained. A wise person would quickly see the contradiction: that we want Holy

Relationship as an ideal — we may even think it's fashionable — but in actuality we don't really want it. As an ideal, we do; as an actuality, we don't. These are some of the discoveries he would make.

And so, the only way that I can know how serious you are about it is from your questions. You should take advantage of this opportunity to find out more about it, to go more deeply into it. I don't doubt your integrity and I don't doubt your sincerity. But there is a lot more that has to be done. It is not just to be wanted. It has to go even beyond understanding. It has to come to something that is realized so that we can finally recognize the truth. And when we do that, only then are we part of that which is timeless.

When we recognize a truth, there is no personality, there is no "you." Separation ends. Truth or Love are Eternal Laws that are indivisible; and we are living at a level where everything is divided. So, there are many questions that can be asked.

Perhaps by now we have discovered that no matter how much anyone teaches — even if the teacher is an authentic one as we have seen in the case of Mr. J. Krishnamurti — it is still up to each one of us. We have sat in his holy presence; we have heard his eternal word; but it doesn't seem to make much difference. It's not possible to listen to someone because we don't have "the ears to hear" what that person is saying. Knowing what is involved in this should be of great interest to you.

We have made the decision to live by Holy Relationship and it is essential that we do. But the fact is that we are caught in the middle — we don't know what Holy Relationship is. This we must realize. At least we can meet this way, without options, really wanting to come to realized words.

> *Student:* What does Holy Relationship involve?

Holy Relationship means that you see your brother as the holy Son of God. That's the fact about him. You may say, "How can I see him as a holy Son of God when he does this wrong, he does that wrong." That is true, but it is true only from your old point of view.

Now that you have made the decision to live by Holy Relationship, you have a totally different kind of responsibility. The responsibility is to undo what you believe. You can no longer believe the other person is this way or that way. The decision is that you will not rely on that as a fact. It is just your opinion and therefore, you can find the strength within yourself to deal with your reactions and cope with your views. Insist to yourself that your opinions cannot be true about your brother. Or, they are true only within your present thought system which is at the level of the body — and nothing that is of the body's thought system is true.

According to the body's thought system, what another does is right or wrong. According to *A Course In Miracles*, it is not. The Course teaches us that we are the Sons of God. It teaches us that,

> *I am not a body. I am free.*
> *For I am still as God created me.*
>
> *I have a function God would have me fill*[2].

Each day's Lesson in the *Workbook For Students* gently demands that every hour, or every half-hour, or every fifteen minutes, that we come to the determination to bring to our remembrance that knowledge of *A Course In Miracles*. We begin to see there is a deliberate action to be taken by the person who is determined to bring *A Course In Miracles* into application.

> *Student:* When the Course says that what another person does is not real, that I can understand mentally. But to come to the vitality that can bring it into application, would it not require an act of active attention all day long so that I can consistently apply that?

You see, we are trained to do things because we want something. Every one of us. I do wonderful calligraphy because I want it to look nice. Everything that the body's thought system knows is, in one way or another, a form of wanting. It is a wanting all the time. Are we seeing that that is the root of it? Our thought system circulates around the wanting. And as a result, we don't have the energy to come to Holy Relationship because we think it is something we have to *want*, and therefore, put energy into it.

> *Student:* That's true. The motivating force for me is that I want it and I try to get it.

Alright. Now please see this very central point. We make a decision to live by Holy Relationship, to live by forgiveness, or to live consistent with the Will of God. Can you see the wanting implied in all that? Then you discover that you can't get a hold of Holy Relationship; you can't get a hold of forgiveness. You would say. ''I want to,'' and then you think the wanting makes you sincere.

A Course In Miracles, on the other hand, does not encourage the wanting. And it is very difficult for us to accept that there is something that exists that requires no wanting. It would bring about a revolution in you, a total transformation, just to know there is another way that has nothing to do with wanting. Do you know anyone who has gone into this deeply — that the problem lies at the level of wanting? How can you want what already is? You may see this for a moment, but that doesn't mean you are going to put your wanting away.

The ancient sages said that one must come to detachment and renunciation. What they were to renounce was more than objects, pleasurable relationships, certain sensations, feelings. What were they detached about? What wantings did they put aside?

You may be saying to yourself: ''If they had to put wantings aside, I wouldn't want to be in their place.'' Would this approach not start more conflict in you? It would start suppression on one side and wanting on the other. This I want; that I don't want. There will always be an opposite. And each opposite somewhere is a wanting.

Wanting is the central issue then. That we have to understand. It is *the* common factor, whether you want God or whether you want gold. The goal may be different but the wanting is the same.

We come back again to the fact that our whole thought system is built on wanting. What, then, does it involve not to want? What would it be like not to want — to be innocent, innocent of all wanting? What purity that would be! Would you have a problem? Could you have a problem if you did not want anything? Does innocence have a problem?

A Course In Miracles is an entirely different thought system. Now I can say this and you could feel good about it, but unless you come to gratefulness for what the Course offers, you will not take the next step. The next step is to see that *A Course In Miracles* cannot be based on wanting because if you came to it through a wanting, you would be conceited. You would believe you had come to it through *your* achievement.

We have to make these discoveries. You would be thrilled — freeing yourself from all the illusions and the insecurities and the unfulfillment. One moment in which you have realized the truth would undo all your unfulfillment. That one split second of innocence would be like nothing you have ever experienced before in your life! It would be a contact with eternity, a freedom from wanting. You couldn't want it because wanting evades it.

Similarly, you cannot *want* Holy Relationship. If you do, you have turned it into special relationship — instantly.

> *Student:* Why is that? Is it because it would then be self-centered?

Yes. Then you are trying to conform to an authority you have imposed upon yourself — a juicier wanting.

> *Student:* Something to add to the ego's image?

Yes.

A Course In Miracles revolutionizes one's life. It does not allow you to do anything that is of past concepts or ideas because these have failed. How can you, hearing this, still go on wanting your old concepts? Is it not important to you to renew yourself? Perhaps you don't feel the need because the means of renewing yourself is again a wanting. You would be using the same thought system based on wanting.

Why can't we discover these deceptions? If you did, you would touch upon an energy that you never knew before. And it would come to you unasked. It does not come to you through wanting.

> *Student:* I have observed that the wantings come because I believe so deeply and firmly in a sense of lack. My Course Lesson today is, *Light and joy and peace abide in me.*[3] I stay with the Lesson but somehow the belief in the lack in myself is so much stronger that I can't come to what the Lesson is saying.

That's what your belief tells you.

> *Student:* But I don't know how to shift the belief.

You don't need to know anything else. Please listen to what I am saying. We want the opposite. Is this getting established? I say, the want for the opposite is identical; it just has a different name. You have given names to feelings, objects, abstract thought. Can you want something that has no name? Are names not manufactured by your thought? The opposite has an opposite name, doesn't it? What difference does it make? It's just a shift from this name to that name. And right now we don't even know what special relationship is and what Holy Relationship is.

What do you think the opposite of special relationship is? Holy Relationship is *not* the opposite of special relationship. Holy Relationship is not the opposite of special relationship because it has no wanting in it. You cannot reach it and touch upon it through a wanting.

So, what would you say Holy Relationship is that is not the opposite of special relationship? Are we beginning to see in a very simple, friendly way that that which does not have an opposite must be whole because it cannot possibly have conflict? And therefore, if it doesn't have conflict, neither could it have a wanting. Could you just see the beauty of this? It doesn't have an opposite, therefore it doesn't have a wanting in it.

Could we then see that we cannot "get to it" because then we would be making of it an opposite? That's an obvious wanting. That's quite clear. It also becomes clear that wanting is the only thing we've ever known. From childhood we have been told by parents, education, religion, social culture, that we have to do something to "get it," and the wantings are strengthened. Yet wanting is a total denial of truth, of God; a total denial of love, of anything that is not of time. Why don't we see this?

You would again say, "I don't want to." And then you would say, "I want to." I said, but they are both the same. You have been telling lies to yourself. One day you make one wanting a little more prominent; the next day, it's a different wanting. But you're back still with the wanting. No shift has taken place. The wanting hasn't changed.

A Course In Miracles points out that there is nothing to want. There is nothing to want but you and I have become victims of wanting. That's the only thing our brain knows. It knows fear, insecurity, animosity, danger, jealousy. Why don't we want to see this? We have been provided with a step-by-step curriculum which is Divine and holy and has other blessings upon it. And we still adamantly want to deny that? Have you ever thought about it, that in this New World, *A Course In Miracles* would be given? Has it ever occurred to you? It's beyond the reach of imagination. Nothing like it has ever happened and we want to reduce it to our wantings?

Have we ever given thanks for the action of God's Plan for Salvation? Out of your gratefulness, rather than your wanting, would be born a different thought system, one that doesn't want anymore. It's just grateful for the given — the given breath, the given daylight.

> *Student:* I can't respond to the questions you have asked but there is something I have been pondering that relates to wanting. It is said that *A Course In Miracles* came into being as a result of two people coming together who felt, after being disillusioned, there must be a better way. How is that not a

> wanting? What is that energy they brought that apparently is not a wanting?[1]

Well, what do you think? What is the fact of it? Just start simply. They saw the fact that they weren't getting along and felt there must be some other way. And that other way they didn't know. Whenever *we* want something we know it, we have a name for it — the name of a feeling, of an emotion, of an object. They did not. That's how simple it is.

"There must be another way." But they didn't say, "We'd better read this or that or so forth." *There must be another way* didn't have any wanting, any name in it except the statement of a fact. And this they dealt with.

Have you ever dealt with any situation in your life and seen only the fact of it? Did you see there was no blame in what they did? When you can't blame, you can't want. Then you have opened yourself. And that takes a lot of energy — in the true sense.

> *Student:* Everything seems to come from my knowing. Knowing is what projects the wanting because I know I have to do this.

You have a name for what you want. We have said that our thought system is based on wanting. Wanting always has a name. Alright, then don't believe in that name. In actuality, there are no names. There are only names given by wantings.

> *Student:* You have brought it to my attention but I still keep coming from my knowing. It still perpetuates. I

hesitate to say anything because I know that even this is a wanting.

Oh yes. Please listen. If you step back and say, "This is all from my wantings," that's a wanting too.

Student: How is that a wanting?

Because "to step back" has a name. "Stepping back" is not without a name. It's not innocent; it has its own activity. Is there anything that has a name that doesn't have an activity? So, are you stepping back then?

Student: No.

Alright, then why don't you find out that "stepping back" is still an activity and you're caught in it. If you were earnest, you would.

So, "stepping back" has a name and it's an activity. Therefore, it's a wanting.

Student: It doesn't seem so much like a wanting.

Of course, but it is.

Student: By definition it would have to be.

It is. That's a fact. The fact has the energy, but it's not a wanting. So then find out: What is the action of the fact? Because that's what *A Course In Miracles* is. It is the action of the fact — the fact of being free from wanting. That's a miraculous thing! Miraculous. And you still want me to give you a name?

The fact *is* the energy. It is the energy that is not of thought. Activity, wanting, stepping back — all these have names and goals and pursuits. Therefore we can say, as a fact, that that is the energy of thought. The energy of thought is all we've ever known for the most part. And with that energy we usually want something.

So then, we have said there is the energy of the fact that we have seldom, if ever, known and it has no wanting in it, but it has an action. What would its action be?

> *Student:* For it not to have a name it would have to be an action.

Do you know the action?

> *Student:* I don't know the action but I can see that far.

Yes. So you see, the energy we know is the energy of thought. We can also say it is the energy of the body because it mainly functions through the body's senses — to procreate, to defend itself, to sustain itself. Then we can also say it is strictly special. Can we see that special relationship is strictly personal?

> *Student:* Yes, very much.

And therefore it is personal because it is divided, separated. There is division. As long as we do not have the energy of the fact, we will never know what Holy Relationship is because in Holy Relationship there is no opposite.

> *Student:* It will remain the energy of thought?

Yes. Special energy is the energy of thought. Holy Relationship has nothing to do with thought. It is the energy of fact, or the energy of truth

— whatever you would like to call it. These are just names. I would like us to come to the actuality of this.

> Student: To ask what is the energy of truth is again asking for another name. The answer could only be the action or the state itself, is it not?

I only hear special relationship speaking, wasting thought energy. It detests innocence. It hates stillness. It is an enemy of a fact, a constant evasion.

We do not know what Holy Relationship is. That's a fact?

> Student: Yes.

But we do know that we do evade Holy Relationship. We evade by confining ourselves to special relationship. It is *you* who evades the Holy Relationship even if you don't know what it is. Why?

I am saying there is something you are doing. For that you are responsible. See the beauty of it. It's not something you don't know or something that is outside of your scope, outside of you. It is activated by you and therefore, you are responsible.

We can put aside Holy Relationship for the moment because that is not in the realm of wanting. That's clear. Then why do you maintain special relationship? Why do you constantly sustain it when you see that it is limited?

> Student: It has been said before that if we see something clearly, then that is an action in itself. So, somewhere I must not see it or I see it partially.

You may not want to see it. Seeing it clearly is the seeing of the fact. The seeing of the fact has no contradiction, no duality in it. Therefore the energy of the fact is superior. Would we say that? Then are we evading the fact? And if we keep on evading it, then in that isolation from one another, which is the maintaining of special relationships, we create a civilization of hate, fear, and the efficiency of selfishness. We then — you and I — are promoters of insanity. We cannot remain indifferent about this.

> *Student:* No one wants to remain with insanity.

We don't like insanity but we are promoting it. And because we are promoting it, we can end it also. It is an internal issue. Helplessness, lack, and all the rest of it have no meaning if you want to end it. It is when you don't *really* want to end it that you become helpless. You say, "It's a lack. I am unfulfilled." Or, "I don't know what to do." And I say, you need not know. It is your knowing that is your bondage. So why look for a "how" or another knowing? This is how we have deceived ourselves and continue to deceive ourselves.

> *Student:* I would have to come to a point of seeing the futility of living the way I am living.

But does one ever see? The very phraseology of wanting to come to it is to be questioned.

> *Student:* I have an image in my mind that certain things are necessary.

Alright. I say, question that image.

> *Student:* I don't see how it is possible not to have that?

Please see that the energy of the fact, the energy of truth, does not enter into the realm of thought. We want to first have an image and then fuss about it, try to examine it, understand it — all of that. I see you have gone astray.

> *Student:* When I am asked the question, ''Why is it I can go on and on deceiving myself?'' I begin to wonder about that myself.

What is it you really wondered? Let's wonder now, together, for a minute.

> *Student:* The first thing that occurs to me is that I am not wholehearted.

Why? As two friends, you and I, why are you not wholehearted?

> *Student:* First I see there is a certain amount of laziness in what I do every day. That takes some of the energy away. And I am sure I only see that partially, too. As I spend more time thinking about it, I can see many more areas that it involves. It's as if there's always more to the picture but I stop short and see only a couple of areas.

Yes, but don't you know that thought cannot see more than thought? It will add more names; it will get more complex. What would be the right use of this horizontal thought, the body thought? We are not totally eliminating the body thoughts. Shall we say that? But what would be the right use of the energy of thought that we know? Start with the known. What would happen if we made right use of it?

> *Student:* One thing that seems fairly obvious is that you would have more energy because you wouldn't waste so much.

Yes. Now let's continue to observe like you have just done. You would have more energy. Why? Having more energy, what would that mean? What would it do?

> *Student:* I probably would not get so caught up in the endless chatter of my thoughts.

You would not pay heed to them. You would not even care whether they are there or not. That's good. Could we say, then, that seriousness is having more energy?

> *Student:* Or responsibility, is that it?

Yes. Then what would you discover next?

> *Student:* If you had more energy when you were more responsible, you would discover that the thought and the energy must be the same. And therefore, the less thought you use, the more energy you would have.

Yes. What is the effect of that energy then?

> *Student:* It should be an accumulative process in the sense that the more energy you have, the more thought you could do away with.

Right. So, the more energy, the less the thought, the wider the gaps between the thoughts. The right use of the energy then slows down the thought. That's a fact. Once the thought is made slower, then what is the quality of that thought?

> *Student:* It's not so scattered. It gets more
> into focus. The energy is purer.

And that is a process one would go through to
meditation. Would you agree, then, that it's very
essential to have those periods of quiet during the
day and at night? Thought is stimulated in a world
of pressures. Do you know how much energy one
single desire burns? Do you realize how much
pressure one single desire produces in the brain? It
makes us insane. Can you conceive of a brain that's
not the least pressured by any desire? That would
be innocence!

So, are we seeing that the right use of the
energy of thought slows down the thought and
then introduces something else most of us have
never known before. And what is that?

> *Student:* That you don't have to do anything.

Yes. It gives you a gift of awareness rather than
thought. First, thought became slow; now it
becomes subordinate. This is inner awakening.
And it is possible for every person. If it is authentic,
you would know it. What would you know? You
would discover that you are no longer interested in
the things that have names, that distract you from
it. The wisdom would be there to see that what
distracts you is unessential. It is false.

The awareness would bring about an inner
correction. Then all you do is correct. Or rather, the
energy of the fact corrects. It corrects all of the illusions, all the concepts, all the fears, all the
knowings of thought. It cleanses itself and you're
not *doing* anything, so to speak. And then you, as a
human being no longer standing in darkness, can

share with the world something that is not of the energy of thought.

So then we read:

I have a function God would have me fill.[5]

You begin to see the truth of it. In a world where man stands in darkness, the function would be independent and it would bring something that is not of the energy of thought. And what would that energy do? It would help bring the brother to the fact so that he too is introduced to his awareness. That's what *A Course In Miracles* imparts.

A teacher of *A Course In Miracles* then is one who has seen the limitation of thought energy and its frictions. He slows down the thought and comes to the energy of awareness that is of stillness. It witnesses but is not affected by anything external. Somewhere he has discovered that thought itself is external because it relates only with external things. These things no longer have a hold on him.

Awareness is independent of the external. To awareness, thought is external. When a man sees thought as external, then he must be with *what is.* He would have great appreciation for *A Course In Miracles* because it is based on fact, not on belief. It doesn't teach; it corrects. Each Lesson of the Course imparts the awareness that corrects.

> *Student:* Somewhere in my mind, there is a holding on to the validity of thought and I don't really take that step. I am not free of that holding on.

Let us say that thought, no matter what it tells you or makes you feel, is the one thing that you have to correct. In fact, it is the *only* thing you have to correct. If you're interested in correcting, would you be interested in believing anything other? Would correction ever let you believe anything you say to yourself?

Student: Not if correction is the intent.

Let us stay with what we know so far. We have seen that the energy is there to be responsible, to have discrimination, to make right use of thought. We have never known those potentials. And in the end, thought is going to try to limit it somehow. No need to.

A Course In Miracles points out something wonderful. It says if you can't get past that last step, then you need to learn. And you have to teach in order to learn. And that brings one to relationship rather than to isolation. See the wisdom of it, the compassion of it! It leaves one breathless. One would get so inspired! The perfection of it!

So then, you would make right use of the energy and come to Holy Relationship. The correction takes place of the thought energy that lives by special relationship, personal relationship. The energy undoes that and relates you with the brother through Holy Relationship.

Student: So then, what is Holy Relationship?

It is a state of peace in which you don't want anything.

I will not value what is valueless.[6]

All that we now know values what is of

thought. In Holy Relationship, what is of thought has lost its meaning. Whenever thought comes up, the correction can take place. Then one is in relationship. Not till one is with Holy Relationship does one know what relationship is; that it is within the One. Holy Relationship exists when you'd rather give than to have. This transformation takes place involuntarily in oneself. It takes place in you without your knowing. It has enormous energy. It's main energy is that it gives rather than wants. What a transformation this would be — of having to give! These are not just ideas. What an opportunity!

Student: I can see that would be liberation.

Yes, what a joy to be liberated from all that one knows. When one is aware, he is aware of the intrusions of the past upon the present and the energy of the present undoes that. He sees that thought maintains special relationships, while the energy of the present maintains Holy Relationship. ''I am interested in you because I love to give.'' ''LOVE YE ONE ANOTHER'' becomes a reality, a fact. Can you imagine anything more joyous, more sane, more pure?

And yet there is no wanting in it at all. Because it receives, it gives. And the more it gives, the more it receives. You can't even call it ''receive'' or ''give.'' It's independent of thought. It is an energy that invokes in a person discrimination between the real and the false. That energy has to come first. You become responsible for what you say, what you believe, what you think, because somewhere you know it's all of thought and therefore it's not real.

This sense of responsibility recognizes what is of thought. *It* can say, "Thought is not real. If it's my opinion, my opinion is also unreal." It can go even further and see that *that* opinion is not real.

In the slowing down of the thought process, a discrimination is born. You become more and more energized because the energy is not being dissipated. You have acquired a discrimination by knowing that thought is useless. "This is just a habit; this is just a tendency." You're becoming wiser because you are getting to know yourself. And nobody else can do it for you. Then, you would value sitting quiet in the morning and evening.

> *Student:* What helps me to initiate that, to maintain that?

Sanity. Seeing the insanity is sanity. And you say, "That's what has always made me mediocre."

> *Student:* Wanting to sit quiet to get there would not do it either.

No. I said, become aware. When you sit quiet, you sit quiet to be aware of what's going on in you. You develop discrimination. The more discrimination you have, the more you will undo the thought, isn't it? It's quite obvious. The more discrimination, the less power the thought has. And out of this conservation of energy, you awaken something else in you.

If the person is serious, then there are certain things he has to do. He has to make a right living; he has to conserve his sexual energy; he has to eat the right food; he has to establish a rhythm which is consistent with this awakening.

> *Student:* What would bring in that serious-
> ness? Is it in staying with it that one
> becomes more and more serious?

The seriousness will come into being as you begin to see the false as the false. You will not want anything anymore. You will begin to see how it makes a mockery of you, leading you astray here, there. And now you say "no" to it. Non-cooperation with that which dissipates is a stand of sanity in the midst of insanity. And we must take that step.

> *Student:* This seems to imply time.

Please see this. In order to keep the thought energy going, you eat three meals a day. Only your thought is alive while this other part of you is like dead — thought is alive but there is no real *you*. Why do you want to support the thought and not wake up? When you sit quiet, *you* are coming to life. Thought becomes dead and you come to life.

> *Student:* What is the image then?

Look how simple it is. Any question that arises out of collective consciousness is not a question at all. As long as you are part of collective consciousness, there is no "you." There is just a name. It can be Richard, John, Frank — whatever. In order to find out who you are other than collective consciousness, it would be better for you to sit quiet for a while. You have been a slave for too long. And now you need the Moses who is inside of you to set you free.

> *Student:* I have been sitting quiet and I try to
> do this, but it seems very slow.

Well, is thought faster?

> *Student:* No, it doesn't work either.

Please wait a minute. You say it is slow. Is the thought faster? Could thought do anything? Sitting quiet may be slow, but the other doesn't move at all.

You see, we are undisciplined people. Insanity is undisciplined. It can't make right use of the energy. And it is your responsibility and my responsibility to make right use of the energy that thought dissipates. No one else can do it. It's not good enough to say, "When I sit, I'm not quiet." Or, "These thoughts bother me," and so forth. Then admit you are not serious. Are you going to be defeated?

Right now you are just an echo of the collective. Can you see that?

> *Student:* Yes.

Doesn't that bother you?

> *Student:* It bothers me more now, but other times it doesn't bother me very much.

When one is lost, it doesn't. That's why we need to do things that have honesty and give expression to something other within us. The whole lifestyle has to change, isn't it? But it *is* possible.

We have to trust. We have to trust in awareness. We need to question thought and learn to correct it within us with the discrimination that sees what is unessential. Don't give it the energy. Slowly, slowly, and you will see what will happen.

I would like to go just a little further into something very much related to our relationship with *A*

Course In Miracles. The knowledge of *A Course In Miracles* is of ultimate laws, or Absolute Laws. We don't know what Absolute Laws are. And so, we don't really know what the Course is saying.

The Course is a different thought system. When we bring it down to the level of the body's thought system, we cannot know what the Course is saying. Then *we* have to do something about it. You can't hear these words and then read the Course the same way. It is of Absolute Knowledge; we can't interpret it. The minute we interpret it, it becomes body knowledge.

So, we are getting down to some key things. Let's forget about the learning; let's begin with correction. Correction is made possible by awareness, by attention. What is of collective consciousness is learned and trained and computerized. And we see that that's not it.

The True Knowledge of *A Course In Miracles* is of Absolute Laws while other knowledge — which is of the relative plane — is not direct, but of interpretations. Now, we don't know what the Absolute Knowledge is, but we do know that our knowledge is that of interpretations. We interpret and then we think we know and claim we understand. What we think we know and claim to understand is of interpretation. It's not True Knowledge. Can we undo that and see that it's only interpretation? That's our responsibility.

Then we can also say that what is of interpretation always has an opposite. We are with special relationship and we take on to live by Holy Relationship; but we don't know what Holy Relationship is because it is of True Knowledge. So then, find out what interpretation has led you to take this on? Find out what your motivations are. Is it a wanting?

You will soon discover that we cannot possibly be true to ourselves as long as we live by interpretation, as long as we think we know, as long as we claim to understand. That is the deception that needs to be undone.When we undertake to live by Holy Relationship, we undertake to undo that which has an opposite, that which is relative, that which is an interpretation.

We don't know Holy Relationship but we do know personal relationship — our preferences, our likes, our dislikes. We can certainly know that. Would you then not value *A Course In Miracles* that provides the help? Come to some gratefulness. Be glad that the help is given and cooperate with it.

So then, once again, we see that while our knowledge is of the relative plane it is not direct but of interpretations. Thus we think we know and claim to understand something that we don't, in truth.

True Knowledge, having no opposite, would be application, wouldn't it? Application means there is no opposite. Then that is True Knowledge. We don't yet know what that is, but we do know the relative and we will not let it take over. So you take a stand against that which you can undo. You take a stand to correct it whenever it regulates you. There is nothing to want in that — but there is a responsibility. And a joyous one.

Our thought system itself is inadequate to know Absolute Knowledge because it has and refers to names. Relative knowledge is made up of names it has given to objects, to ideas, to feelings. That's the only knowledge it has of the external world, so to speak. Therefore, it is limited to the five senses. It is not related to that which is eternal, to the Absolute. And as long as we are preoccupied with this, we are evading that which is Absolute.

This knowledge of names is abstract thought. It is not direct. It is something we are conditioned by. You smoke, you light the cigarette. First you hated it, then you develop the habit, and now it controls you. We are programmed that way too. We must see the necessity of undoing because responsibility demands it.

Deception has to be seen the instant it occurs for correction to take place. If we don't see it the instant it occurs, we will make an idea of it and then we're back with the relative knowledge of time. The action of awareness is instantaneous. If you say, "I want to think about it," or, "I'm no good," you have gone astray again. Don't wallow in it; you'll keep yourself busier than before. Stop right then and see: "Look! I am back again with the thought dissipating the energy, and all I want is to change my opinion." The changing of opinion has no transformation, no truth in it. It is still of the same relative plane.

So, can we take things on that way? Obviously, it would have to be an instantaneous and incorruptible action independent of the body thought. When you *see* it — that you are back again in the relative — that seeing has the power to end it. And there is no wanting in it. It is instantaneous. It just is. It comes if you are there to receive.

CHAPTER EIGHT

8

"TRUTH WILL CORRECT ALL ERRORS IN MY MIND"

How simple things are. Very simple. Very direct. And yet we can't seem to understand.

Could we just consider for a moment: without *A Course In Miracles* would we know where to turn? Every single way we turn would lead to belief, wouldn't it? We believe in sin; we believe in guilt; and we will probably never know there is something beyond relative knowledge. Isn't that simple? Is that debatable? No matter which way you turn, hardly anyone knows anything other than belief.

With *A Course In Miracles*, what *not* to do becomes absolutely clear. Is one grateful for that? How grateful can you be that in this lifetime *A Course In Miracles* is given, or at least, that you and I are born at the time when it comes?

Somewhere in each person, no matter where he is in the world, the questions arise: "Who am I?" "Is there a God?" "Is there something more?"

We see this in primitive man. He thought it was in the thunder, in the lightening, in the rain. Some worshipped the sun; others, fire or water, the rivers. Others have put their faith and belief in someone who had the gift of medicine or in someone who had clairvoyance — the supernatural. And they followed him. Throughout the centuries, man has worshipped.

And now we see that it has all been based on a belief that we need to improve ourselves. That was the lot of man before *A Course In Miracles* came. And still one is not elated?

Can you say, "I would have never known! I would have deceived myself. Everywhere I turn I would have been deceived. A guru would deceive me; a professor would deceive me; a university would deceive me. No matter which way!"

Then why isn't one feeling: "I'm almost liberated by knowing that *that's* not it!" Why isn't one grateful for that? We usually start from the premise of our being inadequate, of our being nothing, that we've got to do something and then we can "get there." And in that deception of seeking, one goes on and on projecting, trying to arrive. People have punished themselves trying to meditate endlessly. Some people stare at the sun and blind themselves; others sit on boards of nails trying to find God.

We are so blessed that finally something is given that is not a belief. Don't you see? That now you can't be deceived anymore by anything outside of you. Nobody could take you over. Isn't that something, that a man walks the earth who can't be deceived? That is better than any education you could get anywhere! Why isn't there a kind of gladness inside to know that you need not be deceived by anything your brain, or anyone else's brain, tells you to do. You won't go for, "This is going to do it!" anymore. It's simple. Clear. It's like having the eyes to see and therefore, you never fall into the pit. That kind of sight has been given.

We see there is only one issue and the issue is internal. It's in me. It's in you. I can't do it for you, and you can't do it for me because the issue is not external. We thought that by doing this or doing that we would get it, and now we know none of that works. We but deceive ourselves. It's an internal issue. It's an internal step.

Then we see there is unwillingness in us — that as bad as the deceptions may be, we still prefer them to truth. We know they are not real but somehow we are so conditioned we don't want to face ourselves. Unwillingness is going to say, "I'm not ready yet. I still like the external." Isn't that the problem? Do you see how simple it is?

A Course In Miracles tells you: "Nothing is outside of you. You are perfect. You don't have to undermine yourself. You don't have to call yourself a sinner, that you're wicked and no good. You can say you are all those things but they are not real. You'll just get frustrated and blame yourself or blame somebody else; and you will be unhappy most of the time. Why? Why do you love sorrow?" *A Course In Miracles* says:

Truth will correct all errors in my mind.[1]

Isn't this what we are talking about? If it is

truth, isn't it already correcting something — that you can't be deceived externally anymore? The key is in your own hand. *A Course In Miracles* **is** the Thoughts of God and it bypasses everything: the clergy, the gurus, the psychics. It is given directly to *you*.

You may think, "Well, how am I going to come to clarity?" And the Course says,

> *If it helps you,*
> *think of me holding your hand*
> *and leading you.*
> *And I assure you*
> *this will be no idle fantasy.* [2]

Or,

> *I will be healed*
> *as I let Him teach me to heal.* [3]

When you read this, He is already there with you. He is with you. The key is given you. You say, "Well, the key is there but I don't know how to open the door." And He comfortingly says, "Look, I'll hold your hand."

Somewhere we have to be willing to *be healed as I let Him teach me to heal.* The issue is: we don't *want* to be healed. Listen to the arrogance of the ego — the arrogance of unwillingness! We would rather be unwilling and sad than be grateful and happy. Gratefulness is difficult for us and sorrow is natural. That's insanity! It prefers destruction rather than life. It prefers lies and deception rather than truth. And you and I have to correct its insanity.

Could you begin to see that a large part of the

errors have already been corrected with the blessing of the Course? You can't be so easily deceived; nobody can sell you some belief system. You are free, totally liberated because the external won't distract you. You know the issue is in *you*. And something direct has been *given* you — the light of truth in the words of the Course communicates directly with you. Wouldn't you give thanks to God for that? Wouldn't you give thanks for this one truth? At least it is put into right perspective.

> *Student:* As I hear you speak, I'm aware there is such resistance, such unwillingness in me.

Very well, then leave that as a fact. You don't have "the ears to hear"; you're unwilling; you don't want to be healed.

> *Student:* But I thought I did.

Alright. So then the next time you think about something else, you'd better not trust that either. Then are you not being healed? Did you get that? How swift it is!

The next time your thought comes in, you say: "Listen, I can't trust thought." What has happened? . . . You have brought your mind to silence because you question relative thought. That's all. You're not seeking anymore. There is no more seeking in it. Something has happened, that now you question. This questioning brings an awareness, a light you did not know before.

Truth will correct all errors in my mind.

The Course is not talking about plans, other people, or big things. The errors are in your mind and that is where they need to be corrected. You don't need more learning because that will merely confuse you again. Can you imagine, *A Course In Miracles* puts an end to learning!

> *Truth will correct all errors in my mind.*
> *What can correct illusions but the truth?*

That's true, too. Only truth can correct illusion. We are in illusion and truth corrects it. What is difficult about that?

> *And what are errors but illusions*
> *that remain unrecognized for what they are?*[4]

But you can recognize them any time; you can see what the motive is behind them. The very fact that an error is made means there is some motivation. And you can undo it by questioning it. A miracle takes place in the undoing. This is, after all, a course in miracles.

> *Student:* I have never really understood what the Course means by a miracle.

A miracle is a moment in which you touch upon that which is eternal, that which is of love, or that which is God-created. That contact takes place independent of your thought process, or of the thought process of man. What we call a miracle is a contact with your Creator, with the Timeless, with that which is of certainty. And *that* insight is independent.

> *Student:* Are you saying that insight is the same as a miracle?

You can replace the name: miracle or insight. Either way, it undoes all that is external.

> *Student:* Does it undo the external by changing
> one's awareness or by changing the
> outward situation?

The outward situation is only your own misperception and that gets altered by the miracle. What
you call "outward situation" is something that *you*
have projected and you exaggerate its importance.
But to the miracle or to the insight, it's unimportant.

Either you go towards thought — which is
misperception — or you come to a moment of clarity
which is not your projection. The miracle comes and
frees you form the illusion, from misperception. It
liberates you from your own beliefs and projections.
In fact, a miracle liberates you from your own
thinking.

The correction that takes place in you is that you
see the illusion, the fallacy of the external. An illusion
is neither big nor small. Illusion is illusion.

A Course In Miracles defines a miracle as a
correction. And it brings light into the mind.

> *Student:* So then a miracle is a correction that
> takes place in my mind?

Where else could the correction take place? Have
you ever asked yourself: "What is the content of my
mind?" Does your mind not consist of what you put
into it? Are you not preoccupied with that?

You see, if you put a problem into your mind,
then you're preoccupied with the problem. You
want a certain car and therefore, you put that idea in
your mind. And then that yearning, that desire, is
what you become preoccupied with.

A wise person, on the other hand, never puts anything of the external into his mind. He lives in the world without wanting, without fear, without cravings. He has an inner contentment and has that to give. He lives by:

Peace to my mind.
Let all my thoughts be still.[5]

Can you please see that each person is responsible for what he puts into his mind? If you put hate in your mind, you'll start fearing the opposite.

> *Student:* Is love something that I put into my mind?

Love already is. Whenever a miracle takes place, you see with the eyes of Love. And in Love nothing is separated. But we put other things into our mind, and therefore, we never get to know who we really are. When we put hate into our mind, we also find means to promote our belief: newspapers, radios, televisons, etc. We spread the poison of our hate and fear of someone till we have even biased a whole nation.

> *Student:* Well, I'm not the only one who puts things into my mind. Society, education, my family, people that I've known — they have all put things into my mind.

We have to see that you and society are not separate. This is the deception we live in. When we see that you and society are not separate, a miracle has happened for you've seen a moment of truth. In that moment, the separation ends between you and that which is real.

What is real cannot be threatened. Love is never threatened. If you are a man of Love, you will never put any doubt, hate, or fear into your mind. You keep your mind immaculate, uncorrupted.

> *Student:* But what if my mind has already had those things put into it?

Then it's your responsibility to undo it. And for that, you will need the miracles.

> *Student:* So then, the miracle isn't something that I do?

No, a miracle is not something you do. But as you begin to question your beliefs or what you've put into your mind, an awakening takes place and you become responsible. You say, "I want to live a life that has rightness in it." And out of rightness comes gratefulness for what is there.

> *Student:* What do you mean by rightness?

Rightness has no duality in it, no opposite to it. Rightness is not personal. It is Absolute. The minute you are with the Absolute, a miracle has taken place.

Rightness has power. Lincoln was with rightness. Gandhi was with rightness. Mother Teresa is with rightness. And that's what they extend. Rightness has love behind it.

So, we come back to the content of the mind, which is Love. When you put anything else into it, you're responsible for contaminating yourself. We *do* put other things into our minds. We have misperceptions. We divide everything, get caught in forms. But Love has no form. Clarity has no form. Truth has no form. A change therefore is required. You must make a change within yourself, an internal change. You question the content of what you have put into your mind. You question that. In this questioning is the strength of integrity that helps you to undo.

We all need to undo a great many concepts, fears, and doubts — the many, little knowings that have become our bondage and by which we live. We are always so ''sure,'' and yet we are divided, separated. A miracle, then, is that which ends the separation for that moment.

How great is a miracle! And this is what *A Course In Miracles* does all along: it frees you from misperception, from separation. Its function is to bring man to peace within himself. Therefore, it liberates him from dependencies.

If you don't have peace within yourself, your life becomes an indulgence, constantly preoccupied with yourself, with personal activity. And it is meaningless. This thing to drink, that thing to eat; this worry, that suspicion. On and on, all day and all night. There is no space within nor without — a self-preoccupation that is endless.

And the Course tells us:

> *I will be healed*
> *as I let Him teach me to heal.*[6]

You will be healed because you have come to trust. The mind that can trust never places any doubt, any suspicion, in itself. You and I have a relationship with the One in charge of the process of Atonement. Having become receptive, He would talk to you.

Do you think that by living *A Course In Miracles*, that you would not be related with the Christ? Do you think that by living what the Course imparts, that you would not have a relationship? Would He not correct all our misperceptions, whatever we think we have made of ourselves? And do you have a relationship with the Course if that trust isn't there? Is there anything trust cannot do?

When there is trust, one puts away all alternatives. You are blessed. When you read the Course, it is His direct Voice speaking. There is no speculation in it. You can be grateful for that. And it's needed.

We limit ourselves but He is not limited. Therefore, don't impose your limitation on what you do. You are an heir to that which is unlimited. You represent the unlimited; you represent God's Plan for Salvation. Would you think in terms of limitation then? Your whole perspective would change.

Why should you be in conflict? Why do you fluctuate in doubt? If we could overcome wanting, then we have trust, don't we? And He said, "I'll take your burden. Leave that to Me." He'll correct the errors of the mind.

Truth will correct all errors in my mind.

You can trust that because the Course has made it clear that the mind is the only place where the correction needs to be. When you've dedicated your life to Him, do you think He will not help? So then, why not come to trust?

There is a difference between belief and trust. Trust, like faith, is direct. You've understood something. Even at the relative level, you've understood it clearly; and you give your life to that. Would you not then be protected, healed, cleansed?

> Student: I see I have to first recognize that the trust is needed. The trust has to be developed in something other than in myself or in my own thoughts.

Yes, we don't have the trust but the need to trust is essential. See the wisdom of it, the necessity of having a relationship with trust — to have a relationship with the One Who is in charge of the process of Atonement!

> Student: What comes to mind are the words of Jesus, "I CAN OF MINE OWN SELF DO NOTHING."[7]

These are the words of a mind emptied of everything. Therefore, it becomes the Mind of God. We are all a part of the Mind of God, but we cannot recognize it as long as we continue to fill our head with other things. And those need to be cleared, undone, because they make of us something other than who we are. We need to awaken to our potential. We are not little. We are as God created us. To know the real joy of it! To be whole! Anyone can do it. Just don't underestimate yourself.

Miracles will surround you if you do not believe in your helplessness. Trust only that which is real. And know:

> *Nothing real can be threatened.*
> *Nothing unreal exists.*[8]

CHAPTER NINE

9

WE MEET
TO UNDO

Where does one begin and what can one say that will make a difference? We have heard so much. It doesn't make much difference what one says anymore. What you are, you are. What I am, I am. We listen to all that is shared; we agree with it. But somehow it doesn't seep in. We like it, but we don't hear it. We listen, but we can't hear.

> *Student:* I was just thinking that perhaps there were things I was being able to hear and understand. And each time it comes back to this — that I've been deceiving myself again in one way or another.

Alright. Let's start right there. It's probably the best way to start because you are making a statement of how you feel and that is very beautiful. It doesn't have the condemnation of self, and it doesn't try to cover up. Most people either cover up with enthusiasm or they get into self-condemnation which is beside the point. Hardly anyone has the ability to reveal himself to himself. We're always covering up.

It is good to hear someone speak of how he feels. That's essential. "I'm not sure of myself. I deceive myself." I say, thank you for expressing that. We can deal with it. You're in the living moment and you're saying exactly what you feel.

We, for the most part, are hampered in being ourselves. We have enthusiasm — "I like this. That's great!" But it's like the media that takes one thing, one trend, and goes on and on with it. We can become nationalistic and that goes on and on. We don't have to "think" anymore. We just go on being that.

So, I'm very glad when somebody says, "Look, I'm not sure," or whatever they feel. I'm thrilled because it's something direct. We have forgotten how to be direct. Because of this, we are easily influenced. A person comes and starts preaching and we like that because he's strengthening our prejudice. Do we not validate those who confirm our beliefs? Are they not our heroes?

We seldom get down to a basic issue, a determining factor. You'll say, "Well, that's troublesome. I'd rather be in the sleep of forgetfulness." And *A Course In Miracles* says:

> *Let not my mind deny*
> *the Thought of God.*[1]

Can we see that the human being is constantly denying the Thought of God? *We* are denying, and therefore, it's a deliberate action.

> *Student:* If it's deliberate, there must be a
> way to undo that.

Of course. But it *is* deliberate. The prayer we have been studying tells us:

> *The sleep of forgetfulness*
> *is only the unwillingness. . .*[2]

. . .*is* only *the unwillingness.* Unwillingness is very active. It's something *I* am. All I live is unwillingness. All I do, *deliberately,* is to deny the Thought of God.

No one can overcome unwillingness and come to the Thought of God unless this is seen as a fact. Do *you* see this as a fact?

> *Student:* It makes sense.

Yes. Therefore, we are irresponsible. And we don't mind being that way. We are going to remain irresponsible. This irresponsibility is the deliberate choice of each person. We can go to churches, to workshops, to lectures, but it doesn't mean anything. *This* is the central issue.

> *Student:* I can see that the normal teaching of religion or the teaching of anything, for that matter, is a pretense.

Yes. So-called teaching is a pretense; undoing, however, is much more valid. The function of *A Course In Miracles* is to undo. The key to God's Plan for Salvation is undoing because in the undoing there is insight. Insight is independent of thought and it cleanses the mind of all past experiences, not just your individual dogmas and prejudices. It cleanses your very cells and purifies you.

And why are we meeting here? To undo. To recognize that we are constantly denying the Thought of God, that we love the unwillingness and cover it up by pretending that we are willing to change or to heed.

Can you be that honest? Make that demand of yourself, that you will not be dishonest in anything you say. That's a good place to begin. You become responsible for what you say. What would you say to the One Who is in charge of the process of Atonement? A lot of phraseology? When you recognize that you can't do that anymore, your relationship becomes direct. It's a direct relationship with an elder brother, so to speak.

This is why we were saying that one who preaches is pretentious because he teaches what is of thought and its ideals. Its knowing is not a knowing at all. That's a pretense too.

So then, we see that *A Course In Miracles* comes and it undoes the pretense, the knowings. Its function is also to undo insecurity at the very root level; that you come to self-reliance so that it undoes your dependence. Are you interested in that? You are dependent. How can you be non-dependent? *That* might well be relationship!

A Course In Miracles brings into application in one's daily life something that is consistent with the spirit of undoing, with becoming self-reliant, with coming to trust in something other than the brain that denies the Thought of God.

> *Student:* May we discuss the issue of the protection of my thoughts? If I said it was deliberate, that *I* am doing this, it would be that I understood that I could undo it. But I don't see that I'm deliberately protecting my

> thoughts. I see the reasonableness of what you have said, but at the same time I seem to think that if I said I saw that, it should be undone. And I don't feel that it's complete.

That's beautiful. The minute you see it, you undo it. That's so nice. But let us see. We don't know what unwillingness is, or what willingness is. We can suppose willingness would be of the Absolute in which there is not the opposite. But it is important to start from where we are.

We are at the level where we use thought to communicate. At the thought level, then, we can come to some kind of communication. That communication would turn into dialogue if there is a student. The student wouldn't deviate from the subject while the non-student's attitude would be to say: ''Well, never mind the communication. I agree. Leave me alone. I want to sleep. I agree! It's all great. Thank you!'' The non-student doesn't want to get into that dialogue.

It is in dialogue, however, that the energy of sharing takes place between teacher and student. This energy that takes place between the two goes beyond so-called verbal understanding. Anyone who is a student has to go beyond instruction. What would that be? It would be a state that doesn't have verbal interference in it. And it would be your own. Both people have worked, but then it's your own clarity. It's direct. Your clarity and my clarity are no longer different. It's shared.

We see in principle that the only thing one can do is undo, unlearn. It's like clearing the way. And somewhere one finds the strength of rightness. It doesn't matter what you do then, so to speak. You move from rightness. Rightness has the strength. We have not paid much heed to it any more than we have paid heed to the Course. And now this has to change.

Are we getting to know something about the action of God's Plan for Salvation, or the action of *A Course In Miracles*? It has to share. It's not going to move from insecurity but it is productive. Truth cannot be contained; it has to be shared with a brother. The Course has that to share.

> *Student:* I understand you to say that the function of the Course is to undo. . .

To undo dependence. May I share something very interesting? I was told that I am a non-dependent person, that that's my function. My function is to be non-dependent. And the energy, the blessing — the energy of the blessing is given to be with that function. Blessing is an energy. Every function has the blessing and the energy of it. When you're blessed, you're energized.

I am blessed with the function to be non-dependent. And by so doing, I discover what it means to be *independent*. If I were to say, "I'm independent," that would be arrogant. But my function is to be *non-dependent*. That's all. And Life helps. As long as I am true to being non-dependent, I'm with my function.

> *Student:* As long as you live from moment to moment, you are staying true to non-dependence, staying with your function?

Yes.

> *Student:* Then it's a continuous action?

Right. And therefore, I discover that that is what is meant by being independent. To be independent — I could make into a goal. But to be non-dependent — I have work to do.

> *Student:* Self-reliance, then, can be made into a goal or it can be on-going. Like you say, there is work to do and it's not an ideal.

Exactly. That's the difference. One is a function, or work, and the other can become a goal, or an ideal. It sounds very good but without the undoing you can't come to it. So then, I have to find out what it is that my mind is constantly denying.

> *Let not my mind deny*
> *the Thought of God.*[3]

How we accept the denying as being normal! And then we think, "Well, if God takes care, we don't have to do anything." But there are things we have to do.

> *Student:* There's a tendency to think that undoing means "not doing." But that's not energetic as you've spoken of the function to be.

Yes. Because you have to share. The Law is there is One Life and within the One Life there is the sharing that is of Love. That's the Law of Completion. If I'm undoing concepts, I share the undoing of concepts. What does the world need to be freed from? Commercialized action, being a mercenary, having no work of one's own. When the understanding of the One Life becomes part of your conviction, perhaps you would write differently, you would speak differently.

> *Student:* What is the difference, then, between undoing and asserting an understanding or questioning how to go about something? These don't really seem to be undoing at all. The responses I give seem to me to be either questioning how to go about something or asserting an understanding of something. Neither of those seem to be undoing.

Put them into application, they will undo.

Look, I say to you that you are to lead a non-commercial life, you are to be self-reliant. You say, ''But that's not undoing.'' I say, ''Try to do it!'' It will be by undoing that they become active. They become real and productive. Undoing is not just some statement. It is part of action. You have work to do. You'll have to undo everything that makes you dependent. It would bring the action of undoing with it.

> *Student:* I'm looking for instances in my mind, or in my awareness, of an undoing taking place when you ask for my understanding.

Can you do anything without first undoing insecurity? If you're always insecure — which we are, if you're always dependent — which we are, how are you going to undo that? Everything we do is born out of fear and insecurity and self-centeredness, isn't it? You can continue that way, but then you're ''doing,'' not undoing.

That's why people theorize a lot. But *A Course In Miracles* is not theoretical. It says, ''This is the Lesson. And that's all you have to do.''

In my defenselessness my safety lies.[4]

Once you've mastered that, you take the next step. Nothing is at random.

I hope this doesn't get too intellectual. We *have* to undo insecurity. We *have* to undo dependence. And we *have* to be productive.

> *Student:* All of that makes sense.

Good. Because otherwise, we'll just philosophize.

> *Student:* Internally, there is a lot of commotion that goes on but it doesn't have as much effect now. I'm not as afraid of it as I was, although it's still an issue to deal with.

Alright. You say you're now less swayed. As long as you're swayed, you have to undo. Just take on that responsibility. You can end it for all times — right this minute. Or, you may not end it. As long as it's there, one has to undo it.

I want to take it away from the philosophical. For me, the thing is very simple. It's this. I want to introduce you to what the function of God's Plan for Salvation is according to the Course. *A Course In Miracles* undoes at a totally different level. It says,

> *Nothing real can be threatened.*
> *Nothing unreal exists.*[5]

Do you know how many thousands of people there are who are aware of the Course, who have heard of the Course, who have read the Course?

They can read the Lessons but somehow they can't undo the actual. They can say of the Course, ''Ah, this is wonderful!'' But they don't know where to begin to undo, to live the Course. And then, after a year or two or three, they want to put the Course away because nothing happened.

Somewhere deep down there is a feeling, ''If I had somebody to help me, some place! I'd be doing something meaningful!'' Who knows what is meaningful or productive or self-reliant? *A Course In Miracles* offers the possibility of inner transformation and then you can be a strength to another.

> *Student:* I have to look at what it means to be helpful to others.

Sir, ''being helpful'' is as big a pretense as so-called learning. But you *can* do something that leads to self-reliance, something that's not totally based on commercial interest and nothing else. Your whole motivations have to change. Because the motivations have changed, you're helping yourself to undo the dependence or the illusion of helping. There is some kind of questioning because your life is dedicated to undoing your motivations and your illusions of helping. You are then part of the extension of an action. It's something far more. There's a joy. And it's new.

In the undoing, there is work to do. Therefore, it's not a goal or an idea. And as I undo, I can extend the undoing. As I undo, I can help another to undo. It's so beautiful. There is not even another somehow.

The work of undoing is blessed. If knowing this doesn't help, I don't know what would. The work of undoing is blessed. That's the work of *A Course In Miracles*. It undoes insecurity and brings you more and more to self-reliance. It gives you space to undo. That's your expression. So you extend undoing. And your work is blessed.

> *Student:* I can see undoing in myself, but if I see something outside of me and I recognize it and back away from it, maybe that's not undoing. There seems to be a difference between undoing inside myself and. . .

But you have to undo to understand it. Why are we now making an ideal of undoing? Don't you see what I mean? We have to undo.

> *Student:* Undoing within myself and undoing what I see externally. . .

It's the same thing. Because when you undo within yourself, the "you" is external too, don't you see? The energy, however, is not external. The energy is the blessing that helps you to undo. For that you can be most grateful.

What a beautiful thing, that the blessing is in the undoing! This ought to change your life! Know that when you undo you're blessed with the energy to undo. You couldn't do it otherwise. No one can undo without the energy of blessing. No one.

> *Student:* I feel a greater appreciation for what is being shared. But I am somewhat confused — not about what is being offered but about my finding refuge in believing that I can somehow embrace the opportunity, or rise to it, and come to something new —

> believing that I can do it. There is no question in my mind that there is nothing more meaningful to be a part of.

Yes. You see, we want to be appreciative, and to a degree we are, but we don't want to undo. We think appreciation is an expression of undoing. But beneath it we say, ''Don't bother me any more.'' This is the trap we fall into. We fall into appreciating. I say, you have to undo. What is it that you are going to undo?

Then you will get the full benefit of this meeting because its function is to undo. The undoing has the blessing; being appreciative that you are here, or liking it, is depriving yourself. Then one is appreciative for one's convenience and not appreciative for the undoing. I want the appreciation to be of the undoing.

We are getting a glimpse of what is required to come to a religious mind, a mind that wants to empty itself. Tell me what you don't appreciate about yourself and let's undo that.

> *Student:* I don't quite understand what you are saying.

I am saying that one can appreciate and one can like, can even assume and feel and be convinced, but how are we going to make sure that that is not the phraseology with which unwillingness sustains itself?

> *Student:* The unwillingness is obviously there. So then, it doesn't matter how it is going to manifest? It doesn't matter what one says then?

Exactly. That's the dilemma. The unwillingness can sing songs and write poetry. We have to deal with the unwillingness because we have to undo it. At least just to question whenever we say things, "Is it unwillingness becoming poetic?" Just that.

It is the undoing that is blessed: the undoing of dependence on the external world, dependence on politics, religion, etc. Undoing is a call to wisdom — to an ethical, productive life — and having something to give that is not of concepts and ideas.

One has to undo within oneself and we can be grateful there is *A Course In Miracles* to help us do so. Gratefulness comes, and we can approach the Course with reverence for it is a Divine action of which we are endeavoring to be a part.

These are some of the discoveries that one makes. It changes one's voice, gives one the strength. Then you are in a better position to undo — everything. Because you have undone, you might be able to help others to undo. Undoing is blessed. The "doing" is not. Can you see the beauty of that?

>   *Student:* *If* the undoing is not just an activity.

Yes, because that is the way of the world. The undoing is, that you have to undo within yourself first. Until then, leave others alone. Until then, you are like the rest of the world, giving others but illusions, earth values.

>   *Student:* I understand that it is really a
>   pretense to try to make corrections
>   in others if they are not made inside
>   myself.

There is nothing you can do except undo in yourself first. Then whatever you would do would also be undoing. So, let's start to undo. Could you give your energy to undoing in yourself and not bother about changing others? Once you start thinking about changing others it's one step removed from the issue. We like being removed; that is our unwillingness.

Unless we ourselves change, unless we can undo and come to the peace of God, we will not be able to do anything for another. Do you value the peace of God?

Student: Yes.

Then undo anxiety and extend peace. Don't use anxiety and worry as an escape, as an indulgence, because it is only evading the undoing within one's self. If undoing is the most important thing, then you are blessed with the energy of undoing.

CHAPTER TEN

10

THE BEGINNING OF SELF-KNOWING

We have been talking a great deal about how to live a life consistent with self-reliance, having something to give, and coming to intrinsic work. We have also said there is a different kind of intelligence than the one we have known so far — something new.

You see, the brain is not intelligent. The only function of the brain is to protect, nourish, and procreate the body. We have romanticized about it and made it into something it is not. And with this has come much suffering. The price one pays for pinches of pleasure here and there is sorrow. Where there is pleasure there is sorrow. And man is in a state of sorrow. He always finds some other factor outside of himself to blame or to react to, to acquire or to possess. That's all the brain knows.

Now, if we see this, the very seeing of this fact indicates there must also be another intelligence. That intelligence can only come when there is trust in something other than the brain, when you have been disillusioned and seen the limitation of the body senses, or of thought. That would be religious. Religion is not a dogma or a belief. Religion is a state of being. It is a state of being independent of brain thoughts.

All another can do is to make it clear to you. And so we meet in this atmosphere, in a one-to-one relationship, where we can value that which brings us out of limitation. We are endeavoring to come to this other intelligence. If we can cooperate in that, then this meeting is blessed because it will flower and bring us to a state outside limitation.

So far, wherever there has been limitation there has been personal life wanting improvement. Please try to see this for it is a wonderful, rational step. Where there is limitation, the brain wants to improve itself. That's the illusion of the brain; it is not the intelligence of the mind. The mind does not accept limitations to begin with. The brain does. The brain has been imitating the mind's function and we've all been deceived. *A Course In Miracles* calls it the *sleep of forgetfulness.*[1]

Whatever is of the mind recognizes no limitation; whatever is of the brain always wants something else. We can say that what the brain knows is unfulfillment. It knows the hunger of the body, it knows the need for sleep and shelter, and so forth. And that's the level where mankind is today. Unless man takes a step beyond this, he remains at the physical level — the animal level.

The animal also has a brain to think but its senses are far keener. The animal is also less destructive. Man's unfulfillment is unsatiating. He even has armies to kill other human beings. Please don't be so shocked to see that that's the way we live. The animal is limited to body senses and man has become limited to body senses.

Man does not sense the wholeness, the completeness in himself and he endeavors to *get there*. "If I could have these twenty acres of land." "If I had more people working for me." It goes on and on. Man has invented the monetary systems, the political systems, religious beliefs and concepts — an abstract world.

In the animal world there is nothing abstract. Everything is direct. The tiger is hungry, it searches for food; the lion is sleepy, it sleeps; the monkey sees danger, it either runs or climbs a tree or hides. Everything is direct. Instantaneous! How beautiful to see wild animals. How they have survived!

Are you familiar with the animal called the badger? He is ferocious! Now the mountain lion comes, and what do you think is going to happen? They are both face to face. We know that the mountain lion can take care of the bear, he's so swift; but he can't do much to the badger. Have you ever asked yourself how that species ever found its ways of survival? How did that body find ways to survive? How does the badger manage?

Well, you must see how animals kill each other. They go for the throat, whether it's the tiger, the lion, the wolf. Then look at the rattlesnake. He starts rattling his tail to make the other animal think that's where his head is. The animal goes for the rattling tail and he for the animal.

There is a knowledge of survival innate in animals. And that is how they developed skill, speed, fangs, and so forth. Otherwise they would have deteriorated and died. They would have become complacent like people in the affluent societies. Is our culture not plagued with the highest medical bills in the world? Hardly anyone dies a normal death. We have hospitals to pay. Big, big bills!

The badger, now, knows that the killing takes place at the throat. So he has made himself very low and the mountain lion cannot get under him to grip his throat. By the time the mountain lion tries to do so, the badger has the lion's leg in his sharp, razor-like teeth, chewing away.

The function of the animal is to bring the other animal to crisis. When the mountain lion is in crisis, he is not interested in attacking the badger; he's just concerned about getting out of the situation. It's too painful. While he was free of pain, he could think freely. Now the badger has got him — just like the corporations and offices have got man. The mountain lion is not concerned about killing at that point; he's concerned about survival. Are we not all into survival? That's where our brains have led us and now we are slaves of survival.

So, we see that the brain is connected with the body; it has to take care of the body; and then it is limited to the body. It enjoys eating, it enjoys sleep, it enjoys procreation. And for procreation, animals can fight and kill each other. And there is always something else that wants to live off them so they keep themselves alert.

The body has developed its own survival mechanism. The survival mechanism then can also bring about the exploitation of another. Animals do not exploit each other. This is particular to man. We need not go further into this if you have understood that our brain only knows its limitation, survival, and self-improvement. You see, nobody tells animals what fashions to wear; they are the way they are. But we have public opinions which control us.

Man is controlled. The animals are not. And can you imagine that they even cope with the seasons — the heat of summer, the cold of winter. How nature takes care. In the Serengeti, almost every year there's a fire and it spreads for miles and miles. It kills the ticks and other things that are a nuisance. It's amazing how nature has a hold. Behind the scene, there is another intelligence. And then it rains and there is water in the lakes, in the streams. When this cycle ends and the rivers begin to dry up, the animals migrate in different directions. For centuries upon centuries they have followed the same rhythm, the same pattern. During summer they are here, during winter, there. Do you see how they rotate?

We want to get stuck in one place, and therefore, we need to have blankets to get through the winter. The degeneration of man began when he discovered agriculture because he then got stuck to one place. And we think that that is when progress began. That's the kind of silly thing only the brain can conjure up.*

---

*For further clarification of these points, see *From The City To The Vedic Age Of Shining Beings Extending The Will Of God* by Tara Singh (Foundation for Life Action, 1983).

Now, understanding the nature of the brain, can we see that when someone becomes ambitious it's from limitation? Or that you could say you're going to "do good" but will step on the face of anyone who stands in your way to do so? That's the nature of the brain. You become like the badger.

Do we see that, with very few exceptions, everyone has lived by this brain that takes care of the body? And those few exceptions, whether they be Socrates, Lao Tzu, or Joan of Arc, usually got into difficulties? Mankind has become the biggest *herd.* You can see the inevitable end of it, that mankind will destroy itself. That's what it is already doing. More prisons, more mental hospitals, more drugs, more wars, more violence. The unhappiness is mounting because we are further and further removed from nature.

What is the purpose of nature? If you saw the perfection of a flower and saw that it was unlimited in its perfection, your vision of its perfection would relate you to its unlimitedness. It would take you out of the brain to some other faculty beyond the brain, a different intelligence beyond the appearance.

Beauty is not only of things external, of nature. Beauty is of the spirit of man! How wondrous is the man who never reacts, who is never affected, who is always himself. We don't know what it is to be ourself. Only that which does not change is itself. The brain can never be itself because it is forever changing. You see, what you put into the brain is what it becomes. If you put insecurity into the brain, the brain is insecure. If you put fear into the brain, it is afraid. If you put into the brain desire for something you have seen, that image will eventually lead you to that store.

The brain by itself does not exist. It is what you put into it that brings it into existence. The brain, *A Course In Miracles* says, is neutral. One man can become virtuous, another can become wicked. Some are trained to be Americans, some Canadians. If no one had put that into the brain, we would not have known we are American, Indian, or Canadian.

This vulnerability of the brain has now become advantageous to modern science. Outside influences can put almost anything into our brain and most people have very little power against it. We start taking the medicines they recommend, eating the foods and buying the clothes they advertise, joining the armies, paying the taxes. Anything we do is no longer our own. We have not yet had a voice of our own to put into the brain. Therefore, the brain is not our own. That's a shocking statement! I hope we can get this clear. Insist upon coming to clarity about it!

The problem is in the brain. The brain is ever changing. The wise person never relies on people who live solely by the brain because they are always changing from this to that. A person can assure me he will not do this or that thing again. I say, very well. I don't have to disbelieve or believe him. I just don't put anything another tells me in my brain because he's going to change. He says it; I don't deny it because that'll also be brain activity.

> *Student:* When I'm listening to someone, isn't that also putting something into my brain?

Try to understand what I am saying. Either the brain is listening — and therefore it is still — or the brain is interpreting and therefore it's not listening. You are going to listen to what you interpret, isn't it? So then you didn't hear what I have said.

> *Student:* I heard only my interpretation of what you said?

Yes. The brain merely interprets. In that way, the educated person and the illiterate person are both the same. The animals do not interpret. They sense: ''There is danger.'' But they don't use thought. It's direct. And the response is direct. So then, we can say the animal doesn't interpret.

I am saying that the human brain always interprets, that it can't listen because it has to be still in order to listen. If it became still, then your brain and my brain would no longer be in the way. We would be part of the One Mind. Then whatever I would communicate to you would be of the Mind, not of the brain. Whatever you receive would also be of the Mind. When both of our brains are silent, we are both in the same state. It's instantaneous. Heeding takes place when the brain isn't interpreting. As long as the brain is interpreting, we are limited to the body. And we are all body-bound, are we not?

Now, we come back again to this other intelligence we have been speaking of. Obviously it's not of the brain. If I told you this other intelligence is love, well, you still are not listening to what that is. You know the word but you don't know the actuality of it. To know the actuality, you have to get past the brain activity. We can perhaps introduce this other intelligence if you listen attentively.

A Course In Miracles states,

> *By grace I live.*
> *By grace I am released.* [2]

Grace is not known to the brain. And we have seldom ever lived by grace.

> *By grace I am released.*

We need to know the grace that up until now we have not known. That's a fact. We have not lived by grace; we have lived by the brain — that means by fear, insecurity, advantages, and all the rest of it. We have motives, we think other people have motives. We're afraid, we know the other person is afraid too. And then we can happily accuse each other. We see the false in the others, but we could not have seen it if we did not have it to begin with.

I hope all this then brings us to gentleness, to forgiveness. If you're really listening, then these are things you would discover — that you have to be limited in order to accuse others of their limitations. So then you grow in wisdom; you leave the other alone. If wisdom is ever to be, you start taking care of yourself, of your own issues.

Wisdom is the beginning of self-knowing. You no longer seek to know anything outside yourself. And what would you know? You would see the limitation of the brain. You won't condemn it, you won't accuse it, you won't adore it; you just see how it functions. This witnessing brings awareness into being. What is the function of awareness? What is its action? Why don't you ask that kind of question? Why do you assume you know?

The brain does not know what awareness is. It doesn't know what grace is. But we can now, slowly, come to the recognition of awareness. The action of awareness is to undo that which is of the brain. The brain has its limitations, its "knowing" that comes from limitation. And awareness undoes it. That's its only function.

Can we see that in order to be released, we need to come to the intelligence of awareness; that no matter what people say, without awareness their words are not true? They are giving you more beliefs, making you more dependent. Can you see this as a fact? Do we want to be released?

> *By grace I live.*
> *By grace I am released.*

We need to first be released in order to live by it, don't we?

> Student: It makes sense that I have to be released first. But how do I do that?

The brain must always have a "how." Awareness doesn't have a "how." It is still. Now tell me, what do you understand the action of awareness to be?

> Student: Well, I can repeat what you have said, that the action of awareness undoes the activity of the brain.

Yes. But have we understood that in order to come to, *By grace I am released*, we will need the awareness that undoes? Then what is awareness? How does awareness come into being? Where do I buy awareness? What mantras, what penance do I have to go through to earn awareness?

If I said to you, "Awareness has to be self-reliant," what would you do? You would say the same things. You'll put something else into your brain and be busy. You'll conclude something and remain in the limitation of the brain: "I can't do it." You are going to conclude something in order to remain where you are, isn't it? Then you are not interested in being released. As an ideal, yes; but that is just nonsense.

> *Student:* Could we go back to the question you asked about how am I going to get awareness?

We said that the brain becomes what is put into it. That's simple and clear — for all times? Then I hope you won't ever put conclusions, fears, selfishness, or limitation into your brain. You are responsible for it. You may say, "Well, give me something that doesn't require responsibility." That's what every brain is saying. But I said that awareness awakens one and you're in the sleep of forgetfulness. You're quite content there. Isn't that true? This is for those who want to be released. That zest, that passion has to be there.

> *Student:* Is there a relationship then between grace and awareness?

The awareness clears the way. The awareness awakens.

We are "asleep." Could we agree to that? That we are in the sleep of forgetfulness? Awareness makes me aware that I'm asleep. Then what? Then you're becoming aware of your sleep and how, in sleep, you become self-centered, you become forgetful of God, of forgiveness, of love.

Awareness, if it is real, won't let you slip back into sleep. But the minute you have concluded something, you are back in sleep. Every knowing of the brain will put you to sleep.

> *Student:* Even my agreeing then is a step towards sleep?

Right. But if you and I were students, we would observe what the brain does. Anything the brain presents to itself — as a question or wanting an answer or concluding — awareness would start undoing. So, you become your own pupil and your own teacher.

To be truthful, the teacher is never external to you. That's why when a so-called teacher draws attention to himself, he has violated something. The teacher is always internal. No real teacher has ever been external. Not one of them has ever started a belief system or a religion because that would be of concepts.

So then, the minute we conclude anything, we have concluded we are limited and cry, ''Help me get out,'' isn't it?

> *Student:* When I say to myself that I must watch what I put into the brain, is that a conclusion?

No, it's not a conclusion if you won't put anything in the brain. But that requires you be responsible.

> *Student:* So then a thought comes up and I recognize it as a thought and just leave it there?

Something like that. But you see, when you ask me, then I become the authority. It has to be your own discovery. If the thought comes up that you left the water boiling, alright, go and turn the stove off. At some level, we need to use thought. But when we start with, ''This is Canada, this is democracy, this is communism, this is Hinduism, etc.'' — it all becomes abstract.

The brain has a function. It can learn about easier ways of cultivating, finding better fertilizers to grow things. The brain has the capacity to know that topsoil is needed to have better crops. Things like that. These things are not abstract. You fall in the mud, you go and wash yourself. There is no problem in it. In direct things, there are no problems.

So, what is the new intelligence? The intelligence is,

By grace I live.

Living by grace, you will be released by grace — from littleness, from worry, from anxiety, from insecurity, all the external pressures that the brain has enslaved you with.

Now you are mostly living the fear and the insecurity that are part of your brain. Fear and insecurity may not be true! But you never question it. Can you tell somebody that nationalism is not true? People are so indoctrinated they won't listen. And just like others are convinced about some things, you're convinced about other things. Everyone's brain is conditioned. There is no individual self. We need awareness to undo the conditioning. That would be natural, wouldn't it?

The action of awareness is that it undoes. For instance, you want to kill a snake and someone tells you it's not poisonous. Then you wouldn't want to kill it. You see, first you bring it to awareness, then you drop it. The danger comes in with survival or jealousy. If you think someone else is going to deprive you of something, it endangers you. These are the psychological things we live by. But grace is not subject to that, it just undoes all of it.

To live by grace is to live by:

"In God We Trust."

And I say that as long as you have not become aware the brain is not going to allow you to come to trust. There is no way the brain will allow you to do so. You have to face this. And yet you must also see that *you* have to do something about it. Nobody else can help anymore than this. Giving you some "method," some "technique," would be to indoctrinate you with a belief.

So then, what is this state of awareness? Let me put it this way. To know the state of awareness directly is to come to that one moment in which the brain is not active. Awareness is then the light of the mind. When the brain is still, then *it* is. When the brain is active, there is limitation. The action of the stillness of the brain is the awareness that undoes.

> *Student:* Is that what happens in the moment of recognition?

Yes. Awareness is an action. Action is an extension of the mind. And about this, you need do nothing because it is the action of blessing. God's Plan for Salvation is blessed.

Student: What do you mean by "blessed"?

That which does not have any opposition, that which is never exhausted, that which is unchanging and has its own vitality of extension. Efforts are not required. When you're limited, you have isolated yourself from it and then you use the body like the animal does — to survive, to procreate, to secure territorial rights, and all the rest of it.

The energy of blessing, however, only extends. In order to be part of God's Plan for Salvation, we must be an extension of that blessing. It would transform the world, not only you. When we bring it down to the brain level, it doesn't work. And thank God! Because if it did work, we would think our *efforts* did it.

It's very clear that if we want to be part of God's Plan for Salvation, then we have to come to "In God We Trust" — the energy of blessing — and that we would not intrude upon it. But since our brain doesn't allow it, we have to do "something." And that "something" is to become aware whenever our brain moves, concludes, pretends to know, becomes afraid or optimistic, and so forth. *You* have the responsibility. Once you take on that responsibility, the awareness brings you more and more to the remembrance of grace, to the remembrance of God, to the remembrance of the One Mind. And each one of us has that. We can recognize it and "come home."[3]

I take it that now, after it's explained, you can be glad it is brought to your awareness. If we can't come to the awareness together, there is little likelihood that on your own you would even want to come to awareness. Then, in this togetherness, the teacher becomes, for the moment, external in order to introduce you to your own light of awareness. He doesn't start religions, he doesn't start communities. He remains self-reliant, non-commercial, having something to give — always — even to his so-called "enemies" because he never gets down to the relative plane.

Awareness, then, comes to a brother who tries to impart that to you and says, *"You* have it." He imparts Divine energy and nothing in the world can affect it because it is not subject to the brain. How can it be affected? It's not subject to the brain, therefore it will always have the energy of blessing.

God's Plan for Salvation will never know failure or success. These are relative words that have no meaning. As part of God's Plan for Salvation, you do not seek success — nor evade failure. Anything that is of relative knowledge has no validity whatsoever. You would use the brain in the right way, rather than misuse it in a psychological way.

To use the brain in the right way means, for example, that you cook the food by being present with it. And that food becomes blessed. If you cook the food with worries and anxieties, it won't be. If you cook the food while your brain is filled with desire, it won't be. You can't justify or glorify desire. It has nothing to give. It seeks its own amusement.

Gratification has all kinds of names. Yet HE has said,

"LET THE DEAD BURY THEIR DEAD."[4]

The quality of food we prepare would change because we have discovered,

> *By grace I live.*

And it is:

> *By grace I am released.*

Everything is given. It is not your brain that has brought you here. And if you still go to the brain, then no communication has taken place.

> *Student:* The way I understand what you are saying is that there are pieces of knowledge that I have stored in the brain which we call ''relative knowledge,'' and by which I approach the world. How I use that relative knowledge determines whether I'm coming from awareness or whether I'm limiting myself to just the brain.

I don't think we ''come from'' awareness. Awareness would undo. It would be very different. It would be new so we cannot say we'll be ''coming from'' awareness. We have no right to define awareness without knowing awareness. Because then we are speaking from brain memory. To define awareness without being in awareness, you'll have to find another blind person to agree with you. Talk to me about the brain because that you know. But you will see that whatever you discover about the brain isn't interesting at all. It's limited.

When awareness is in action, it doesn't see any merit in what the brain is going to say. The brain, on the other hand, describes awareness without knowing it. Similarly, one cannot say, "I love." Or, "I trust." We don't know what that is. When you know it, you extend it. Blessing is to be extended because that is what it extends. When you extend blessing, then you have it. When you know what peace is, you extend peace. When you don't know it, you talk *about* it. That's the preoccupation of the brain.

Can we see that the brain is the block that prevents us from knowing what the action of awareness, or what the grace of God, or what "In God We Trust" is? We don't know what God is. We don't know what trust is. The brain cannot know. No matter how long or how hard we try, the brain will never know. It can go on for a million years.

Hearing this, right away you *want* to know it, isn't it? That's always the impulse of the brain because it never knows satisfaction. But it also doesn't want to end. It doesn't want to end but it is always wanting, always insecure, always pretending to know. You become aware of that when you begin to undo.

What we are talking about is the need for you to have the discrimination: is this of the brain or is this of grace and awareness? If you *really* saw that it was of grace, then already it has extended itself to you and you'll continue to extend it no matter what happens. How do you understand this now?

> *Student:* Anything I say is going to be of thought. I'm trying to understand what you are saying and in order to do that, I'm trying not to interpret, just listen.

Will you succeed in that?

> *Student:* If I succeed in that and try to tell you about it, then have I not brought it down to an idea? Would not the actual succeeding of it only be demonstrated by some action I don't know?

How do you feel *now?* Just be simple. Because "I don't know" is also a knowing. How do *you* feel?

> *Student:* I feel very alive and very attentive, just listening.

If we are attentive, attention would lead us to awareness. Giving attention is already asking for more energy than the brain is used to working with. Attention then demands that, isn't it? The brain has enormous energy. It has kept man in his predicament for eons. But it also has the energy to see its own deceptions. Can you imagine that? And we want to remain asleep and be irresponsible. We'd rather get a job and have a boss to tell us what to do.

There is a tendency in man not to use the energy he has. That tendency is getting stronger and stronger. We read newspapers, chew gum, smoke cigarettes, all kinds of things. The tendency to be lazy or to be stimulated with ambition and greed is exactly the same. It can become very efficient, but that kind of efficiency also becomes vicious.

Attention, however, is something that demands more energy than we usually give to anything. So, first we start with attention. Attention is borderline to awareness.

The action of awareness is that it takes the pressure off the brain. It brings us to:

> *By grace I live.*
> *By grace I am released.*

Does this free you from pressure? In order to live by grace, we have to take the pressure off the brain. And the brain is so frightened, so insecure! Can you see how much stimulation, how much tension there is in the world today? Man will destroy himself because he cannot stand it. The politicians who make the decisions are more pressured than you realize. There is neither space for attention nor for awareness. And so, we always ''know'' how wrong the ''enemy'' is!

In order to survive this insanity, awareness is necessary to free the human brain from its pressures. If you have heard what I have said, then the action of grace has already taken place. How are we going to live by grace and be liberated by grace if that cannot be communicated?

This natural process then also brings us to decision. You may say, ''Look, I can't come to it.'' Or, ''I don't want it.'' Or, ''I want it.'' Whatever. But, being responsible, you *have* to come to decision — that you would not pressure your brain with anxiety or with fear.

As long as your brain is pressured, it is not going to be able to say, ''I live by grace.'' When you live by grace, you would never know what failure is. You would never know what success is either. You don't relate with anything the brain says. You do what you have to do because there

would be something else that we don't know now.
You would see meaningfulness in it. Your "doing"
would be an extension.

> *Student:* Perhaps one of my difficulties is not
> understanding how much I need to
> know *right now.* I was following you
> closely through the discussion of the
> brain and stimulation and how
> degenerated it has gotten. And just
> about everyone is caught in it. But
> trying to understand awareness,
> and grace particularly, I fall short. I
> want to know it but I get confused.

Well, of course, we get confused because
awareness is not of the brain.

To put you at ease, I think that first we need to
understand a principle. And then, if you are sincere
about it, you may get more attentive. So we start
that way. There is no such thing as failure anyway.
Neither is there such a thing as difficult. It's only
because we think there is something "easy." But
"difficult" and "easy" are both nonsense. They
are both illusion. It's a dream. HE has made us
perfect. Nothing can contaminate that. We are fully
protected because the energy of God's Love is
what we are. Do you think it's going to change?

A Course In Miracles is given to liberate man.

> *There is no death.*
> *The Son of God is free.*[5]

It's an unbelievable statement! So powerful! The
body dies but you don't die. It's like taking off your
shirt to take a shower. Why do you limit yourself to

the body? Let's start understanding this principle. It would make you somewhat responsible.

So now, to use the word "understand" — "I understand" — would be an action of grace. When you understand, that understanding is because you have understood grace. If you've understood how *bad* you are, that is not understanding. It will only bring guilt into being. We already know how bad and how small and how terrible we are. What's the sense of learning more of it? That we know. Don't bother with it.

Understanding is when you have understood that grace works. Everything is alive because of grace. No tree would grow without it. There is nothing else but the action of blessing, the energy of blessing. And somehow, what we have called "understanding" has put us in the limitation we are in.

Why can't we rejoice that we are part of God's Plan for Salvation and we don't have to worry anymore? That takes the pressure off, doesn't it? Please see it. Just the wisdom of it. We said that the pressure has to be taken off, didn't we?

Student: Yes.

So then, let's be at ease. As the pressure starts diminishing, I don't have to worry. It's my brain that limits me, that worries about the future. But there is no such thing as "the future." You're never going to eat "in the future." You're always going to be eating in the present. Are you ever hungry *tomorrow?* You're hungry *now.* Can you imagine that time is also an invention?

So, we come back to the principle. Understanding a principle means I understand something that puts my brain more at ease. I don't quite know what grace is, but I see a certain limitation. And the friend is saying, ''Don't be frightened by it. I'm with you. We'll deal with all the monsters that are going to scare you. They're just projections.'' Don't you feel stronger that way, that nothing can touch you? You won't be afraid — ever!

The principle is that we have understood the brain has a function and we have limited ourselves to that. Now, isn't that some kind of relief? Also, we begin to see there is some other action that is always taking place; otherwise, no rain would fall, no grass would grow, you and I would not be here. This action *extends.* And somebody calls it ''the action of grace.''

> *By grace I live.*
> *By grace I am released.*

Therefore, no brain activity is necessary. Do you not feel a little more relaxed knowing that no brain activity is needed?

And then we say:

''In God We Trust.''

You don't have anything to fear if you trust in that action. If you trust in God — God meaning extension of grace or the energy of blessing — then you have nothing to worry about. So then, what's your problem? It's your *habit* to worry, your *habit* to be in anxiety. That's all you have to deal with. The other is already perfect. Alright?

Now tell me what bothers you, that you think you need to deal with? Let's see if we can bring awareness and attention into it. Is that fair enough? How do you understand it?

> *Student:* Well, what has helped just now was making the principle clear. That to try to know what grace is is getting into brain activity again; trying to know something that can't be known.

Yes.

> *Student:* I see that I can know the limitations and not to be afraid or identify with limitations.

Right. So then the wise doesn't teach anything that the brain can know. The known cannot know the unknown.

> *Student:* One of the sources of anxiety is wanting to know the unknown.

Yes, of course, but whenever it would know, it would still be within the known.

> *Student:* I'm beginning to see that.

The brain activity cannot know. The brain has to be still to know that which is unknown. Is that established?

> *Student:* Yes.

So one can't say, "I know grace and I know trust and I know God and I know love and I know peace." It's an untruth. And untruth does not have the power to extend.

God's Plan for Salvation has the power to

extend grace. But we don't know what that is. And when we say, "I know it," it becomes a belief. We still don't *know* it. And the whole world is caught in belief and making it real. Each person struggles to make belief real, till finally he dies. Would you believe that? Is that not insanity?

> *Student:* I see what you are saying, especially about the future and how we project our limitation or lack of something into the future.

The other name for limitation is "lack." Where there is limitation, there is lack. They are both synonymous. We've been preoccupied with the activity of lack and limitation. Could we say that? That's a fact.

So now, what are you going to do? If you've understood it, then in the understanding of it some action takes place that is not of the brain. You see, awareness undoes. The action that takes place in the beginning is that of awareness, which brings about the action of undoing. All that is needed is to undo the concepts of the brain. Then there is space for something else. We don't know what that is. But we *must* undo.

> *By grace I live.*
> *By grace I am released.*

Are you seeing now how the two are combined into one? From childhood our activity has been born out of lack and limitation, and our relationship with grace has been virtually nil.

> *Student:* The issue is what one does with the space.

I'd rather say it this way — if you and I can agree — that whatever we have been doing has been out of limitation and out of lack.

> *Student:*   Yes, I can see this.

From childhood it has been so and it continues even now.

> *Student:*   I can accept that.

And you can continue this way for the rest of your life! But you will be promoting limitation and maintaining lack. This awareness must evolve something within. What are we going to do now? Is that not a reasonable question? You are responsible. What are you going to do? Would you not admit that whatever you have done was born from a lack? So now, if you've understood it, what would you do? What is your responsibility now?

> *Student:*   I have to pay attention to what my conditioned responses are. That's the only thing I can do because wanting it to be some other way is still the same.

Yes. It's no different because it is still from lack.

> *Student:*   Yes, that seems to be the only thing.

The awareness of this, without effort, would come to you. You can now say, "I don't know what to do, but I certainly can't go on the way I was!"

> *Student:*   Yes.

That's some step! You see, fear would only intensify the lack. But we say, "My God, I'm glad I know what *not* to do!" That's about all one can learn. That's all a teacher can share. Anyone who tells you what to do is again maintaining the lack. So then, we've defined what a teacher is.

> *Student:* It makes things simple — that there's no reason to worry. That's clear and either I do it or I don't, but to worry about it just makes me stay in the same place.

Let's say you're very thirsty but you've seen a spider in your tea. You can't drink it anymore. Something like that happens. You come to some kind of dismay, some kind of crisis even, that you regret having wasted the last twenty years. There is hardly anything you could put your finger on that was worth much. The more you see that — not with effort, but normally — the more you would be careful not to continue wasting your life.

This is why we said earlier there is only one decision one makes in life, and that is the decision to end! The decision is always to end the past, the habit, the momentum. You take the step irrespective of what happens because you are no longer afraid of consequences. Therefore, you are courageous. You are yourself! Are you afraid to be true now? Can you afford to be true, or would you go for the convenience of "I don't know"? Where are you now?

> *Student:* I don't really have any words. I don't feel afraid in this moment the way I usually do.

At least not as much as before.

> *Student:* Yes, but I don't totally feel comfortable either.

We don't quite trust ourselves. No one can trust

the brain unless he is really insane. Insanity lives by the brain. Look at the manifestation of insanity everywhere, in your own life, in every life. So, we're getting to know the *known* better, aren't we? And what it is.

> *Student:* When the brain moves now, it's not so much a threat. It's something that is known. And when I see that it's the known, that to me is understandable. Since I can't know the unknown, that keeps me from having to seek and strive and push and effort and everything else that I've been putting into it. It helps considerably in being more relaxed.

Yes, and also to see that what we have known is born out of limitation. We die just knowing limitation.

> *Student:* I'm having difficulty in being able to stay with that point.

Yes, because we don't have "the ears to hear."

> *Student:* It's very difficult just to stay right there with it.

Do you know why?

> *Student:* No, I don't.

Because we want to forget that. We want to evade the truth. If we did not want to evade the truth, we would stay with that point. The only activity the brain has known for the most part — psychologically — is always to evade the truth. But now, at least, we're not afraid to see that we are part of limitation and that whatever we do is born out of insecurity, out of fear. At least we're not afraid to see it. We can watch it. Just let it be. Don't even try to stop it because if you try to stop it, you're again getting involved.

But what if you were just to say, "I don't have 'the ears to hear,'" and you observe that. You don't do anything about it. Then you're with awareness, are you not? And we don't stay with it because we want to run away from it, from the truth. The brain activity is always going to evade the truth. Its activity is that of evading, that of seeking. They're both the same. And neither will stay with it.

Would you now stay with it? Either you would forget it, or it would come to your remembrance again. And that's what *A Course In Miracles* does constantly: it brings the awareness to our remembrance. It says:

> *By grace I live.*
> *By grace I am released.*

We then forget it. But the Course tells us to repeat it again; and something happens. Perhaps some time during the day, you will heed it if you do it right. Can you imagine that? You'll have miracles and come to a Holy Instant — whenever you heed it. That I guarantee!

Something else would happen; it's the unknown that would allow you to stay with it, with the actual. So then, when you say those words,

> *By grace I live.*
> *By grace I am released.*

your words are true. When you hear them as true, you'll stay with it — even for a short moment. Your whole relationship with the Course changes, especially now that you know you have been busy out of lack, out of limitation. Some awareness is clearing the way. And you can give yourself a little more to the Course. At some point, you would see, the truth will reveal itself because it is inherent in *A Course In Miracles*.

Now I'd like to go on. We have understood a principle and I will repeat it. We know that ours has been an activity of unfulfillment and limitation. And it's still liable to go on but at least now we know it. We are also capable of knowing the truth of the words of the Course. We can evade it. But we can also observe how we evade it, that the brain is not interested. The brain is interested in its own activity, either of seeking or of evading.

Then you see that the brain activity is what really keeps us limited, consumed. And that's the block. Some day you may want to scream, ''What do I do? It doesn't leave me alone! I can't get away from it! Not in sleep, not in bathing, not in running! What do I do? It goes on involuntarily.''

And then someone says: ''Alright. Just be aware. Leave it alone. The more you want to suppress it, the more you want to do with it. . . They are both the same.'' You begin to discover this. Now, at least, you are not opposing it. You are getting yourself somewhat free of conflict. As the awareness comes, the conflict begins to minimize. Isn't that a beautiful gift of awareness? What a relief it brings!

Awareness makes change possible. Without it, life will pass us by. We *must* come to knowing the deception and the limitation of the brain — as a fact, not as an idea. We must come to self-reliance and to knowing:

> *By grace I live.*
> *By grace I am released.*

We can't go on doing the same thing we've been doing all our life.

"In God We Trust."

Without coming to this trust, we are enemies of our own selves. We *have* to discover the trust in order to extend that. If we came to trust, everything we need would be provided. That's some statement! Everything we need would be provided if we came to trust. If we don't, then we are violating the energy of blessing that goes with it. We have everything to gain if we could come to this. That's why I'm struggling so hard to make this principle clear.

The energy of blessing will accompany what you do. Otherwise, you're evading what you thought you wanted. The self-centeredness would continue and you will not be very happy with that. If we cannot come to trust, it's because we don't want it. At least this is made clear. As long as we are acting from limitation and from lack, and therefore not from "In God We Trust," it is not going to work. That is what we want to correct.

If we make the inner change, there is no such thing as lack anymore. Problems only arise because we can't make the internal change. And this is an opportunity for us to come to inner correction.

How beautiful to be able to say:

By grace I live.

What does that mean? It doesn't know failure. It doesn't know success. It is intrinsic. It is self-reliant. Therefore, it extends. Then what a gift we have given to ourself and to the world!

Make contact with *A Course In Miracles* and there will be no struggle in life. It provides the opportunity to know the fact that it is blessed and has the energy; therefore, it knows no lack. It ends all duality, all inconsistency, because it doesn't believe in anything that is relative. It trusts God! No matter what happens, even if you were to starve, you would never project anything of thought and not undo it. That's what I call trust in God! For you, nothing else exists — nothing that your thought can imitate and project and scare you with. You would never give it validity.

It is the individual who gives it validity. And you, as an individual, are responsible to undo it with the awareness that it is not real, for:

Nothing unreal exists.

and:

Nothing real can be threatened.[6]

That's all we need to come to. We no longer have options. We need to take that stand. We have to put an end to this brain that rules our life because it is not real. Take that stand — that whether you live or die, you have no choices anymore. You've come to a decision.

I would like to end this meeting with one other principle. Let us say that there is God, and God is unknown. He is beyond thought, beyond knowing, therefore of stillness. And out of that stillness, out of that wholeness, an expression was born which was the extension of Love. That extension of Love, then, is the extension of God — His Son, the One Son.

At the physical level of manifestation, this One Son divided himself, so to speak. But the memory and the truth of His real identity still remains intact in Him. Perhaps we can understand this through an example. If you put water in ten bowls and put them on a table outside when the moon is up, every bowl will reflect the moon. Yet there is only one moon. Similarly, the One God is in everyone. As long as we are looking at the ''bowls'' — the reflections — there are ten moons; but when you look up at the source, there is only the One.

That One Son who is the extension of God tries to bring others to the awareness of who they are — that we are all One. That is the action of the Son who comes to awareness, to realization. He brings others to that awareness. That is his natural function. That is also the basic principle of *A Course In Miracles*. When you undo, you are consistent with its laws.

If you understand this as a principle, you too have the same function — the function of bringing man to awareness, of bringing man to the recognition that it is lack that binds him. The awareness, then, starts removing the blocks to reality. This is everyone's function. As long as you stay with that function, you will never know insecurity. That function is protected; it is provided for with abundance; and it knows no limit.

I hope this gives you vitality and inner clarity so that you can say, ''Yes, I have taken this on. And by this I will live.'' By what?

> *By grace I live.*
> *By grace I am released.*

There is no substitute for it.

CHAPTER ELEVEN

11

IT IS TRUST
THAT FREES THE MIND

During the years I spent in silent retreat, I learned a lot of things. What do you think one would learn when, for three years, you have been silent? What are you going to learn? Something very few could learn.

One thing I learned was that if my mind was really silent, no one would dare to approach me. Nobody. It was amazing to discover that. If I was with a silent mind, I could walk through the crowds on the beach or in a grocery store — you can't avoid being with people — but not one single person ever became curious. I wasn't shying away, but not one person intruded.

Another strange thing was that people needing directions, however, would always find me and talk to me. I said to myself, "Good God, with all the people around, they come to me!" They'd want to know where Ocean Avenue is or where this road leads to. But I never felt I was "talking" in directing them because it was meeting a need. The need and the silence became one. Can you imagine!

Now, you might say there is a contradiction here. But at the relative level there is always going to be contradiction. Don't ever expect it to be otherwise.

Why don't we want to see that we have never known anything other than contradiction? Why is it we are not interested in finding this out? Why is it I am the one explaining it? Are we seeing what I am saying? Certain things can come into being only when there is mutual interest.

At the thought level contradiction is inherent. So don't even try to come to a state that doesn't have contradiction in it. Is there anything that you can think of or that you have ever done that did not have a contradiction in it?

Contradiction cannot be eliminated at the thought level because thought itself is in contradiction with reality. And you're trying to now find non-contradiction through means that are contradictory. Are we seeing it? We have to overcome this. Then you would ask intelligent questions. They would be intelligent because you would have done some groundwork, become aware of other factors.

One can give a certain kind of insight into this but it's your interest that has brought you to that point. You see that thought itself is in contradiction, personality itself is in contradiction. "How do I end contradiction?" And I would say, "Well, you need to come to self-reliance. And in order to do that. . ." Are you seeing how the question would change?

You, as Richard or you, as Connie, are a contradiction in life — to the wholeness. Have you ever felt that? Then you have a job to do. You want to solve it at a third rate level where it can never be solved. But this requires transformation in your life! You just want to solve something "out there." The person who wants to solve it "out there" is not a student. It can't be solved "out there."

Being separated is a contradiction and the thought that separates and yet wants to end the contradiction is also a contradiction.

When you go to a wise person and ask, "How do I get out of this contradiction in life?" he'll tell you you have to come to self-reliance. You have to come to self-reliance because otherwise insecurity would get you. There are rich people who have millions of dollars and they are unhappy. Their sleep isn't any better. Probably worse. Having money and having ranches and having this and that isn't self-reliance nor does it end contradiction.

The self-reliance we are talking about is something different, and you haven't tried to find out in what way it is different. Unless you come to self-reliance, you are violating a Divine Law which is that you have a function for which you came. Until the issues of insecurity and survival are solved — in a clear way — you cannot end the contradiction. And if somebody says: "I'm going to give you a pill and you will have nirvana," you will be dependent on the pill or dependent on the person who gave you that pill.

The self-reliance we are talking about is the most sacred action in life. Something that seldom takes place in the world. We haven't understood it in its depth and we haven't yet made any effort to do so. Not that we are "bad" people. The multitude or the collective is just not interested. It's quite dormant; it doesn't want to awaken other potentials; it wants to understand at a superficial level.

That understanding is again a contradiction. But here we meet to *end* the contradiction — once and for all and at every level. Are you interested? Are you really interested — not just in "learning" what I say? If you're interested in "learning," it doesn't work.

I'm not going to teach what I knew yesterday or even five minutes ago. I want to share that which awakens in me — a truth, a clarity — in this moment. Can you share that? Have you the "ears to hear"? Have you the ability to end your interpretations? I will not teach; I will share that which is *now*, that's not mine.

I have to come to a state of non-contradiction to transmit non-contradiction to you. If you can't heed or you keep on interpreting, and so forth, we haven't taken the step. We just want the net result. "Give me nirvana." Or, "Give me non-contradiction." I say, "Well, you have to put some energy into it. You have to be serious about it. You have to be interested in it."

Am I making this clear? I wonder if I am. . . I wonder if you will ever know that I am talking about something totally different than what you think. I am talking about a fact — a fact in which there is no contradiction. Otherwise, it won't be a fact. Are we seeing it?

You take the fact and make it an idea. Then how can you and I relate? You make it an idea; you

bring it down to the brain level. I need to end that –
and you need to be the student. Are you seeing it?

Student: I think so.

Each person brings it to the idea level and then
you think you have learned. I want to burn your
learning! It's a trap! Where there is learning, it is an
evasion of fact. A fact requires transformation and
we are playing hooky. Fancy what kind of a
student would have to be a student now! The doors
are open; no need to get up tight and tense and
say, "Oh, I'm going to do this and that." You can
do whatever you like, but it's a reaction. The fact is
not of first importance to you and you would have
never known it. Not one person would have
known it.

I wonder if the people who are going to read
this sharing will ever know it? They may be thrilled
— by what? By the idea. Ideas can be taught. It's
like man who can either use science to end wars, to
end hunger in the world, to love mankind, and to
end nationalism; or he can continue to abuse
science for the privileged. The stupidity of
education that doesn't educate in the real sense! It
merely trains the brain, it doesn't awaken it.

Either we share that which is not of personality,
neither mine nor yours, or we keep on believing in
"learning." Therefore, we don't have discrimination. Learning can mislead you, as it has. It's the
learning that is the curse. Learning can be a good
thing *if* you have learned that it only goes so far, or
at least you have learned *about yourself,* that you're
constantly with words, you're constantly satisfying
yourself, getting frustrated, and this goes on and

on. We have to learn about ourselves and realize that we can't listen.

We are talking about learning which, like science, can be abused. People can remain nationalistic or divided into religious beliefs: Catholic, Protestant, Hindu, Sikh — and thus, become mindless. Learning can be abused, has been abused, and will be abused even more. And someone says: Learning is not valid; it prevents the awakening. It's your responsibility to see that and then meet the situation.

What is awakening? Awakening comes to the fact. It outgrows the idea, seeing the falseness — that it is abstract and is not real. Then you can heed the fact.

The fact is not mine, nor yours. The fact transforms life and your contradiction is ended, your insecurity is ended, your problems are no longer. You acknowledge no lack. You will never use thought to limit your life, your existence, your glory. And then, your very presence upon the planet is a most sacred event.

That's where we are heading; that's what is already here. How little heed we pay! Does it make any difference? Does it make any difference to know that thoughts are manmade, that you can make contact with the fact?

I am as God created me.

I wonder if *you* are going to listen to me or the Course and outgrow ideas and share the fact with me? You see, the past is of idea and that which is not of time is the fact.

Somehow Life has brought us together — each one of us. This is no accident. Every encounter has meaning, but at a different level where the externals are no longer that important. We are trying to change the external with the external. It's like cooking a meal without a fire. Something else is needed to know what the Forces are that brought us together.

Those Forces are not of thought. The Course says the things that happen are not by chance. And we say, "Well, I know that as an idea." Again, to know that one has to outgrow the idea because if we understand it as an idea, it still isn't real. At that *other* level it is possible to understand. And maybe at that level it doesn't have the same kind of detail; it might have a different kind of depth. Are we seeing that?

> *Student:* Trying to understand it with thought is not possible. That's what I understand.

And you want *me* to explain it to you at the thought level of understanding. I said, even if I did it wouldn't make much difference. But there *is* a way. There is more. We have a responsibility to another purity, to different values.

But for us, there is negativity, there is limitation, there is lack. Is that not what we know? People who have an understanding of ideas have lacks and limitations. They'll say, "What can I do?" It's going to come to that; it's inevitable because the idea has that limitation.

I don't want to do anything that has limitation or

a sense of lack. I will not. And I'm not afraid. So then I say, that's self-reliance. It is something very different; it has no contradiction. I may die today but it doesn't matter. The Life behind the word one has spoken that is true would still be here. See how free it is from the externals? So, one comes to that kind of peace. Would you have ever believed you had that opportunity? Could you expect anything more?

Aldous Huxley at one time said to Mr. J. Krishnamurti that for one moment of true perception he would give everything he had. One moment! And you are not going to let go of anything to be with that moment. Why? Why don't you want to know the fact? Why don't you want to know that which is boundless, that has no lack? Somebody has cleared the clouds and the cobwebs for you, to present it in the simplest possible, conceivable way. It has no dogma, no belief, no big thing. It's presented to you at your level in the clearest possible form so that you can understand the clarity and the beauty of it.

Why are you reluctant to take the step? You have only to take one step — and something else has taken a million steps to meet you: Life!

Tell me, could you want it any simpler? Do you want it any simpler? Then why is there this resistance to change? Why is the unwillingness still alive in you? Why? This is a one-to-one relationship. Has it ever been offered to you? What are you going to do? How are you going to cover this up, that you had this opportunity?

I have no expectations. I am with the fact. The fact has no expectation because it doesn't have a lack. I don't have a vested interest. If I did, it would mean that there is a lack. But this is a blessed opportunity, a Holy Instant in which we meet. How are you going to justify this?

> *Student:* First, I know I have no alternative.

Is that true?

> *Student:* That's the truth.

Then you have no conflict, sir. You see, at the relative level there is always an alternative. Can you then tell me that, being at the relative level, you have no alternative? It wouldn't be relative if we didn't have the alternative. God gave man free will. He either stayed with it — and therefore had no alternative — or he was in the alternative.

> *Student:* I recognize that there are those alternatives. I am attempting to put them aside when I recognize them on that level.

What if it doesn't work at that level?

This is a very beautiful question. Are you seeing the beauty of it? I hope you do. We can say *A Course In Miracles* or God's Plan for Salvation doesn't work — but is that true? In reality, is that true? For you it may be true because you are still with the relative. You don't accept it; you don't want to receive it. That's different.

Are we seeing it a little differently, more profoundly? You may say, ''Well, it doesn't work.'' You would probably blame yourself and then that will fade out and the relative would really intensify itself. At the relative level, you can become very pious for a moment.

Where does this exist in the world, that you could say one word and it is met with compassion and brought to truth? Where in the world does that exist? Is this not one-to-one relationship? The difficulty is that we don't come to gratefulness.

What is shared has the unlimitedness in it that deals with the limited view — the freedom, the space, this other thing that takes place and that can only be related with gratefulness. So then one speaks with exuberance. It is the gratefulness that touches others, not the stories we tell. The stories are only means. What we share is not the story but this other thing that is beyond the human being — the sharing of the freedom of the moment, something else that inspires one. One is inspired by what that moment must be that makes all our knowings irrelevant.

Why hasn't gratefulness touched you? Why? What it would do! What cleansing it would do! It would cleanse the world, leave aside your life. You would be inspired beyond ideas. What a benediction that is! Gratefulness is the one thing that helped me. Appreciation, being inspired.

Why do you want to stick with ideas? Why would you not want to take that step from idea to fact? Idea is of someone else and it influences you. It's not your own. And the fact is something you and I can share which is not personal.

> *Student:* I know that I'm not going to stop in the attempt. I'm determined but I don't have an answer as to why I don't take the step.

I would listen to the question differently and I would listen to the answer differently. I would not make it personal. I would deal with the forces that prevent one from getting past interpretations and wishes and wantings. Undo that! And in that moment you are a student. Are you seeing this vast difference? We are talking about a different thought system — to think objectively. Therefore, it's no longer of personality. That's what we are trying to come to now.

> *Student:* I don't understand the force that you speak of in any real, profound way at all, the force that's essentially behind resistance. I understand it from the effect it has inside of me. But it seems futile to deal with it at that level.

Then why are you dealing with it? Then don't use the word "futile." See, you cannot have judgment. Are you getting some idea of how profound it would have to be? When you say "futile," you're judging something. And then you're in contradiction. Why don't you see the contradiction?

In the end you have very little to say — anyone. When you have reached the point in which you have very little to say, what you will say will be *yours* rather than mere echoes of other people's concepts with which we are contaminated. Are you seeing that?

But I am saying to you, personally, that you have to be comfortable with being helpless. You have to be patient with yourself and fall in love with your helplessness. That's for *you*; it's not for everyone else. Because if you don't, then the frustration is going to destroy something. Is that not the basic issue for you? The frustration will take over. I want you to always be at peace and in love with your helplessness.

> *Student:* That would have never occurred to me and I can see that it's appropriate.

Don't make helplessness an idea though.

> *Student:* I don't think so. It's easy to interpret what is said and not have to change. As long as I can interpret it and listen to myself, then there is the resistance to change.

Yes, but there is one thing we don't want to understand because it's simple. We don't want to understand that being brought to the awareness of a fact is a blessing of God. Just knowing that. Then leave it alone. "I can't get it" or "I'm going to get it" — don't get into that. Then you are grateful. "My God, how blessed I am that this is pointed out to me." *That* awareness — that you are grateful for the fact being pointed out — has its own action that we haven't yet realized. It's the action and the gratefulness of awareness that will bring about some other transformation within.

The awareness is that: "I can't say anything. Whatever I say is futile. But I've heard something!" Then give it the space. Awareness will bring you to an awakening. It has its own action. Don't run to thought and say, "I like it" or "I don't like it."

We will begin to see how an involuntary action of Life takes place because we are grateful and we are with that awareness. And something else happens.

It's like the dawn within one. And it's not of thought. Then you are grateful if you have heard those words. That's all. But the minute you want to go back to yourself — that you can change, you're going to change, you can't change — I say, you're back again. You have made John alive and not gratefulness alive, not awareness alive.

> *Student:* It doesn't seem as if I can leave it there. I can't stay with that; I've got to have an answer.

Alright. You touched upon something very beautiful: that insecurity wants an answer. And politicians give it to you, gurus give it to you, and you're a slave forever. The fact is that we don't need an answer.

> *Student:* How can that be?

You will see. The fact is, we don't need an answer. Would that not be more self-reliant? The need of an answer is a lack and a dependence. See that. See the beauty of the fact that we don't need an answer. As long as I think there is an answer, I think I am inadequate. It's a hard thing to break but the fact is there. Let it be. It's a seed sown.

To take the answer away from a man is to liberate him. And I would not replace this freedom with an answer because I love you. That's why it's not commercialized. Answers are commercialized. Every phoney guru is selling answers, isn't he?

> *Student:* It's difficult to say anything after that last comment.

Then you have mastered reaction. When you

have mastered reaction, when you have seen the falseness of reaction, you would walk a free woman in the world of insanity. Bring to your remembrance that reactions are unessential. They only degrade a person.

> *Student:* I don't know what to say either. One thing I would like to explore is why the gratefulness doesn't inspire me more? Why don't I come to some energy with that because certainly my life has been deeply affected and changed in many ways, in a positive way, by attending these sessions.

Yes, but then why can't one be grateful that finally this thing is becoming the focal point? Say, ''I'm grateful for this because without *my* having this, I won't be able to help my child.'' Teaching is not going to work with your daughter. She is too smart, too quick. If you confront her with a challenge, she is going to try to evade it with thought, and so forth. She needs for *you* to know the truth of gratefulness. Then in some way, it would extend and bring her to a more serene state rather than her getting so stimulated. She is growing up very fast and we need to introduce her to what gratefulness is. We can't introduce her to a gratefulness of ideas. Think about that, how essential it is.

Become aware that you need to be more grateful and then find out what the other needs are. We have seen in today's session that one person has frustrations; another reactions. What are *your* other needs? If you have true gratefulness, it will overcome them because they make one dependent on the past, on others. Let gratefulness flower in you.

Student: Gratefulness for what unfolds?

Yes. It's a discovery of how blessed you are. If I tell you, ''Be grateful because I gave you a pair of shoes,'' that's not gratefulness. Gratefulness comes from:

I am content to be wherever He wishes.

No matter what the situation is. If you have to cook out in the rain, you remain grateful. There is no alternative.

Student: You have introduced us to so much and I feel blessed in what you shared today.

What did I share? That's what I want to know. Don't talk *about* it: ''I am grateful for what you shared.'' I don't know what I shared. I don't want general statements that are complimenting. I want to see how you face what was shared. Is it a burning coal in you that doesn't allow you to sit quiet?

Student: What meant a great deal to me was hearing that self-reliance is not possible as long as there is the reaction controlling me.

You use the word ''possible.'' In what way is it possible? Perhaps we can all benefit. One person has discovered that it's possible. What is *that* discovery? Then you will be sharing something, wouldn't you? Everyone here is wounded, they are on stretchers, and you say you have found the aid that makes it possible. We need it quick.

Student: I don't understand.

I am saying that the word ''possible'' is an idea,

and therefore, it need not have been said. But if it's a fact, then that's what we need.

> *Student:* What I had said was that, from what you were saying, self-reliance was not possible as long as there was reaction in me.

Yes. Now I am saying, in what way is it in application in you? Can you truthfully say that it is still an idea and not a fact? Then it gets down to the core of the issue. Can you say, ''I like what you said but for me it's an idea, not a fact''? You might even admit, ''Somewhere in me there is no real intent of knowing the fact.'' Then we are dealing with the issue of unwillingness — something concrete. It would be honest, not trying to appease the situation.

> *Student:* I don't know what to say.

Alright. But I won't let you off so easily next time. ''I don't know what to say'' will be an expedience then. What's good one time may be bad the next.

Mr. Krishnamurti used to tell a story about a rich man who died and went to Heaven. Peter is at the gate and says to him, ''There is an alternative to Heaven, you know. Maybe you'd better have a look at it before you come here.''

The rich man said, ''What is that?''

''Oh, just try it. Push that button.''

So he pushes the button and, instantly, he went down. And, you know, there were gardens, flowers, the most select wines and women, music. He wallowed in it awhile and went back to tell Peter.

''I like the alternative.''

So, he pushes the button again. Right down he goes. Now this time he lands and there are two husky people at the gate, no flowers, nothing, and they beat the dickens out of him. He said, ''Hey! Why? Just two minutes ago I was here and everything was fantastic! What happened?''

They said, ''You were a tourist then.''

So, you can't come back to ''I don't know what to say'' next time.

> *Student:* It is moving to see how, in a relaxed way, you take away what the brain projects inside as an alternative.

Has it been taken away?

> *Student:* Well, it has because I don't know what to say.

At least we are getting an idea that we can't just say ''take away.'' That might be so, but if yours is not taken away, then it is not so. So self-reliance may be real, but as long as you have lack and you are dependent, for you it's not so.

> *Student:* I see that there is no other way than the undoing of the thought.

I would still not say ''There is no other way.'' I would just say, ''Yes, I can be grateful.''

Who is next?

> *Student:* I'm still very struck by not having to have an answer — that we are not in need of an answer.

Yes, but wait a minute. We are not in need of an

answer. That's beautiful. Then one is inspired. But we can't go back to the same place we were ten minutes ago — there are two husky people!

We can't use not needing an answer as an idea. If it is real, then it is a gift.

> *Student:* That's the removal of the problem-solving mentality but yet to really do that is another thing altogether. It's how one lives.

Work with that. It's much better than reaction or pleasing somebody with how much we know. It's all false. Now you are dealing with *you*.

> *Student:* I was struck when you said to be grateful for the fact that has something to offer — whether I have received it or not. It occurred to me that I haven't received it; that's the only fact that is true for me. It's hard to come to gratefulness in that way when I keep with the lack in myself. I'd really like to know what gratefulness is without it being relative.

Well, perhaps you could discover how you keep the lack intact within you. You need to learn that. The lack bothers you so much that you really intensify it.

> *Student:* It clouds everything over.

You're not even being nice to yourself. How poisonous is negativity. It's really something. How it poisons one. It is the opposite of gratefulness.

Negativity can only exist at the relative level. Why not just see what is there — what actually is? That cleanses one of negativity.

Student: Are you saying that there is a way of seeing lack that will dissolve it, but the way *I* see it intensifies it?

Yes. But please listen. I don't think anybody sees anything because seeing, in its real meaning, is direct. Our seeing is seeing through thought. As long as I am seeing through thought — I look at another through thought — I never see *you*. As long as I am seeing through thought, it's going to be relative and I'm going to limit it to my opinion.

So, the word *seeing* is to see something directly. And most of us don't do that. When you are negative, then there is more thought. When you are grateful, there is more space. We are saying, "Look towards gratefulness."

It's not my need that you think this way or that way, but it certainly is yours. When you have recognized that, you will also see the unwillingness in you about which you have to do something. But if you are always finding negativity, then you are denying yourself. Therefore you don't want to change. And you then say, "I can't change." You will have to deal with your negativity and your unwillingness. You are directly confronted with it.

There is a Zen proverb that says:

"When the archer misses the bull's-eye, he finds the cause of the error in himself."

The minute you say it's the fault of the bull's-eye, you're not going to find the cause of the error in yourself. If we could only discover that that's one of the factors of our unwillingness! It's a means of postponement. It limits you to time. And at the time level, you can project a tomorrow and a yesterday. Therefore, you never know what is present. How deceptive the human mind is! How it finds ways!

I don't want to know what's wrong with "another" because you are looking through thought. I want to deal with *you*. Like when Jesus was saying, "You are a hypocrite." They didn't want to deal with that either, did they?

How serious the issue is! It's going to take everything to deal with that issue. Those things are within us in our very cells.

> *Student:* The main thing I wanted to say was not having to have an answer was so meaningful to me because I'm always wanting to have the last word. And I try to prove something.

I don't think it's so much needing to have the last word. You are a little too convinced about that. I don't think that it's the last word with you. You say things in a most spontaneous way, more than anybody else, and that's a beautiful thing. A person who wants the last word would be so wrapped up they would have no spontaneity in them. So just forget that. Don't get the second thought into it. Now, will you leave it alone?

> *Student:* Yes.

The question still remains: why is it that one would rather stay with ideas — which are of the world, which are unreal, which know no love — and not be with the fact that *A Course In Miracles* or God's Plan for Salvation offers?

> *Student:* With me it's just laziness.

Yes, that's a very basic thing. What do you think would help?

> *Student:* I don't know. I've been working with my thoughts. I sit quiet to try to follow them through and I've come to the awareness that I can't stay with anything at all. I can't find a subject that I'm interested in. It just keeps changing.

Sometimes I have many thoughts and I'm not in the mood to see them all the way through because I get tired or lazy. I have all those things.

> *Student:* I always give into that thought, to the laziness.

Oh, I love doing that too! But the point is that I can then read something from *A Course In Miracles* and something happens. Just one line.

I am as God Created me.[3]

I've seen it a thousand different ways. How it renews me. It's never renewed me the same way.

I am determined to communicate one thing: that when anyone reads *A Course In Miracles*, he invites the Presence and that Presence goes along with his reading. But if you read it in that moment of laziness, He would come but you won't be there.

I'm saying that for me, just the reading transforms something. It's another energy. So, instead of going back to, ''I know I am going to fall asleep,'' or, ''I am going to get disinterested,'' or, ''I won't stay with it,'' something new takes place.

It does something. And therefore I have discovered that the Presence is there; the power of the truth of the Word is there. And so instead of using your words to go back, why not have the words that have no contradiction? Are we seeing this?

Student: No, I'm not quite clear.

Instead of your trying to think something all the way through — why are you this way or that way, and so forth — that those words you're going to think about are dead. They don't have the vitality and they will make you more lazy. If you read the words of the Course, *they* have a vitality and a power because they don't have duality.

Student: Yes, I see that.

That would inspire you and give you vitality.

The most important thing is to get to know yourself but there are times when you need more energy. Like we need food to energize ourselves. So why not read something and stay with it and see if you can come to the awareness of what those words are saying? Try it.

Student: I'm afraid of that space.

Which space?

Student: Of not knowing, of not having an answer.

Isn't everybody? Now that's very beautiful. The unknown is a great scare. We'd rather suffer, we don't want the unknown. Isn't that something? This uncertainty, the unknown, is very scary.

Student: You have offered to each one here something unique to that person's tendency or situation. To me the session has been an example of what the one-to-one relationship is, that even in a group meeting, what is shared is unique with each person. That's beautiful to see.

And also basic issues, without the alleluias. It's almost inconceivable that there are only ideas by which we live. And there is the fact, the unknown. I have to die to the ideas. If I *want* to know the fact, that very wanting to know the fact is also an idea. Can we discover the energy of that fact?

Student: We don't take that step.

We don't even come to gratefulness. Look how swift that action is — that all the time there are those moments of awareness and we go on with what we *want*. The idea limits us. We also see that whether Moses is impeccable or not impeccable, it doesn't matter. The way we see it is not what it is anyway. So then, why not deal with the negativity and see, ''This affects my consciousness. I am responsible for *this*. The situation may be something other than what I see.'' How much healthier that is!

It is absolutely necessary to come to gratefulness. That's why the intellectual experts, whose minds are so crowded, can't be inspired. Or if they are inspired, it's about something they bought: a painting, a vase, this, that. It's always associated with self, with objects. And gratefulness is something that doesn't have that.

Gratefulness is not for *things* of the earth. It could be for human kindness, it could be for someone who inspires something other within you. Gratefulness is what you receive by having perceived it. Having perceived. Then it's not an object, is it? It's your own richness you are getting to know. Do you see how beautiful that is?

Can we be grateful for just *seeing* a flower? Can we be grateful for seeing an action that is free of motives? That way. That gratefulness would purify us.

> *Student:* I can understand that gratefulness is not when I've done anything to approach it. It just is there.

Yes. It happens. It's independent of thought. And that's beautiful.

> *Student:* My whole life has been an evasion of that. It seems that I am always trying to get away from "me." It's an issue for me. And somehow I am not measuring up to it. I am resisting it.

Again I say that negativity is also self-condemnation. And that contaminates a person, alright? Your condemning yourself also contaminates the situation. Can one stay away from that?

> *Student:* I don't know how to do that.

You see, we can learn about ourself just as easily as about someone else. I think the one who is going to appreciate won't be condemning himself as much. The minute you condemn yourself you are back with lack and limitation.

> *Student:* I can understand that but it's always an active thought. It's always, "There I go again." And it's the same thing.

But are we also seeing something new that we have shared, you and I, that there is self-reliance, one-to-one relationship, all of these things? That's very inspiring. That in this day and age it could take place! This inspiration has something uplifting because it's more of the spirit than of thought.

So then we say that you must always remember you are as God created you. Don't say, "I am not this." That's not a fact either. You don't have the right to condemn yourself.

This is the new thing. This negativity has to end — whether it's negativity towards someone else or towards yourself.

> *Student:* I've read this in the Course, but in life it has never been presented to me as it has here. It hits me but it never really *inspires* me.

It might. It might. Who knows the power of this moment, of these words that we are sharing. It might.

You see, we have to come to something the ancients knew. They taught the child to have reverence for parents so that there was someone they would not contradict. That requires some self-control.

Do you remember the story of my visit with the saint? I thought I was selfish, and indeed I was, but my contact with one person for whom I had reverence helped me to overcome it. That one could do so! My whole belief system, everything came to an end because of that reverence. I touched upon a strength in me that could end the duality, end the concepts. I was introduced to a confidence that was in me. The confidence must have always been there but it was used for mischief. And now the encounter takes place because I have reverence for one person. One person!

So, the child was taught to have reverence for his parents because they meant well for him. There was a good relationship. They listened more and therefore developed character. There were certain things they might want to do, but because of the reverence, they heeded.

Then later, once that had taken place between the child and his parents, the parents introduced him to a real teacher because they had prepared him. The child could trust the teacher.

Today parents have very little relationship with their children in terms of reverence. Therefore, they can't find a real teacher or a school that would be different. The parents, like the child, have remained insecure. And so they find teachers to train their child with skills to get a job. The whole value system has changed.

In ancient times, the child was brought up to have reverence. Now we don't have reverence because we can contradict the parents and declare our independence: ''I've got a job at the gas station.'' What is vertical has almost totally been taken away.*

So, I'm saying that it's important to have reverence for *A Course In Miracles,* for God's Plan for Salvation. Don't you see? Maybe it has something authentic. And in order to know if it does or not, you need discrimination. So back you are with yourself.

---

*For a detailed discussion of the issues involved in parenting, see *How To Raise A Child Of God* by Tara Singh (Life Action Press, 1987). (Editor)

What discrimination it would take for you to know if it is authentic or not!

What discrimination would it take for you to know that you have to have reverence for your parents? You are not born by accident, so to speak. A child may want other parents but there is another Force that's in charge. The lessons are there to learn. You are born to make those corrections within yourself. And you can't make the corrections within you unless you have reverence for the parents.

So then, the problem is over with. You don't contradict them. Do you see what I mean? The right relationship takes place and they find you a teacher who is going to teach you something beyond the manmade because they prepared you.

The only necessary thing is having discrimination, isn't it? And today, man doesn't have discrimination; it's not necessary anymore. The only discrimination you need now is: this is America, that's Canada. Communists are bad and the capitalists are good. That's not discrimination.

Discrimination is a necessary thing. Do you agree with that? This other Force we have been talking about, we don't know; but it is an action that we can all observe. Awaken your discrimination so that you establish a direct relationship with it. It is discrimination that determines for you whether a situation is authentic or not. *You* are responsible for discrimination.

Then, if you're negative about someone else, you have to take care of the negativity within yourself. That's discrimination! "I'd better leave the other person alone. I'd better do something about my negativity." Something else takes place. Can you see that we are not "teaching"; we are changing the direction so that each person can discover his own potentials.

> *Student:* That's where it ends for me — coming back to finding the error in myself.

But when you find the error in yourself and you stay with the error, I don't want negativity to come into it.

> *Student:* What's the difference?

The difference is that one is an observation and the other is a blame. Can you be a witness and not blame?

Do you see how quick that is? He asks a question and immediately it gets answered. When a student can ask a question it gets answered this way — if the fact is there, *it* does it. Now do you see the value of asking a question?

> *Student:* When you speak about negativity and discrimination, it makes me feel as though the negativity in me is not having the confidence of knowing I have discrimination. Perhaps if I could just trust, that would eliminate a lot of the negativity as well?

It's very difficult to trust. Very difficult. But it is trust that makes the mind free, and not education. Look how profound that is!

IT IS TRUST THAT FREES THE MIND,
NOT EDUCATION.

So, trust is a very difficult thing. As long as we are identified with the body, we cannot know trust. And you say, "That's all I know." Then maybe a brother called a teacher could help because you would not deviate from the subject of trust. Without trust, fear comes in, laziness comes in — all these things.

Any one fact, any one basic word could relate you to everything else. If you could learn what trust is, you wouldn't need to know another thing in the world. You wouldn't know insecurity, nor lack. One thing. Just one thing.

If you don't trust, how are you going to trust *A Course In Miracles* or God's Plan for Salvation? Your trust would merely be a belief. We are trying to say that it's very important to come to discrimination, to trust. You can't be casual about it.

Trust is absolutely necessary. It's the only solution to the vibrations of our modern age which are so disturbing. Man today can barely soar beyond the business mentality. Can you imagine? Business is a very low standard. You want the furs, you kill the animals.

Do you know how many pigeons there used to be in America — the long tailed, large pigeons? One naturalist has written that for hours and hours you couldn't see the sun when they flew. They were all killed. And the cruelty to the buffalo. Whether it's pigeons or buffalo or Indians or gold mines, it goes on. Everywhere in the world it's the same.

There is one saving grace:

"In God We Trust."

That can change — transform — that impurity, that vibration.

So we are back with trust in God, aren't we? And just to see that is inspiring. The forefathers had placed "In God We Trust" on every dollar bill because that is what will take us out of the business mentality and bring us to trust. Both are on the same note. Which do you choose? A fact or an idea?

If it's brought to idea, then it's limited again. Can one touch upon that which is beyond thought, beyond ideas, and be inspired by that other something that brings gratefulness with it?

I hope it has become clearer: that we need to see the fallacy of ideas that prevent us from coming to fact. Fact is not of time. Fact is not personal. Ideas are personal and borrowed and they limit us to "me and mine." *A Course In Miracles* is based on something that is not limited to "me and mine." It is timeless; it doesn't know lack. Therefore, we have to first see the fallacy of ideas and step into fact by using the fact. By coming to the fact, the ideas will resolve themselves involuntarily.

Can we remember that? Seeing the fallacy of the idea is already making the fact alive and active. That's what is doing it.

Thank you.

CHAPTER TWELVE

12

THE SURVIVAL
OF LITTLENESS

We have talked about objective thinking and the need to have discrimination. They are very subtle. They are not for the mundane nor for those who are too ''educated,'' so to speak. They are for those who are responsible for how they live, for what they do. The casual person who is just interested in ''me and mine'' is not concerned with objective thinking or with discrimination. He is not going to stop at anything; he's already blinded; his questions are already answered, don't you see? You can't explain subtle things to him.

But a wise person looks at things differently. We may see all kinds of paradoxes or contradictions in a situation which at another level don't exist.

A very nice lady came for lunch today and was asking about certain things we are doing that are, let's say, ''good business.'' But the fact is the

Foundation for Life Action is not a business.* Why is it not a business? It is not a business because we extend what we are doing. Then you say, ''Well, what's the difference between business and extending?''

Business and commerce might be different but no one would put business and extending in the same category, or say there could be a misunderstanding about them. They are so far apart. Then what is the difference between them?

We are extending because we are interested in what we are sharing, as students. We want to share this and because we live in the world of today, we also need money to pay for rents and so forth. If we were a business we would be thinking about money. But when we are extending, it's already something that is here, that needs to be shared. Are we seeing it?

Let's say John has clarity; he has evolved himself. He has ended his duality. Then he must share. He *must* share. He is not doing it for business reasons. Out of this sharing then, he would want to extend.

The difference between extending and business is that extending is a total action. It has a wholeness to it. You cannot extend something that is not whole. Business, on the other hand, is an

---

*The Foundation for Life Action is a federally approved, nonprofit, educational foundation which makes available books and audio and video cassette sharings related to *A Course In Miracles* and to the expression of wisdom throughout the ages. The Foundation is also a school for training teachers to bring *A Course In Miracles* into application. (Editor)

expedience; you want something. Are you seeing the difference?

To extend, it has to be whole. You can't extend a partial thing. It extends because somewhere it relates to what is of eternal values. There is no way you could say, ''Well, let's just have it for ourselves and not extend.'' You cannot stand in the way of total action.

Could anyone of you have said what the difference between business and extending is? We are defining what you may think of as a paradox, or what the world may think of as a paradox.

Having understood these things, you can share further about what *we* are doing. You can share further with the lady or with anyone for that matter and bring *them* to: ''Don't *you* want to be an extension? Don't you want to quit the job situation? Don't you want a different lifestyle?''

When you answer a question another person asks you, you are not going to stop short because you've got to extend. The question has entered a different realm. If you give a casual answer, you are not extending. Are we seeing it? Anyone who asks you a question is ''hooked'' — *if* your life is an extension — because the minute you explain it, you'll say: ''Now what are *you* going to do with it? Make it intellectual?''

What we are saying is that you can't be close to a person who extends without becoming responsible yourself. He is going to demand that. See how much further we are going? That's *your* responsibility. So then whatever you do would be extending and making the other person more responsible for his life because you are responsible in extending. At no point are you going to deviate from love or extending.

It's like the cheetah that comes into view and is seen by the herd of gazelles — they run in every direction. People might all run away from you! But be it so because you can't be anything other than that — always making it possible for the other person, that he can be responsible. And what are his justifications? "How can I make a living?" Or, "What can I do?" You'll say: "These are questions that are not real. You have just accepted them as real." That way.

We don't know the power of the word because our words have very little meaning. Do we know what truth is? Our words are words of expedience for the most part. We talk about freedom and no one is free. Doesn't that shock a person? Hardly anyone is free from loneliness, fear, selfishness, insecurity. And yet we believe we are free.

We must be very serious about how we live. Just take account of what it is you have learned in a real way. What have you learned? If you have reverence, you won't waste. Have you mastered any single thing? Has your wastage of water been cut down? That you would not waste at all? Does that make any difference to you? Have you learned anything?

We use all our energy to limit ourselves, don't we? All of us. All the so-called intelligence, all our knowing — it's all to make ourselves more narrow-minded. That's what a horizontal life is, you know, more nationalistic, more ambitious, and so on.

We have developed efficiency. We can travel on planes from here to there. But we have also strengthened the "me and mine" more and more.

Everything to limit yourself. You were educated to limit yourself: you became more selfish, more dogmatic, greedier. Do you know what I am talking about?

Your politics, your education, your religion has made you "small" — and it never occurred to you. You worship this littleness and then you want to protect it. And it gets more and more intensified. So, what have you learned?

The wise man does not make survival his first concern. Have you listened to what I am saying? Did you then discover the littleness of being preoccupied with survival? That issue is more prevalent today than it was even fifty years ago.

Can anyone of you say that you have taken advantage of these sessions? Not once did anyone come with a question that burns within! You have been presented with the fact. Has this occurred to you? Is this something startling? Have you valued one truth, one fact? Once you leave this room, it's still partly with you; by the time you are outside the building, it's gone. Is this not a fact? What are you going to do with this?

You don't even know that there is a difference between business and extension. When you extend you can only be whole. It's a total action. Therefore, it revolutionizes life because it is in relationship to the earth, to your neighbor, to yourself, to your wife, to your husband, to nature, to everything. Have you seen the wonder of it? Do you ever let it expand outside of your littleness?

It's like a balloon: you put a little more air in it and it gets a little bigger, but it has an enormous limitation. And you are glad that it could go this far.

Man has used his energy and his physical senses to make himself little, more confined. Not just by dogmas and belief systems, but at every level. Do you think that a saint who is unlimited could fit into anything? Has it ever occurred to you? Supposing someone gave you a hundred thousand dollars, what would you do? Intensify your littleness? Think about it, will you please? And you come to *A Course In Miracles*, God's Plan for Salvation, and you don't want to leave your own plan of littleness? Talk about freedom and you're not free. What prevents you from being free? Have you ever dealt with that?

What deals with the littleness is not something that one has learned. What deals with it is the awareness that you have made yourself narrow-minded — being aware of what is! Then out of that awareness something else takes place. Have you ever sat down and dealt with it like that?

> *Student:* I think all of us would agree with what you say. And yet that doesn't effect a change either. I feel a sense of withdrawal even more when I hear it because it seems more futile, more out of reach.

Yes. One loses confidence. There is a certain span of time for adequate response.

You know, in a country like India, people could leave home and go search for God. They were very sincere when they started. I met many of those people; they were burning, sincere. They would not have left the comfort of the home otherwise. Young people, kings, queens. It's something! Thousands upon thousands of people left.

And then somewhere they lose confidence in themselves. They have tried this and tried that, and then this and then that — and they lose confidence. They may not even be aware of it. They get down to more of a sub-level and then their real nature is there. The motivations come in, "I'd better beg for food from there," or "Those are kind people." Don't you see? The motivations come in and you're a slave of yourself. And you left home to be free!

People who go to monasteries give their whole life. I am sure that there is a sincerity in it, but at what point do they lose confidence? They pray and Jesus doesn't "do it," or Mohammed doesn't "do it," or Nanak doesn't "do it." You can't tell anyone because they will mock you if you go back. Perhaps one of the things that keeps a person there is that he can't expose it. And it could go on. You know, you make it convenient because you have brought it down to where you are comfortable.

One is comfortable being narrow-minded, self-centered, small. All of one's energy goes into it. The smaller you make yourself, the more energy you need to spend to retain it.

And now, having a profession has become a necessity. Therefore, you can be owned; you're just a number. And the computer has taken birth. It is the artificial, mechanical intelligence superior to the human brain.*

---

*For further discussion on man's present condition in the world and the consequences of his dependence on jobs, see *The Future Of Mankind — The Branching Of The Road* by Tara Singh (Foundation for Life Action, 1986). (Editor)

> *Student:* I can see that in smallness I dissipate all my energy.

How nicely said. That's nice.

> *Student:* It seems that the only alternative is to reach out to something higher. Something that inspires me is the only thing that really stops that. But once I am in it, I continue that and it's like a locomotive within.

That's all the ''locomotive'' knows. So we have become creatures of habit. Who is going to break that habit of making himself little? Who? That person would be a student. That person *is* the student. In littleness one dissipates one's energy, isn't it? Each one of us is there. And our energy goes into maintaining our little, narrow-minded selfhood.

> *Student:* Is that littleness then more than just fear or a kind of feeling? Is it also if I think I'm a certain type of person or if I have a certain type of direction? That could be limiting as well?

Yes. That's what we are trying to say — that the littleness then projects a bigness. So the bigness is also little because it's born out of the littleness. It's a projection from the littleness. And *that* requires a university education. Beyond the ''becoming,'' we know almost nothing. Only littleness is interested in becoming something different. But it's never different, it is still littleness.

Do you think this is going to make any difference to you after two hours? Or two days? Nothing seems to hit one!

Littleness dissipates man. It dissipates all the energy and you have nothing left. You can't meet a challenge; you evade the challenge. More and more the human being is getting exhausted — less ethics, less conviction. He is becoming indifferent. "What can I do?" The monster of helplessness.

The littleness has ambition on one side and helplessness on the other. But they are merely tentacles of littleness. And you have been with *A Course In Miracles,* God's Plan for Salvation? What if you *really* heard it? What would you pay for it? The only price you can pay is to break the bondage of littleness. Then you would have something to give to the world. But can littleness ever give? Could it? Is littleness ever free of motives?

So, we said all of man's energy goes into maintaining the smallness, the littleness. You probably never thought about that. Now it's presented; what difference does it make?

Well, let's take the intensity away so that you can breathe better. I remember one time I had a terrible, feverish headache and at about twelve o'clock all of you were to come. I didn't have the energy to do anything that I could do to get out of the headache. It was maddening. I knew certain things to do to get rid of the headache but I couldn't do them. You see, it takes a longer time and you don't have that space. And you're in great anxiety: "What am I going to do? They are going to come." And so forth. The few hours you have, you feel terrible. You really feel the intensified pain of littleness.

And so you watch how everything that one has done has been to energize the littleness — the wrong living, the wrong thinking. Is that going to occur to you? That it's wrong living, wrong thinking?

Well, I know that before twelve o'clock I am going to be out of it. That's all. I was in great pain with the headache. Have you ever known that kind of headache, that you can't even open your eyes? But I said, ''I can't. It is so, but that's not who I am.'' And a few minutes before, or half an hour before, I am totally out of it. Not one of you would ever know.

There is something that doesn't accept littleness as real, even though it becomes a physical reality. But the physical is not real. And littleness has no power. As if there are other blessings, other forces, something else that has no name. You can call it grace, but we don't know what that is.

When you are true to something, littleness can't touch you. When you are true to something, there is no littleness and therefore, you have something to give. There is some exuberance, some joy in you. The pain and the littleness don't contain you.

You have no idea how much vulnerability suffers. The vulnerable person is tossed around. That's why nobody wants to be vulnerable. You want to protect it. And the minute you protect it, you intensify the littleness. We don't know any other means.

Tell me, if you were not little, would you defend yourself? Would you know to lie? Would you have a problem? If you were not little, would you justify? Have you ever thought about what littleness does? You live by it throughout your life. Haven't you watched what you do — how you protect yourself?

Do you know the word "vulnerable"? Have you ever tried to question the meaning of,

In my defenselessness my safety lies?[1]

Have you read the Course? Can littleness read it? If littleness read it, it wouldn't be little anymore. See what this beautiful lesson says:

*Let me recognize the problem
so it can be solved.*[2]

Have you ever come to that point where you want to recognize? Have you made any attempt to just recognize? The problem is the littleness. Shall we stay with that?

When I first came to America, I moved from the Plaza Hotel in New York because all my money was gone. I stayed with a family in New Jersey and this good friend of mine said, "You know, the graduating engineering class needs a speaker and they are going to pay this much." I had never been on a stage in my life. But, the thing that really got me was that it was three weeks away. That's what got me. Life can really trap you! Like Hemingway said, "I can do anything tomorrow."

But the "tomorrow" came. And I was shivering. All of these people! I wanted to go to the bathroom and never come out. I wished that my leg would break. I wished that my uncle were there. Anything. You don't know what to do. I have been through those situations.

And they are raving about this man. Oh Lord, you never hated anything more than praises for you at a time like that. And my turn comes. Oh, it is something! You have to go to the podium. And one factor — they are all men except for one woman, and I don't know what to say: "Ladies or gentlemen. . ." You want to do it the way it should be done and you don't know what to do. You feel so inadequate. Now I can say it doesn't matter, but at that time. . .!

So, I stood there; I couldn't say a thing. I froze. Nothing would come out. But it didn't last long. I spoke even though I was stunned. (Can you take charge of a situation? Are you going to do that now? It's just a matter of how long you would allow littleness to control you. At what point would you be loosened of it — and be with what is?)

Now these are graduating engineers. Do you know what saved me? I saw a fork and I said, "If I look at a fork, it leads me all the way back to the engineer. There are two forces in this world: one of God and the other of the engineer. The ship I came in, this microphone — are part of the wider role the engineer has played in evolution. Will he betray science now or use it to the advantage of man? That is the point where we now stand.

"Would you be true to being creative, to being helpful, using things for facilitating and making the human being more dignified? Or are you going to betray and go towards one dogma or another and build armaments? What is the engineer going to do now? What is he going to build? Bridges? That would be wonderful; they are needed. Or is it going to be war planes to destroy what he built and what God created?"

That is where you start. And somehow you get an ovation at the end. So, you have to deal with things. I would always sympathize. I know what it is like. Is that fair enough?

Now that we have this background, we come back again to business versus extension. What do we learn? We learn to eliminate that which is unessential. Can you come to that discrimination and see what things are unessential? You become strong because you are dealing with facts, with that discrimination.

As long as it is not to maintain smallness, it would work. If the efficiency increases to strengthen smallness, then it is ambition. How can you come to an awakening of other potentials without being ambitious and without being a business? You extend a total action.

We come back to it, that the total action is what extends. The total action has enormous resources. Can *you* renew yourself? Each person wants to but who dares challenge their habits? What would you need to challenge habit? Awareness, isn't it?

What is awareness? Awareness is what was necessary to first see the limit, the smallness — that everything we do maintains our littleness. If you are not at the level of awareness, your enthusiasm or your wanting to do it is already an oversight. You're again settling for things of the brain. Things of the brain can only limit you. And we have said that failures and success do not matter.

Now, how do you understand this?

> *Student:* I hear what you are saying. I only wish I could say something profound.

Well, the thing is that the internal action of correction is difficult, isn't it? So, what are we going to do? Remain little? You would say, "No," but it doesn't mean anything. You see, the answer doesn't mean anything. The only thing that matters is the action.

So, what am I doing all the time? Speaking from awareness, trying to transmit awareness. There is no *teaching* in that. We learn through experience, which is the long way, but awareness doesn't need time. We think we do. This littleness is so convinced that it needs to learn and that it takes time. It believes in "becoming." Awareness is independent of all that. Isn't that a nice definition of awareness? That awareness is not "becoming" and it is independent of time. That's why this is a course in miracles. Miracles are flashes of the grace of God, or flashes of insight.

I think that what we need to learn comes back again to the same question: Are *you* an extension? Then you have the power of Heaven behind you. Can one appreciate that? In order to extend, we have to make inner changes. Inner change means to free yourself from the littleness that dissipates all the energy. You'll say, "I cannot do that."

We must make sure not to be victims of littleness. We must make very sure that we are an extension of God's Plan for Salvation and *By grace I live.*[3] To come to awareness doesn't take time. And we *have* to come to this awareness — the awareness that "I'm not little. I am part of God's Plan for Salvation." Something takes place.

The tendency is for littleness to feel helpless.

So, how are you going to respond to the challenges ahead of you? Every challenge is a challenge to the littleness and to the helplessness.

> *Student:* For me to challenge that littleness, the only way I can is through my faith in the grace of God, as much as I know it.

Well, what I'm trying to say is that it's going to take a bold action for any one of us to break through the littleness. It has to be that bold. If you could take that step — the step is that you would not live by littleness — you've given everyone a gift, including me.

> *Student:* What occurred to me earlier in the evening was the comment you made about how the littler or the smaller you are, the more energy it takes to maintain it. And it really hit me. We may not identify something with ourselves but I can see from my own experience with people who are bigoted that they are just so bound up in their beliefs, whatever they might be. And I can see how it does take more energy to maintain that. When you said that it sort of struck a chord with me.
>
> Then the other thing was when you were saying how difficult it was. And somehow I just wondered: Why should it be difficult? It shouldn't. We're maintaining it. We keep putting the energy into whatever you want to call littleness. It doesn't seem like it should be difficult.

At the level of awareness, there's no difficult or easy. It just is. Therefore, it's independent. But it is difficult at the personality level, at the littleness level. And the only thing the littleness wants is the bigness. They're both outside reality, so to speak. The function of awareness is to expose and to undo that.

I'd like to go into something we were talking about this morning — that perfection is always present, always there. And whenever you become aware of the perfection, that which made you aware of it sees that everything you did is what brought you there, to that point. You see that everything you did — all the mistakes, everything — was necessary. And therefore, all the past is finished and gratefulness comes. There is no more guilt, no more regret, no more past. The possibility of coming to the gratefulness of the perfection is there.

Can you try to understand this, please? You think, "My life is miserable. I've made so many mistakes. I wish I had done it this way and that way." Everyone can say that.

I'm saying there's always perfection in everything because there is only the good. The only reality in life is gratefulness or perfection or love. And then you say, "Oh God, I've known so much hate and ugliness in me and in others, and you talk about gratefulness? Forget it."

And I say: No, because this perfection always accompanies your life. It's like angels are with you. Always there is that light with which God has surrounded you, the other energy of which we know so little. It's like the Life Force itself and each person is surrounded by it, therefore, protected by it.

We have not known that because we are always preoccupied with littleness. So we say, any time you become aware of,

By grace I live.[4]

or,

I am as God created me.[5]

right away you would see that all the bad things you did or you thought you did are finished. Then why do you keep on prolonging this duality, the struggle, and not come to "In God We Trust"? What good is it knowing that perfection is always there? You're already perfect. *You* think you're not. That's the only deception that needs to be removed. Whenever it gets removed, you see the perfection you are and the perfection of everything that's there. As a matter of fact, you see that imperfection never existed. You were the one validating your own images.

Now, if you are a student — I mean a real student, not *wanting* to be a student — then you are already provided for. When you are not a student, you go and work and pay and so forth and you get your relative knowledge.

The one who goes for relative knowledge is only maintaining littleness and dissipating his energy. Is that clear? Can you imagine how the universities flourish? You support them — with your littleness. Isn't that something? The whole cockeyed world!

Relative knowledge doesn't lead anywhere. It's only for the survival of littleness. Can you imagine, everything exists just for the survival of littleness? Once you accept yourself as little, you need to be "religious"; you need to be successful, ambitious; this, that, and so forth.

If you became a student, if you were *really* a student who wants to free himself from littleness, everything would be provided. First, the very teaching, so to speak, would be non-commercial because you are no longer in need of the relative knowledge which you bought to maintain your littleness. The one who has True Knowledge cannot commercialize it because he is part of extension. How can he commercialize it?

True Knowledge cannot be sold. Where there is True Knowledge, there is His Divine Presence also because it's a sharing. And that is protected and provided for. It's a blessed thing. And it is possible any time because it's always there.

Have you ever thought about how significant such an action might be upon the planet? Have you ever thought about how vast and unlimited it would be? If you can't come to gratefulness, you're dead. Have you ever thought about it?

So we say — look how simple it is — that as long as you want to maintain littleness, you need relative knowledge. For relative knowledge, you go to school to be trained. It doesn't teach you virtue or ethics. You can still lie. You can be unethical. And you can do what you like as long as you're at work on time and do the paperwork or whatever it is. If you're a marine, you do what they want. And they don't care about anything else.

But we're saying the student is one who is no longer interested in relative knowledge because he has seen the fallacy of littleness and how it maintains itself. If this meeting could accomplish only that, or just make you aware of it, then you could be a student. It's the awakening of the student in you. It's something within *you*. The seeds are sown. You couldn't fit into anything. You would see that it is pleasure or it is consequences. And you only seek pleasure and success because you're in a state of sorrow. You think *it* is going to do it for you. The Ferrari isn't going to get you anywhere faster but it gives you status.

Status is needed as long as you consider yourself a personality. So then, that's more littleness. What you care about is your "name" — very touchy about it too. Someone is critical of it, you want to sue him. If others don't like your dogma, you criticize them, and so forth.

If you could just know that everything you have done, anything you can learn, whatever you are trained and drilled for, has only been to maintain your littleness! Is that a fact? Are you clear about it? No disputes on that? If this is your truth, if you keep this in your awareness, you won't fit into the littleness. You have touched upon awareness.

But littleness is also a force. It's the strongest force you have, and you find strength in it. It has built up muscles; it knows how to make you feel insecure, how to make you feel lonely. It has projected a tomorrow. Its unreality is what you live by.

Awareness doesn't acknowledge tomorrow or yesterday. Isn't that beautiful. Awareness. The minute you come to it there is no more past. You feel the perfection. It brings you to the perfection, to the action of grace. And you are no longer little, nor are you preoccupied with yourself.

And for such a student all is provided. That means you don't have to have effort. We believe in effort. But it has nothing to do with effort! You would see your own perfection. You would see that the things of time are illusion. There would be only gratefulness. ''My God, I thought I was a sinner and I had done this wrong but it doesn't exist anymore.'' You would see the glory of God, that He doesn't punish. You would remember His forgiveness and His Love.

The student is fully provided. Perfection always is. And the teacher can only bring you to awareness. It's a faculty you have — a faculty by which you will find your own holiness. You don't have to ''become'' perfect; you *are* perfect. What else is there to teach than to make one aware of who he is as God created him? A person who makes you aware of that, is he not going to be provided for when he is an extension? Does he worry about insecurity?

And you, as a student, also become an extension, moving away from deceptions. The extension is protected. And it has so much energy. The whole cosmic world, the universe that it extends, is behind it. That's what God's Plan for Salvation is.

At any time you can come to that. But the ego keeps on postponing and thinks, ''I'm not quite ready yet. I know I'm *going* to do it.'' Make it an idea and you won't heed it as a fact. Why? Can you heed what I am saying as a fact? Have we not presented it that way? We have dealt with fact, fact,

fact. Then why can't you come to the fact? Why do you still stay with the idea?

> *Student:* That question has been going through my mind too. What really is it that prevents it?

We mistake idea for fact.

> *Student:* Yes, I know that I'm not there and I'm trying to see — what is it really that keeps me from that? . . . It's just some *idea.*

And then the idea is that it still wants to do good. Well, let's stay with that. It still wants to do good when it isn't good itself. So, place, person, activity — the experience of that keeps one where one is. Can we then term that the helplessness?

One is helpless, otherwise one would stay with the fact. Helplessness wants "to go and help" because it must have an activity.

> *Student:* I see.

You cannot now go towards helplessness, since this has been clarified, in the pretense that you're "going to help." Why don't you deal with that fact? That fact will require some dialogue — that you have become a student who really wants to know the fact and not the idea. You cannot afford the pretense of "going to help" somebody. Well, if you can't even help yourself in coming to the fact, it's pretentious. You can't be a friend. You still validate that there is such a thing as circumstances.

So, why don't you talk about what *you* are going to do so that you and I can dissolve the "person, place, and activity" that's personal? Why aren't you interested in ending the personal projections and activity? Why? Is it not offered?

> *Student:* Why is it that I can't come to the fact?

Once you are with the fact, you would know, wouldn't you? Now you know that you are not there. And I said, well, these are the three factors that prevent it: person, place, activity. Each one of us has the same three factors. Why don't you want to discover the factor, or unload yourself, empty yourself, expose yourself to what that is? Then it can be dealt with by the awareness of which you and I become a part. I won't say, ''Let that go'' because that's still the opposite. But you and I can come to awareness. That is offered. What could be more blessed than that?

> *Student:* I see that it is possible.

God's Plan for Salvation is upon the earth. Why would one still refuse to do so? Obviously, the ''place, person, and activity'' is still more important and it prevents one from being the student, isn't it? That's your deliberate choice. You give it the vitality and therefore remain little and pretend you want God or awareness or miracles or insight or friendship.

> *Student:* As soon as I look at what the person, place, or activity is, I see that I'm looking for what my problem is so that I can single it out in one of those terms. In some ways I see that almost as fast as I put my finger on it, that's not it. But I don't seem to get anywhere with that. It's

evasive. I'm more aware of it as being more internal. There is something that rises, there is an action of this limiting, this activity of limitation in my own consciousness that, as far as I can see, is solely reactive. And I keep asking myself: Why? Is that deliberate? How am I participating with that?

Reaction is not part of awareness. We can get into a sub-level and then all we know is reaction. But we don't have to be at a sub-level.

The fact is that there is an awareness that's independent of learning, independent of time, independent of cause and effect. You say, "Yes, I understand it but that's not my reality."

Student: Yes.

It's not your reality and therefore you say that that too is abstract.

Student: Yes.

But you can't truthfully say that awareness doesn't exist.

Student: I know there is an awareness but I have not experienced it. I know that there is something other.

Then let us put it in a different way which would be simpler for everybody because this is getting a little bit intellectual. There are *blocks to the awareness of love's presence.*[6] Love is always present, but there are blocks to the awareness of it.

Student: Yes.

And therefore, this action of awareness is what we may call the action of grace.

By grace I live.[7]

Now, "I haven't known that. If I knew it, then the block wouldn't be there." That's what you are pointing out. But you do see that whatever you conclude is not your reality. Whatever you conclude I will not accept as real either. You will have to come to awareness. That's my responsibility — as long as you're willing to expose your conclusion. The conclusion becomes the block, doesn't it? It's my responsibility to remove that block.

And then tell me, why is it we are not grateful for that? There is not the exuberance. How can you ever come to it without gratefulness? How? Ingratitude is what makes us sick with impurities and negativity. And you still say, "I don't see it." You'd rather come to a block: "It's not my reality."

I am not discouraged. I said, if it's not your reality, then it's my responsibility to remove that. So, it would lead to dialogue from where we can end the phraseology and remove the blocks, the conclusions. But you don't say with exuberance: "My God! I never expected that this would be possible! That it's possible for me, it's given!"

You don't want to come to gratefulness. You just worship your ability to not accept it. The non-receiving has been worshipped. You refuse to accept it and you're not grateful. Are you going to have peace with ingratitude in you? Not gratefulness to me, but to the fact of Life. For the air you breathe, the food you eat, the sleep that comforts you, the blood that circulates, the grace that brought us together.

I would be so elated if somebody said to me, "Look. There are these blocks to the awareness and the block is what you conclude." And he said, "I will remove that. That's *my* responsibility." Are you frightened of being grateful? As long as one is not grateful one is with ingratitude. There is no in-between. And then there is the effort. Ingratitude, I was told, is the only sin. That means ingratitude is the only thing that preserves separation. Separation from the One, from the reality of what one is.

I don't need your gratefulness, but you need it. You need it. If you can't be grateful, have it your way. When I say "have it your way," I am saying that's the way of the ego and you want to extend the ego. It's up to you. Another person can't do anything other than to say that if you are fed up with the ego wanting to maintain time, it can be ended. And you say, "I've never heard of such a thing. Is that so?" I say, "Of course. Try it right now. It's possible."

If, with a true heart one accepted that, it would bring you to it. But if ingratitude is there, you never really faced it. You won't try to make the correction inside of you because you'd blame somebody else. That's what we are trying to prevent. No one can criticize what is real and have peace. Listen to what I am saying. You can't point a finger in that direction and know peace.

There is a wonderful story about a man who was very devoted to Allah and he took his son with him on a pilgrimage to Mecca. It's a difficult place to get to because it's in the desert; but they arrived. The father got up very early in the morning to pray. He woke up the son and the son looked around and everybody was sleeping. He said, ''All these people came to Mecca, the holy place, and look, they are all sleeping.'' The father was so pained. He said, ''I wish I had not brought you. For you to criticize, to come to that negativity, that judgment, better you had not come.''

What a beautiful thing! If you didn't come to gratefulness, you would judge. You don't come to gratefulness, and you'd rather judge. What are you going to do about removing your judgment which is the block?

Judgment is a block to the awareness of Love's presence. You don't want someone to awaken you. You don't come to gratefulness for a moment to step out of the littleness. Awareness is also part of gratefulness. You can't be aware and not be grateful. They are both one and the same.

> *Student:* It's become very clear that it's one or it's the other. I mean, there is no in-between.

It's either real or it's unreal.

> *Student:* The closest I can even approach it at this point is with an appreciation of the understanding that's been given.

How sacred is understanding when it is real understanding. Real understanding is what inspires you — just seeing or knowing that there is a block which is one's own conclusion! Even though you haven't come to the reality of enlightenment, but something brought you to the understanding. Your realization of gratefulness brought you to it.

That's why I was told that ingratitude is the only sin, the only thing that causes separation. It separates ''you'' from ''me''; it separates ''you'' from your ''Self.''

> *Student:* Why are we afraid of that? Why is the thought process afraid of that?

You see, the ego is not going to identify with gratefulness or grace. It's going to identify with the body. And that's the block.

We are explaining it all the time in different ways. Do you see the beauty awareness has, what vitality it has? It renews hearing. It can present it this way, that way. It is always new. And you don't want to be renewed?

Has anything ever happened in the New World so sincerely dedicated to coming to new consciousness? Why is it then one still wants to not be inspired?

> *Student:* I appreciate your pointing out that there is no blame in life. That every time I am in confusion, I am not with gratefulness. Thank you for having put so much emphasis on this particular thing in spite of the non-response or the inadequate response. That, to me, is a real example of what gratefulness is — that it continues to give.

You have to tell me, my dear, that, ''I know all

reactions are born out of littleness. I don't understand what the opposite of littleness is, but I will take care of the reactions.''

> *Student:* I feel that.

Good. It's going to take all the strength you have. And then that strength is your bank account in Heaven. Every time we overcome a tendency, it's a gift. Every time we have been good, thoughtful, caring, it's a gift before the altar of God — your treasure. Reaction represents littleness. So right away when it comes, you know where to correct it. What greater gift can one give?

> *Student:* I see that littleness doesn't know gratefulness at all.

Littleness always wants something, therefore, it's always unfulfilled. It always wants something, and so there is no gratefulness. It only knows desire. *Its* gratefulness is when that desire is met. You want to buy a dress or suitcase, candies, or whatever. That's all it knows. It's at that level.

Don't get into littleness. If you do, you will go for urges — for all kinds of things that make you even more little. Can you contain the past urges and impulses and not let them enter into the present?

The littleness lives with its desires, projections, impulses, ideas, opinions. Only that lives. Such thoughts are contaminated. They are a force that brings about war and disaster, the devastation of unfulfillment. There is such poverty. Man is destroying animals. Human beings are destroying human beings. Ingratitude. Insecurity. We want to end wars when the violence is within? The perpetual conflict is within. We think there is "another." As long as there is "another," there will be wars.

> *Student:* I can't deny that it's my littleness, my feelings of having a need, that are my blocks. And that it's the giving that makes life worthwhile. That's been made very clear to me.

Clarity takes away the littleness. Gratefulness takes away the littleness. It doesn't have the same hold.

> *Student:* If I understand it rightly, gratefulness is a true expression of my higher Self, and habits or littleness, however that expresses itself, is what the Course says is the ego or my consciousness.

And that consciousness, or the ego, has a history, can you imagine? And its history, all its memory, is all nonsense. How we decorate it! It's unbelievable! How energetic littleness is.

Everything we know is the history of littleness. It's documented. In a flash of awareness it becomes nothing, for that's what it is. In a flash, it becomes nothing.

> *Student:* I hope I can use gratefulness as a means to undo the littleness.

Just see the littleness as littleness and you are forever grateful. That's freeing one. Gratefulness is active. It's alive every minute.

> *Student:* A few days ago I had asked for some guidance in something I needed to overcome. And I opened up the *Manual for Teachers* at "Judgment." I

wasn't judging myself but I was judging why others weren't doing things that I thought they should be doing. This sharing made me see how small it is to get into something like that. There is enough to deal with with my own awareness.

You see, an elder or a parent or a teacher must make people aware of the littleness. Making another person aware is not judgmental. It could be judgmental if it's a reaction. But it could also make the other aware of the littleness that transpires in him. Do you see the beauty of it?

A wise person deals with littleness; he doesn't become indifferent. He brings it out, he shows you the judgment. One is judgment, if it's a reaction; the other is an action of observation and awareness which you want to share. The subject could be the same. See how subtle things have to be? If I'm accusing you, it's judgmental; but if my heart is of love, then it leads to the awareness.

> *Student:* It depends on how you're really feeling about it?

And who you are. The teacher has to do that. There is such a thing called "order." I don't feel hesitant in pointing things out because somewhere we both see that it's part of order. Once that relationship is established you can do it. I can even scold but the scolding — if you like to call it that — becomes something that's strengthening rather than judgmental. It's a different relationship. It's a very different kind of action.

Student: I feel deeply grateful for your patience and for the love that has made it possible to not lose faith and to bring about changes. What you shared is a turning point for me, that I can't delay anymore. I look upon this time as a golden opportunity. I can't imagine how we have merited it.

I would like to say something that means a lot to me. I hope I can hold back my tears. Christ is in charge of the process of Atonement. And if we appreciate and we are grateful to be in His company, His Presence, then we would feel blessed. It is He Who does His work. It is He Who has brought you here. It is His Love that sustains us. I hope that we are grateful for that. Grateful to Him.

And then we would bring our life into order. You are related to Him. Feel that way. When He says,

If it helps you,
think of me holding your hand
and leading you.
And I assure you
this will be no idle fantasy.[9]

it works every time. I know. There is never any touch of question or doubt about it in my mind. Not now because it happens all the time. That gladness. *He* knows it; I don't have to know it. It makes us almost inseparable. That's so beautiful.

So, can we be grateful to God's Plan for Salvation, for He is in charge? What a beautiful thing that would be!

Student: I see more clearly that without the

internal change, without different values, without gratefulness, this extension you spoke of isn't possible. That without a grateful heart or a certain joy we would become a business.

One reason we don't want to become a business is that we would lose the authenticity that is in us. But as we extend, it's our purity that would extend, that would become Co-Creator. Then it is natural. Please try to see this.

If we become ambitious we could succeed business-wise. McDonald's and 7-11's and liquor stores, all of these have succeeded. So what? You can make all the money you want with any kind of thing that promotes the appeasement of distraction. We know that. But we have seen what business does. It's like living off of each other.

Now extension is related to the quality of our being. To the degree we are pure, we will be entrusted. Your not knowing lack is the strength that would manifest everything to fulfill the needs of others. Can you hear this?

One person can meet the need of everyone Life brings him into contact with. The need — survival, not wantings. One person. *If* that one person doesn't know any lack, any limitation.

It is your purity, your inner gratefulness that merits that. That's what we are going to do: extend. It's not a business.

So, we have to make that inner transformation. We have to come to that inner correction of not limiting ourselves. Your prayers — if your prayers are real — would teach you not to limit yourself.

A Course In Miracles talks about the non-limitedness, the non-lack. How can we be with God's Plan for Salvation and go on limiting ourselves? It's a contradiction. To come to the truth of a state of no lack! How we want to stay away from that. It frightens us. We'd rather expand; we'd rather go towards bigness. But I said, the bigness is still small. Lack is not real. Can you see?

One person like that is needed in the world to help mankind. So put away your littleness and see how we can merit it so that wherever Life places you, you're unlimited. Anyone who comes in contact with you, his needs are met. You may see that the people are hungry; they need to eat. So you multiply the bread and the fish. These things are going to happen. The world is not ruled by manmade rules. It is governed by another power that knows no limit.[10]

And how can one, having heard this, get into one's triviality of problems? Always wanting, wanting. Why be in this muddy mess of ingratitude? Why? Hasn't it been demonstrated that we are sometimes confused, sometimes dejected, sometimes petty-minded, but the awareness comes and we feel cleansed, uplifted?

> *Student:* We are all benefitting from the offer of freeing us from our dependence on littleness and coming to some strength inside. It's been a very important sharing for all of us, to see to what degree we allow the ingratitude to remain.

And that makes us little. Is that a key now? The minute the ingratitude comes, you have made yourself little; you have a lack. That which knows no lack can do anything. These are true things.

So, if our negativity surrounds the earth it is going to bring earth changes and wars and destruction because *it's* alive. That hate and fear and insecurity, that division created by our politics and economy, those things we are taught and indoctrinated with to preserve separation, doubt, suspicion, and ingratitude — all of these are destroying man. And you want to be part of God's Plan for Salvation still retaining that? You can't tell me you have heard me if you are still with limitations.

We will merit and what we merit has no limitation. When you make efforts you become dependent, isn't it? It brings disorder. You have to start with gratefulness. Gratefulness would expand like a rising sun. Your gratefulness would make everything possible. You would be happy people, grateful for the Christ Who is in charge of the process of Atonement.

Do you want to end the separation and come to wholeness? That's the question before each one. God's Plan for Salvation's sole function is to bring one to Atonement — Atonement meaning the ending of separation. And He is in charge.

So, pray and thank Him. Renew that vitality within you — that your life is solely dedicated to coming to Atonement. Your *single purpose* is the only thing that offers it.

My single purpose offers it to me.[11]

Again and again we bring it into focus that the

purpose and function of God's Plan for Salvation — of which He is in charge — is to bring you and me to that which is unlimited, to Atonement. Then we know no lack and we can meet whatever need there is. Because your thought will never be for yourself, you will be extending something that's of love, of care. The power of loving your brother is the only sane thing.

What we are trying to do is to get away from wanting. When you want, you have already denied that which has no lack. And we are saying that the resources are unlimited. Let's overcome the wanting by which we have been living. In the overcoming of it, we will begin to merit. We won't be distracted by our wanting and our lack that keeps us busy and makes "place, person, and activity" important. They have no meaning at all other than in the world of illusion and personality.

When we have seen the fallacy of wanting — the fallacy of "person, place, and activity," that it's just thought bound — awareness comes in to undo it. This great gift of God or the awareness that frees us also brings us closer to that which knows no lack.

This is the way we begin to *merit* rather than to succeed and achieve. Extension demands that I make the correction within myself. Expansion, on the other hand, is an evasion of the real issue. See it as that and you will realize:

I will not value what is valueless.[12]

Let it energize you.
Listen to it.
Hold it for a while.
Keep it in your mind.
Live with it until it imparts its power to you because you gave it the stillness.

THEY WAIT

I did not know Your Voice. And what I heard
I did not understand. There was a Word
In which was everything. Yet all I found
In its immensity was but the sound
Of meaningless contention. I passed by
A thousand waiting angels. And as I
Rushed along vain detours I did not see
The hosts of holiness surrounding me.
Yet I will certainly return. For You
Have promised that whatever I may do,
Angels and holy hosts will wait; the Word
Will hover over me till it is heard. *

*From *The Gifts Of God,* page 33.

ADDENDA

THE SCHOOL
"HAVING THE EARS TO HEAR"

INTRODUCTION

A *Course In Miracles* came to human awareness in 1965 and blossomed in its completion into three volumes in 1976. *A Course In Miracles* is not channeled. What is channeled is a reading of the Akashic Record of what takes place on the planet at the time level. But *A Course In Miracles* is the Thoughts of God. The scribe rose to the State of the Course and met it to awaken us to our God-created Self.

It was the sincere yearning of man that brought *A Course In Miracles*, with its step-by-step curriculum, into manifestation. In the ten years the Course has been with us, it has invoked a gladness in the few who have read and studied it seriously. The sole purpose of its curriculum, however, is to bring us to its application.

On Easter, 1983, the One Year Non-Commercialized Retreat: A Serious Study of *A Course In Miracles* began with forty-nine participants in Los

Angeles.* It was offered by the Foundation for Life Action, a federally approved, nonprofit, educational foundation, at no tuition charge.

The scribe of the Course told me directly:

''The Course is to be lived.''

Following the One Year Retreat, twenty students remained with the Foundation. They have now lived and studied the Course on a full-time basis for almost four years. We have discovered:

The Course cannot be taught.
It can be shared.
Thus the One in charge
of the process of Atonement
teaches both the teacher and the student
while we share.

In His Presence,

> *there will be an instant*
> *which transcends all vision. . .*
> *This you will never teach,*
> *for you attained it not through learning.*[1]

The Course extends
the indivisible Light of Love —
the Will of God.
It is a sacred and holy encounter
to be approached with reverence
and quietness of mind.

The function of the heart is love.
Inherent in each Lesson of *A Course In Miracles*
is the innate power that purifies the heart

---

*The One Year Retreat took place from Easter Sunday, April 3, 1983, to Easter Sunday, April 22, 1984.

and endows the brain
with the light of discrimination.
True Knowledge is beyond the range
of intellectual comprehension.

A time-pressured mind retains
the unwillingness to receive.
We must realize
that unwillingness and helplessness
are synonymous.

The Eternal Word of the Course
bears the Light of His Love.
And without that Light
we continue to seek:

illusions to replace the truth.[2]

Beguiled by ideals, few people in the world have realized what is actually of first importance. What is usually of first importance to us is the fallacy of a goal yet to be achieved. The status quo of what we are attached to and victimized by is the actual, and out of unfulfillment the brain projects an opposite. Thus there is the contradiction. Who can say that, to him, self-centeredness or self-survival or safety is not of first importance?

Without self-awareness, deception becomes of first importance. Who would know the value of awareness which is not learned and effortlessly makes inner correction — instantly taking deception out of the relative, the knowledge of duality.

All through the ages, man has thought he made God and peace of first importance, while the actuality is war. First importance is never dependent on anything external, nor is its God a projection. Eternal life cannot be made into a goal. The few who extend the peace of wholeness have outgrown the limitations of desire.

Who is ready for the internal awakening that is not of thought? Thought must remain secondary for it does not have the vitality to perfect itself. Sri Ramakrishna[3] said, "Only the Will of God is true." Therefore, It is of first importance.

The School — "Having The Ears To Hear"[4] — is an extension of God's Plan for Salvation,[5] consistent with *A Course In Miracles.* It does not,

> *aim at teaching the meaning of love, for that is beyond what can be taught. It does aim, however, at removing the blocks to the awareness of love's presence.*[6]

Hence the School does not teach, for whatever one teaches, in the end, has to be undone. The students the School accepts are those who see that unlearning must be of first importance. He who recognizes the consistency in this will come upon what is of first importance within himself and nothing on the earth could deter him. This is a direct action of grace. Always what is of first importance is beyond the realm of wanting.

The School is for those
who are to live as a guest upon the planet.

> *It can be but myself I crucify.*[7]

Our culture is based on
an ego- and survival-oriented existence.
It is not a culture of humility.

Once humility is gone, no matter what we do,
it is invariably an extension of self-centeredness.
Can we see that each government,
and the very educational system,
promotes our false identification with insecurity?

In ancient times, particularly in the East,
the wise could live by:

"THY WILL BE DONE"[8]

and,

In my defenselessness my safety lies.[9]

Even in the West, Job exemplified a state
not affected by the externals.
Peace, serenity, and reverence are not oriental.
Humility is a law of non-conflict with the Creator.

A Course In Miracles relates with love
and dispels the unreality of fear.
Each person, irrespective of the government,
is responsible to make this inner change.

The School to bring *A Course In Miracles*
into application
ushers in a new thought system
and prepares Ministers of God for the New Age.
The School is limitless
because the Son of God is not limited.

The student is one who can, by the eleventh day,
realize the actuality of the eleventh lesson:

*My meaningless thoughts
are showing me a meaningless world.*[10]

The Holy Spirit accompanies the reader
to help him come to disillusion

and lay down the burden of his own knowings.
This is the pace of *A Course In Miracles*
and the criterion that determines
who the student is.

Only the rare student values disillusion
as the most important factor
in changing one's lifestyle.
He can be relieved of the perpetual sense of lack
by the Holy Instant —
an action outside the realm of time.
This sudden shift from the horizontal to the vertical
is what is needed
to bring *A Course In Miracles* into application.

> *Today I let Christ's Vision*
> *look upon all things for me.*[11]

We look through thought and believe what we see.
This misperception must be undone.
Truth is a direct action of undoing.

The true student who reads this
cannot subject it to his opinion,
for it is not the output of my opinion.
It has taken me forty-six years to understand
the function, potential, and requirements
of the School.
We sum it up by saying
it is a Course-inspired school
that results in coming to Christ's Vision.

It is possible for purity of attention
to come to one mind with the author
so that distance and time disappear.
Nothing can mar the unity
between the student and the School.

If one has read this casually
and has not made contact with this new energy
he will not qualify for the School.
The School is to be consistent
with the Order of the Universe;
therefore, it will not accept anyone
whose life is not in order.
It is something beyond the personal.

THE SCHOOL
"HAVING THE EARS TO HEAR"

The Foundation for Life Action, dedicated to non-commercialized life, has evolved into a School to train teachers to bring *A Course In Miracles* into application.

The School — "Having The Ears To Hear" — is situated at *The Branching of the Road* and deals with the inherent unwillingness in man to accept his true relationship with God.

> *When you come to the place where the branch in the road is quite apparent, you cannot go ahead. You must go either one way or the other. For now if you go straight ahead, the way you went before you reached the branch, you will go nowhere. The whole purpose of coming this far was to decide which branch you will take now. The way you came no longer matters. It can no longer serve. No one who reaches this far can make the wrong decision, although he can delay. And there is no part of the journey that seems more hopeless and futile*

*than standing where the road branches, and
not deciding on which way to go.* [12]

The School is based on the curriculum of *A
Course In Miracles*. *A Course In Miracles* is not a
religion. Its purpose is to bring man to inner peace.
This School is for those who recognize that
bringing the Course into application is the obvious
next step and that undoing the thought system of
relative knowledge is required to realize True
Knowledge. The evolvement of the School is a
unique event, not man projected, but an extension
of the Spirit of *A Course In Miracles*.

A Course In Miracles is the Thought System of
God, the energy of pure thought. Our thought,
which is of the body-ego, is not whole. It is limited
to time and fragments life. Based as it is on fear,
insecurity, comparison, and self-interest, our
thought is useless in coming to understand the true
meaning of:

> *Let me remember I am one with God,*
> *At one with all my brothers and my Self,*
> *In everlasting holiness and peace.* [13]

Thought, the lowest form of intelligence, is not
the means to clarity. Outside the reality of truth,
thought continually projects images of duality. It
must be seen that:

> *My thoughts do not mean anything.* [14]

and,

> *My meaningless thoughts*
> *are showing me a meaningless world.* [15]

for one to be innocent of fear and external imagery
to live by Eternal Laws.

The Course points out:

> *You do not know the peace of power
> that opposes nothing.*[16]

This is consistent with:

> "RESIST NOT EVIL:
> BUT WHOSOEVER SHALL SMITE THEE
> ON THY RIGHT CHEEK,
> TURN TO HIM THE OTHER ALSO."[17]

The world's thought system is divided into geographical boundaries, political divisions, religious dogmas, and economic theories. Thus, there is the accelerated energy of conflict promoting endless violence and wars. All this is the opposite of the Will of God — the creative and indivisible Light of Love.

The vested interest of belief and fanaticism, with its energy of friction, has its own educational system to oppose the law of unity. But the Son of God, who lives by Eternal Laws and Divine Grace, is a stranger to doubt and despair. Not for a moment need he ponder over consequences.

The thought system of the School — "Having The Ears To Hear" — is not of lack. Self-reliance is its natural expression. Thus, whatever we do originates from fulfillment.

For us, *A Course In Miracles* is not religious. Its basic theme is application of the Eternal Laws of Love and sinlessness. Inherent in it is the blessing that accompanies the potentials of its state. It is a spiritual teaching which aims at *removing the blocks to the awareness of love's presence. A Course In*

Miracles brings us to the inner peace of:

> *Nothing real can be threatened.*
> *Nothing unreal exists.*[18]

> *To learn this course requires willingness to question every value that you hold. Not one can be kept hidden and obscure but it will jeopardize your learning.*[19]

> *Forget not that the motivation for this course is the attainment and the keeping of the state of peace. Given this state the mind is quiet, and the condition in which God is remembered is attained.*[20]

"HAVING THE EARS TO HEAR"

During the Non-Commercialized Retreat, now in its fourth year, we have discovered that:

I. Learning the Course is only the first step and comparatively easy. It undoes a great many beliefs and concepts, but learning without application merely remains at the level of perception.

> *Perception is a function of the body, and therefore represents a limit on awareness. . . The opposite of seeing through the body's eyes is the vision of Christ, which reflects strength rather than weakness, unity rather than separation, and love rather than fear. The opposite of hearing through*

> the body's ears is communication
> through the Voice for God, the Holy
> Spirit, which abides in each of us.[21]

> Christ's Vision is the Holy Spirit's
> gift; God's alternative to the illusion
> of separation and to the belief in the
> reality of sin, guilt, and death. It is
> the one correction for all errors of
> perception; the reconciliation of the
> seeming opposites on which this
> world is based.[22]

II. The intimate atmosphere of the one-to-one relationship is essential, for the sharing of truth requires a totally different thought system than the one we presently adhere to. An education that awakens the vast potentials of man's higher faculties *demands the intimacy of one-to-one relationship.* In that deep communication, where two or more gather,[23] is the grace of God.

III. The capacity to accept True Knowledge demands freedom from the pressure of mental stimulation and preoccupation with problems. The *Manual For Teachers* assures us:

> All the help you can accept
> will be provided,
> and not one need you have
> will not be met.[24]

The School — "Having The Ears To Hear" — fulfills this need. It exists for those who, deep within themselves, long to give themselves to a new lifestyle.

Unless one has brought all loose ends to a head, one cannot realize what is entailed in ''God is my first love,'' for it is only the energy of First Thought that awakens the mind to the remembrance of God.

IV. The special relationships of the world are destructive, selfish, and egocentric. Students are to be free of involvement. We have undertaken to love one another and not to have special relationships among ourselves in order to know the purity of Holy Relationship and to undo, with a sense of joy and gratefulness, the misperceptions and deceptions within.

THE NAME OF GOD
CANNOT BE COMMERCIALIZED

Because the Name of God cannot be commercialized and ill-earned money begets other vices, the School charges no tuition. It has evolved its own integrity of:

Having one's own intrinsic work
and not working for another.

Being self-reliant, productive,
and living a non-commercialized life.

Never taking advantage of another.

Living a life free of consequences.

I am under no laws but God's.[25]

Having to give what St. Peter gave:

"SILVER AND GOLD HAVE I NONE;
BUT SUCH AS I HAVE GIVE I THEE."[26]

Gratefulness is everlasting.
It transcends time and is our first commandment.

Those who have heard the Voice of God in the Course have seen the value of miracles in correcting misperception. Thus they come with space within; there are no loose ends in their lives and they can live by:

I will not value what is valueless.[27]

What order and discrimination are required
to awaken from *the sleep of forgetfulness*[28]
and deal with one's own, inherent unwillingness
to realize one's God-given potentials.

The School is a meeting ground, a holy place,
where resistance to correction, unwillingness,
a sense of lack, and irresponsibility
are dealt with.

A Course In Miracles and this School
are based strictly on the Absolute Laws of Life
that are not subject to time or personality.

The School is for discriminate individuals who come:

NOT TO *LEARN.*
BUT TO *BE.**

---

*Refers to the song, "The Seventy," first sung at the Forty Days in the Wilderness Retreat. See *The Voice That Precedes Thought* by Tara Singh (Foundation for Life Action, 1987), page 282. (Editor)

Students will only be accepted who have no other option. The School is not a place where you come to study and then go back to the world of calculations. Doing good and wanting to help are also of the energy of thought and are dependent on people and self-projected activity. The preoccupation of the brain, no matter how good, is externally regulated. The purpose of the School is to share the Holy Instant in which we give as we receive.

SEEKING IS OF LACK.
TRUTH IS AN EXTENSION.

Wisdom is an awakening that refuses to be false.
It makes no mistakes and is free of consequences.
Awareness, untouched by desire and problems,
is blessed by gratefulness.
Who can — who will — put an end
to the deceptions in his life
and bring learning itself to an end?

The School is based on the principle of the Law of Completion. It awakens man from the spell of ignorance and introduces him to the truth of:

Love, Which created me, is what I am.[29]

A Course In Miracles clarifies the Law of Completion in this way:

> *As Heaven's peace and joy intensify when you accept them as God's gift to you, so does the joy of your Creator grow when you accept His joy and peace as yours. True giving is creation.*[30]

One exists only in relationship.
It is when the truth of this is understood
that one is close to the realization of wholeness
that knows no separation.

The One Mind of God,
of which we are all a part,
is indivisible.
It is the creative energy
that ever extends itself.

Within the One, you are free
from the limitation of your own isolation.
For you have discovered
the workings of Divine Protection
that not only make it possible
but slowly awaken you to realize
your ultimate function
as being the extension of wholeness.

The School — "Having The Ears To Hear" — is to bring one into contact with the Self, the Christ within. To the one who is ready, this news of the School will ignite the light of Truth in his mind. This is what is meant by having "the ears to hear."

The purpose of *A Course In Miracles* is to bring man to resurrection, to restore him to the awareness of his natural state:

> *I am not a body. I am free.*
> *For I am still as God created me.*[31]

and,

> *My mind is part of God's.*
> *I am very holy.*[32]

To bring *A Course In Miracles* into application is the ending of relative knowledge. Only a few will listen and it is only meant for the few. Unwillingness, we have discovered, is one of the strongest *blocks to the awareness of love's presence.*[33]

Mere enthusiasm is not enough. There is an inherent resistance within man to change and live by the indivisible law of Love. The School addresses this basic issue. It is for those with discrimination, whose very need has brought the School about.

> "The world situation is worsening to an alarming degree. People all over the world are being called on to help, and are making their individual contributions as part of an overall prearranged plan. Part of the plan is taking down *A Course in Miracles,* and I am fulfilling my part in the agreement, as you will fulfill yours. You will be using abilities you developed long ago, and which you are not really ready to use again. Because of the acute emergency, however, the usual slow, evolutionary process is being by-passed in what might best be described as a 'celestial speed-up.'"[34]

In this phase of "celestial speed-up," the cycle of preaching and teaching wisdom is almost over. There is neither the time, nor the space for it. A true teacher of *A Course In Miracles* brings the student out of endless time to the Holy Instant, where the light of awareness by-passes man's present thought system and instantly dispels illusions without the use of time. The change that takes place is internal and immediately in effect. It does not take place at the level of activity.

By hearing the vertical words that have no opposite, the genuine student, having "the ears to hear," awakens his own potentials and is transformed by his own clarity.

Who would be the teacher of such a School? Certainly not a personality, but the One Who has promised that He would be there in the midst where two or more are gathered in His Name.[35]

> *I am in charge of the process of Atonement, which I undertook to begin. When you offer a miracle to any of my brothers, you do it to yourself and me. . . . My part in the Atonement is the cancelling out of all errors that you could not otherwise correct. When you have been restored to the recognition of your original state, you naturally become part of the Atonement yourself. As you share my unwillingness to accept error in yourself and others, you must join the great crusade to correct it; listen to my voice, learn to undo error and act to correct it.*[36]

The Student comes to be part of God's Plan for Salvation and is solely interested in Atonement, the ending of time.

Only in application will we discover "What Is."
Do we still believe in separation?
Do we react and hold grievances?
Is there anything that affects the love in us?

> *Forgive us our illusions, Father,*
> *and help us to accept*
> *our true relationship with You,*
> *in which there are no illusions,*
> *and where none can ever enter.*[37]

It is the *true relationship* that teaches both the

teacher and the student as they recognize that love is ever present. When they are receptive, His grace is upon them and they are both free of the illusion of time.

The School has to be where *there are no illusions, and where none can ever enter.* Only after the unwillingness is dealt with does the awakening take place, and:

> *From your demonstration others learn,*
> *and so do you.*[38]

Henceforth, the student lives by Holy Relationship and the peace of forgiveness.
He stands in quiet,
the world of nothingness fades away,
and his life is no longer meaningless.

> THERE IS NOTHING ELSE TO LEARN BUT LOVE.
> BUT TO REALIZE LOVE, YOU MUST MASTER
> FORGIVENESS,
> NON-JUDGMENT,
> AND GRATEFULNESS.

The School has no preferences but only the responsibility to make no decision by itself. Only those students will qualify who are meant to be there.

> *Remember that no one is where he is by accident, and chance plays no part in God's plan. . . As the teacher of God advances. . . he learns one lesson with increasing thoroughness. He does not make his own decisions; he asks his Teacher for His answer.*[39]
>
> *And thus it is that pupil and teacher seem to*

*come together in the present, finding each other
as if they had not met before. The pupil comes
at the right time to the right place. This is
inevitable, because he made the right choice in
that ancient instant which he now relives.* [40]

How could the School that makes the Given
accessible charge money for True Knowledge?
Discrimination does not teach. Yet those who want
it and have their own energy are endowed with the
capacity to receive the peace of the Absolute.

It is the creative movement of the Will of God
that knows who is suited for what. Decisions are
made at the level of timelessness. It brings those
two people together who are ready for what the
sharing is to be. In defining who God's teachers are
and who their pupils are, the *Manual For Teachers*
states:

*His pupils have been waiting for him, for his
coming is certain. Again, it is only a matter of
time. Once he has chosen to fulfill his role,
they are ready to fulfill theirs.* [41]

Every person who comes into contact with the
Teacher has a destiny. Either they get ignited and
come to *single purpose,* [42] or they stay in the insanity
of earth values. The *Manual For Teachers* clarifies:

*Except for God's teachers there would be little
hope of salvation, for the world of sin would
seem forever real. The self-deceiving must
deceive, for they must teach deception.* [43]

The teacher/student relationship is deemed by
the wise to be the most significant in life. It is
supreme. Not only does it extend beyond time but

it has the potential to set one free. If you are a student, only then is He your Teacher. But it is extremely rare to merit being a student. So few realize what it constitutes. It is a Law. Jesus, out of the vast multitude, could only find twelve for the three years of self-transformation. His was a one-to-one relationship for the few.

Jesus sought the twelve
awakened enough to be His Disciples.
To them, all He had to say was, ''FOLLOW ME.''[44]
He taught them by demonstration.
Whatever He said was true, untouched by time,
and not abstract.
It became instantly manifest and actualized.

What He taught His Apostles
was the Power of the True Word.
He brought them to the certainty of:
''You can do what I have done and more.''[45]
The Acts of the Apostles in the Bible
confirms the truth of this.
The Apostles had the power to heal the sick,
give sight to the blind,
and bring the dead to life.
The integrity by which they lived
demonstrated what faith can do.

Jesus proved that:

> *There is no death.*
> *The Son of God is free.*[46]

and that Resurrection, in truth,
is the fact of Life.

He has assured us:

"BE OF GOOD CHEER;
I HAVE OVERCOME THE WORLD."[47]

A Course In Miracles emphasizes
the change of identity and corrects
man's false identification with the body.
Now humanity, freed from misperception,
is endowed with the awareness of Resurrection.
It is a fact that took place
in the mind of every human being.
Jesus undid the illusion of separation,
the limitation of belief,
and the fallacy of relative knowledge.

A Course In Miracles is an extension
of what Jesus imparted to His Apostles.
It transmits the same energy to those
who are willing to live by Eternal Life.

In *A Course In Miracles,* Jesus speaks in the first person:

> *Teach not that I died in vain. Teach rather that
> I did not die by demonstrating that I live in
> you. For the undoing of the crucifixion of
> God's Son is the work of the redemption, in
> which everyone has a part of equal value. . . .
> God's Son is saved. Bring only this awareness
> to the Sonship, and you will have a part in the
> redemption as valuable as mine.*[48]

The Teacher of True Knowledge exists for those who have "the ears to hear." In His Presence, the discriminate student, at the brink of salvation, recognizes the benediction of right relationship.

Purification is in the Word of the Man of God. It

is the Word itself that makes attainment of self-knowledge possible, instantly. The Word here shared has the strength of eternity behind it that makes the space.

MY SINGLE PURPOSE
OFFERS IT TO ME.[49]

The Foundation for Life Action provides the means, the support, and the happy ground to bring us to *single purpose.* We have discovered that looking in the same direction and the love and peace of togetherness make life truly productive and meaningful.

The student must have the discrimination to know the difference between the essential and the unessential and the willingness to outgrow what is irrelevant. Bringing order in one's life is the first requirement before having something of one's own to give. Very few students will be selected since it is important that the class size be limited to a small number, where direct communication can take place. Students will have to be totally dedicated to be consistent with God's Will. It has become clear to us that people with unresolved issues are not quite ready to take the step.

The School has to consist of a small, energetic group of productive people — factual and responsible, with professional aptitude and an up-to-date outlook and perspective. This is what it takes to be Self-Reliant and to succeed in Non-Commercial Action.

For us, teaching and learning is a constant process. It continues day and night and is manifest and present in every relationship, in everything we do. *A Course In Miracles* is not limited to a classroom; it is most challenging in its relationship to Life.

Above and beyond it all, the School makes a statement that is powerful and practical: it is mandatory for man to step out of the economic slavery to jobs and come to an inner dignity of his own, where another action can take place.

Those who emerge from the School will share *A Course In Miracles* non-commercially, for the Name of God cannot be commercialized. A very solid foundation is laid beforehand for self-reliance and trust in God.

> *When pupil and teacher come together, a teaching-learning situation begins. For the teacher is not really the one who does the teaching. God's Teacher speaks to any two who join together for learning purposes. The relationship is holy because of that purpose, and God has promised to send His Spirit into any holy relationship. In the teaching-learning situation, each one learns that giving and receiving are the same. The demarcations they have drawn between their roles, their minds, their bodies, their needs, their interests, and all the differences they thought separated them from one another, fade and grow dim and disappear. Those who would learn the same course share one interest and one goal. And thus he who was the learner becomes a teacher*

of God himself, for he has made the one decision that gave his teacher to him. He has seen in another person the same interests as his own. [50]

The teachers of God have trust in the world, because they have learned it is not governed by the laws the world made up. It is governed by a Power That is in them but not of them. It is this Power That keeps all things safe. It is through this Power that the teachers of God look on a forgiven world. [51]

At the end of the One Year Non-Commercialized Retreat, the following Statement was signed by each participant:

As students of *A Course In Miracles*
we are the disciples
of the One in charge of Atonement.
He is to us — Alive.
We think with Him.
Whatever we do is done by — Him.

Ours is the Ministry of Gratefulness.
Together, productive and self-reliant,
we stand on our own feet
to bring the Course into application
in our lives;
and prepare to see man, in Truth,
as the Altar of God on Earth;
and extend to the tired world,
taxed by meaningless work,
the message of — Fulfillment.

We have no projects,
no ambition to own a community

or external ashrams.
We do not commercialize life
nor ask for donations.

Our own sincerity and purity of work
makes our life intrinsic.
We are strengthened
by the power of seeing a — Fact,
and the integrity of single purpose.
We do not work for another
and see no man contaminated
by external unreality.

We have found our — Calling,
having heard the whisper
of Absolute Knowledge.
Gratefulness, Forgiveness,
Non-attachment are — Real.
And Fulfillment already is a part of — Love.

IN GOD WE TRUST.

Our lesson for today is:

My mind is part of God's.
I am very holy. [52]

*　　*　　*

For information regarding the School — "Having The Ears
To Hear" — contact:

FOUNDATION FOR LIFE ACTION
902 South Burnside Avenue
Los Angeles, California 90036
213/933-5591

THE PURPOSE
OF THE
FOUNDATION FOR LIFE ACTION

The purpose of the Foundation for Life Action
is to be with the Eternal Laws
so that it does not become an organization.

LOVE IS ETERNAL.
ABILITIES EXTENDING LOVE ARE BLESSED.

In the absence of Love
abilities become the bondage of skills,
limited to personality.
Among virtuous men,
it is what the human being is that is Real,
and not what he does in a body.

The purpose of the Foundation is to be part of

GOD'S PLAN FOR SALVATION.[1]

Thus it has a different point of reference
than the thought system of man.

Obviously, the Name of God
cannot be commercialized.
There are no fees in what we share.
We do not believe in loss and gain.

Non-commercialized action is provided by
the blessings of productive life.

IN GOD WE TRUST

Those who are with the Eternal Laws
in times of change remain unaffected.
In crisis, it is your care for another
that is your strength.

We have a function in the world
to be truly helpful to others,
knowing:

I am sustained by the Love of God.[2]

My only function is the one God gave me.[3]

Nothing real can be threatened.
Nothing unreal exists.[4]

We are not pressured by the brutality of success.
We are blessed by the work we do.
Gratefulness is complete, as love is independent.

To us, you, the human being, comes first.
Thus it enables us to go past
the conventional opinion of right and wrong
and relate directly to you.

For man is as God created him,
unchanged by the changeable society
that rules his body with its belief systems.

The Truth is a Fact that dissolves illusions of time.
Our function is to dispel the abstraction of ideas
and realize the actuality of Fact.

For,

I am under no laws but God's.[5]

Reverence for Life is of a still mind
hallowed by His Love.
This transformation is what we call

THE PATH OF VIRTUE.

The Path of Virtue is the ministry of gratefulness.

The wise who extends the Kingdom of God on earth
lives consistent with

"BUT SEEK YE FIRST THE KINGDOM OF GOD,
AND HIS RIGHTEOUSNESS;
AND ALL THINGS SHALL BE ADDED UNTO YOU."[6]

AUTOBIOGRAPHY
OF TARA SINGH

Tara Singh, founder of the Foundation for Life Action and the teacher of the School — "Having The Ears To Hear" — spent his early years in a village in Punjab, India.

"I came from a background in India of living in a spacious house with one door, where my parents and grandparents, sisters, uncles, aunts, cousins, and nephews lived together. The one door signifies that our house was not divided and for centuries we had lived in harmony. Wisdom resided there and lifted us out of irritation and reaction. The elders extended goodness and we grew up surrounded with affection and a sense of reverence for life. No one in the family had ever been career oriented. We had agricultural land and were an honored family. We considered ourselves affluent. The one door stood as the symbol of unity.

''The family was religious and even without knowing it, I absorbed the values of the spirit. Some of us extended ourselves beyond the village and beyond the boundaries of self-centeredness.

''During my formative years, there was an innate resistance to imposed, formal education. I sensed that it was not right and felt false submitting to it. It was so much inferior to what one learned directly. *That* I enjoyed and the imposed appeared harmful. The teacher even had to resort to tying me to a tree during the six months that I attended school because I repeatedly ran away to play in the fields or by the village pond. All my life, however, I learned through what awakened my interest. And I later discovered that natural intelligence is autonomous; it can cope with anything and has its own capacity to learn.''

From this sheltered environment, at the age of nine, Tara Singh and his mother and uncles traveled to Panama via Europe to join his father who was in business there. While in Panama he attended school for two years. At the age of eighteen, he and his mother returned to India and he found himself caught in a conspiracy to get him married. Inspired by the family saint, at the age of twenty-one, his search for Truth and God led him to the Himalayas.

''For four years I wholeheartedly applied myself to a religious life of devotion and discipline. I had flashes of insight that led me to question and to undo my own knowing. I realized that Truth is independent of time and conventional religion, and a mind conditioned by religious or secular beliefs is always limited. I emerged from the solitary years with discrimination and the capacity to receive and to heed. Disillusionment brought about a sudden change of value, but to be freed from the mask of pious attitude and to outgrow tradition is an invaluable experience. Now I insisted upon being responsible, on questioning and coming to clarity before getting involved.''

In his next phase of growth, Tara Singh responded to the poverty of India through participation in that country's postwar industrialization. The great beings he met were his best teachers. He was forever affected by how wisely they lived and the goodness they shared.

''There were several wise men of intrinsic life and consistent knowledge who made a strong impact on my life. One of the most extraordinary men was Giani Kartar Singh. I met him on a train at Amritsar on the way to Lahore in 1945. He came and sat opposite me in the compartment. I was in crisis, burning to make contact and not knowing how to approach him. But the energy of first thought acts involuntarily. Gianiji, an eminent man, was the saintly, genius leader of the

Sikhs. His Sikhism encompassed all humanity in its range; his nationalism was unlimited humanism.

"This contact opened totally new dimensions and potentials within me and made things possible in an India besieged by the cruelty of poverty. It culminated in an enormous industrial project at the grass roots level with capital of over six million dollars, supported by Sikhs, Maharajahs, and others, but most of all by Gianiji's impeccable integrity.

"He was a man of renunciation and religious outlook who never had a bank account. The force of his love transformed my life and in his atmosphere, I blossomed. He offered an intimate relationship through which I became a friend of Prime Minister Nehru and other eminent leaders of incorruptible lives. He had said when people asked him, 'What do you see in Tara Singh?'

> 'The word "impossible" does not apply to him. He will not accept second best and this will make him or break him.'

"In 1947, the advent of freedom and the partition of India and Pakistan disrupted the humanistic plan. I was virtually penniless and homeless but felt the need to visit the West and make an individual survey of the impact of science on society before embarking upon another venture. One questioned what part the gigantic, underdeveloped, agrarian society of almost two billion was to play in the Post War period. Would the West heed India's authentic voice — the wisdom of its unbiased outlook — and avert the spread of tension? The media was accelerating Cold War propaganda, and nationalism was being drummed into the collective consciousness.''

It was in the 1950's, discovering that man's problems cannot be solved externally, that Mr. Singh was inspired by his association with Mr. J. Krishnamurti.

''At the end of 1947, soon after the independence of India, I arrived in England and then came to New York to meet with those at an international level who made decisions and determined human destiny. In the West, I met a great many men and women of excellence. Very quickly I came into contact with the mind of the age and found there was little use for wisdom which never makes survival its first concern. Skills had become important and man was rapidly losing his work and becoming subject to jobs. I was startled by the power of the media with its ability to influence collective consciousness, the panic about communism, and the stimulated daily life obsessed with problems. These were just facts, not good or bad, but what was.

''The background of the Sikh religion

prior to meeting Gianiji was essential to the new awakening. Similarly, before meeting with Mr. J. Krishnamurti, it was essential to be aware of world affairs. For me the cultural life of New York City revolved around the work of the United Nations and various philanthropic organizations. I was captivated by the creative spirit of the West. New York at the time seemed like the capital of the world and I was overwhelmed by the music, art, theatre, and literature which it offered. Also, contact with the lofty voices of the forefathers of the New World — Emerson, Thoreau, Whitman, and Lincoln — enriched my life.

''It was in New York that I literally learned to read. Loneliness compelled me to it. Usually the hours spent reading from 8:00 p.m. to 2:00 a.m. became the most rewarding time in my life and this continued for years irrespective of where I lived in the world.

''To outgrow is always blessed — not to get stuck, but to be enriched by the deeper expression of life on the planet. It was a good background to meet with Mr. Krishnamurti and enter the realm of eternal laws.

''It was on my second trip to America, in 1953, that I met Mr. Krishnamurti in New York. In twenty minutes, all that I knew or pretended to know, or wished to do, disappeared. The contact was so strong it put an end to the bondage of my knowing and lifted me to what is not of words. Never could I have conceived the blessing of such a sacred encounter. I remember thinking to myself as I walked through Central Park that it was a blessing to be born at the time that such a great being was upon the planet. The unchangeable light of his word extended itself and still continues to expand its newness in me.

''A few years later, I arrived in Ojai, California, a week before the annual 'Talks' began and met with Mr. Krishnamurti daily. When I attended his first 'Talk' at the end of that week, he looked at everyone in the audience prior to beginning to speak, as was his custom. When his eyes met mine for a fleeting instant, it imparted a joy, a tremendous blessing, and I was given 'the ears to hear.' After the 'Talk' I sat for hours transfixed.

''The next day, when I met with him, I told him that I understood what he had shared beyond the words. We sat in silence a while and then he said:

> 'Drop everything.
> Be still.
> The seeds are sown,
> leave it alone.'

''It took years for me to know the full significance of his words. Year after year, I continued to discover what 'the seeds are sown' meant and the responsibility that Mr. Krishnamurti assumed. The God-lit Teacher imparts the energy that brings one to stillness and the gratefulness out of which the next action emerges. He guarded me directly, and indirectly, from ever getting involved in what was not part of creation — in the end to extend the True Knowledge of eternal seeds with which he blessed me. The energy of gratefulness then enabled me to relate with what is eternal.

''The only true relationship is between the Teacher and the student. It is not between parents and children, nor between wives and husbands. All these fall short of timelessness. It is the relationship with the Teacher that ends the separation and brings one to the Oneness of Life and the One Mind of God. The relationship is eternal and does not end in death. Its action continues as the student harnesses the energy of joyous responsibility and realizes that that which is real emerges out of his own stillness and gratefulness. From 1953, meetings with Mr. Krishnamurti continued now and then. I was not a regular devotee, but he remained my constant companion in life.

''In 1963, I brought all loose ends to a head and had even outgrown wanting to help the world. I had been involved in world affairs, increasing the per capita income of underdeveloped areas.

Through this work I realized:

> Times will reveal themselves —
> that you cannot depend on the
> externals. Without the externals,
> there is no personality and there
> is no relationship at the person-
> ality level. The fear of the
> externals will destroy the
> manmade, external world.

"I felt the spaciousness of noninvolve-
ment with either person, place, or activity
and went to Switzerland to attend Mr.
Krishnamurti's 'Talks.' Early in 1964, I
had an interview with him in Madras. I
said that I had come to give myself totally
to a life of the spirit. He startled me by
saying: 'Go and earn some money.' But I
said, 'Sir, I have made up my mind. I do
not want to live the life of the world. It has
no fascination for me.' He stopped me
short and repeated what he had said
before, 'Go and earn some money.'

"I was under the impression that a
sannyasi who lived a vertical life did not
touch money. The tradition in India was
established that men and women of
renunciation were fed by the house-
holder. I pleaded my seriousness. Mr.
Krishnamurti said, 'Go and earn some
money or I will never see you again.' This
time, the *or else* gave me no option but to
heed. Instantly the duality ended and my
own heeding transmitted a sense of joy so

energetic its profound meaning still continues to unfold.

His words, when heeded, are those
that have no ending.
They light the passage of your life.

''I had only about $20 in all to my name when I started. As I was leaving, an additional instruction was given by Mr. Krishnamurti: 'Do not ever take advantage of another.'

''How difficult it is to end the preference for advantages. One wants to lead a spiritual life, but could this ever be within our present thought system based on motives?

''The words of Mr. Krishnamurti, who was free of personality, and like Jesus and Lord Buddha owned nothing, ordain an action in one that contains the vitality to actualize its completion. This discovery is the blessing. I learned that the action of Life is impersonal; activity is devoid of action. My whole mind gathered itself to earning money and within four months I had acquired sixty thousand dollars.

''In this age, it is difficult to lead a truly religious life without one's own independent means. Without money, one invariably resorts to exploitation and ends up needing people for one's own projects.

''The responsibility for the right use of

money was the next step. What wisdom it would take to make right use of a dollar.

I will not value what is valueless.[1]

"What discrimination it takes to end wastage, deny yourself nothing, nor look at price tags, but be with the essential always."

Subsequently, Tara Singh became more and more removed from worldly affairs and devoted several years of his life to the study and the practice of Raja Yoga and the non-commercial lifestyle of the enlightened beings of the Vedas and the Upanishads. During this time he also came into close contact with the teachings of Sri Ramakrishna and Sri Ramana Maharshi. The discipline imparted through Raja Yoga helped make possible a three year period of silent retreat.

"Mr. Krishnamurti warned me that Hatha Yoga is merely physical and stressed the importance of health and discipline in life. The deeper meaning of discipline that is not imposed but has its own order began to reveal itself. It awakened a passion that had no alternatives. This led me to spend three years in silence in Carmel, California.

"Silence, ever whole, has its own wisdom of non-dependence and succeeds effortlessly in coping with all the essentials without the need of another. It has its own independent existence. Not imposed from without, it is of an inner

yearning to be with the spacious aloneness in which one is related to all that is.
Silence is not isolation seeking some
projected goal of self-improvement.

"As I emerged from silence, I saw that
hardly anyone listens and realized why
Jesus placed so much emphasis on having
'the ears to hear.' Without it, one cannot
communicate. Learning is abstract; it is of
things and ideas that have names; it is
deceptive for it is based on interpretation.
But to communicate and to heed demands
an attentive, receptive, and silent mind.
Self-honesty or truth requires consistency
at all levels of one's being.

"Inwardly, there arose a yearning in
me to be productive. True productivity is
not projected but is independent of the
externals. It is without direction. It can
only be the extension of the Divine Will,
the only Reality."

As he emerged from the years of silence in 1976,
he came into contact with *A Course In Miracles.* Its
impact on him was profound. He recognized its
unique contribution as a scripture and saw it as the
answer to man's urgent need for direct contact
with True Knowledge. The Course has been the
focal point of his life ever since.

"When I discovered *A Course In Miracles*
and read in the Introduction:

> *Nothing real can be threatened.*
> *Nothing unreal exists.*

I recognized the Power of the Word of God in it and also, for the first time, my function in life. A direct relationship with the scribe came into being for which I will be forever grateful. One is grateful for what is timeless — forever the strength and light of your life. This benediction is your constant companion.

"You realize there is nothing to achieve, perfection is ever complete. God's Plan for Salvation is already accomplished.[2] The truth of this is what brings learning *almost to its appointed end.*[3]

"The wise, it is said, remains ever the stranger to doubt and despair."

The Foundation for Life Action, a federally approved, nonprofit, educational foundation, begun in 1980 on the principles of rightness, virtue, and having something to give, started with no money and the conviction not to seek or live off donations. It came to self-reliance by doing workshops and retreats throughout the country, sharing mostly the principles of *A Course In Miracles,* providing an atmosphere of friendship and one-to-one relationship. The Foundation was earning approximately $1000 a day from workshops, retreats, and sales of books and tapes when, at the end of 1981, Tara Singh realized that in order to bring *A Course In Miracles* into application, something other was required than mere workshops and retreats. They had served their purpose.

Since Easter, 1983, Mr. Singh has conducted the Non-Commercialized Retreat: A Serious Study of

A Course In Miracles — an unprecedented, in-depth exploration of the Course at no tuition charge.

> "At the height of prosperity, the decision was made to end workshops and retreats and to begin the non-commercialized action — probably the first time it has been offered in the New World. I was told that the Course is to be lived and spent a hundred days to discover intimately what is entailed in bringing it into application. I realized that the Name of God cannot be commercialized. It is something you receive while you give and fulfills the law that one must teach in order to learn. How can the energy of love be sold?"

Mr. Singh has chosen to work closely on a one-to-one basis with serious students. The program is sponsored by the Foundation for Life Action.

> "For the past four years, *A Course In Miracles* has been shared non-commercially. It is a one-to-one, intimate atmosphere where the 'Given' is made accessible. But it is for those having the energy of the first thought. For us the student is one whose first love is God.

> "The School — 'Having The Ears To Hear' — is in the spirit of the Upanishads and the wise men of ancient India and China — where the Teacher and the student lived together and wisdom was neither bought nor sold. The only requirement was a student with the capacity to receive. Self-honesty and the

passion to know the truth of man, God
and creation were essential, as well as
having no unwillingness that blocks and
evades the holy instant.

Philosophers, educators, gurus —
the interpreters of knowledge —
and others who share their ideas and beliefs,
want to conform us to think in a certain way.

I do not fall into any of these categories.
For me, religious life is not
a concept or a dogma.
It is a state of being.

Absolute Knowledge cannot be interpreted.
It transcends learning.
We can be made aware
of the limitations of our conditioning
and can question our conclusions,
the fallacy of external authority,
as well as our faith in insecurity.

All of this is still in the realm of thought,
adjustments, and changes of attitude.
As long as there is relative knowledge
conflict remains our lot
and we are ever unfulfilled.

It is Undoing by which man is awakened
from the illusion of learning
and the preoccupation
with accumulating information.
Undoing,
by which the awakening can take place,
is of your own energy,
your own internal clarity.

Teaching and learning
are not what the School
— "Having The Ears To Hear" — is about.
The School is for those
who come not to *learn* but to *Be.* *
There is no authority.
It is consistent with
"where two or more gather in His Name"[4]
to jointly explore and undo past knowing.
The School is for those
who refuse to be influenced by another
and realize that only the newness within man
can transform his life.

It takes great wisdom and integrity
to come to a silent mind,
to dispel the insanity of helplessness.
True Knowledge is free of conflict
and acknowledges no problem as real.

I am not here to persuade the student
to think in a particular way,
or to give instructions,
or to conform anyone to any ideals.
The School is based on
dissolving misperception
and acknowledges no problem as real.
We do not direct the student
to follow a certain thought system
or a method of solving problems.

The student must be highly responsible

---

*Refers to the song, "The Seventy," first sung at the Forty Days in the Wilderness Retreat. See *The Voice That Preceeds Thought* by Tara Singh (Foundation for Life Action, 1987), page 282.

to be a participant
of the one-to-one relationship of the School
to realize the clarity
that frees one from dependence.

> *Forgive us our illusions, Father,*
> *and help us to accept*
> *our true relationship with You,*
> *in which there are no illusions,*
> *and where none can ever enter.*[5]

''What we share — impart — is Self-Reliance. To come to Self-Reliance is essential, especially at this time when the monetary system of the world is in control of the lives of men. Since man has lost his work, he has become subject to jobs. Now he must find his own inner calling and come to intrinsic work. The Foundation for Life Action provides a productive life of intrinsic work where one can come to Self-Reliance by having something to give to the world. We undertake to live by Holy Relationship to discover the Self that is not a body. To know:

> *I am sustained by the love of God.*[6]

is our undertaking — to forgive and not to judge as a process of self learning. It is an internal action since wisdom begins with the knowledge of self.''

Tara Singh is the author of numerous books and has been featured on many video and audio tapes in which he discusses the action of bringing one's life into order, freeing oneself from past conditioning, living the principles of *A Course In Miracles,* and coming to inner awakening.

His life is dedicated to:

"I will not be dishonest to myself."

and to the fact that the Name of God cannot be commercialized. His thought system is not of lack. He has no goals, therefore, no doubt.

"God's Plan for Salvation represents humanity. It is not a religion or an organization. Its purpose is to come to inner peace."

In answer to the question, "What kind of life do you envision for yourself?" Tara Singh responded:

"Rightness.

Rightness is independent of personality
and its consequences.
It stands vertical — a law unto itself.
Nothing of the body senses can affect
or obscure it.
Rightness is independent
of the limitations of right and wrong,
thus free of judgment and conflict,
free of lack, of seeking and trying,
free of thought, feelings, and reactions.

Such a man is liberated
from the illusion of time
and its beliefs and concepts.
Ever stable, stately and uninvolved,
he knows no loss, gain, or unfulfillment.

Such a man is an extension
of the grace of God.
He has an atmosphere of purity
surrounding him.
It is a blessing to be in his presence
and to have the ears to hear
his eternal Words.''

REFERENCES

INTRODUCTION

1. *A Course In Miracles* (ACIM) is a contemporary scripture which deals with the pyschological/spiritual issues facing man today. It consists of three volumes: *Text* (I), *Workbook For Students* (II), and *Manual For Teachers* (III). The *Text*, 622 pages, sets forth the concepts on which the thought system of the Course is based. The *Workbook For Students,* 478 pages, is designed to make possible the application of the concepts presented in the *Text* and consists of three hundred and sixty-five lessons, one for each day of the year. The *Manual For Teachers*, 88 pages, provides answers to some of the basic questions a student of the Course might ask and defines many of the terms used in the *Text*. (Editor)
2. ACIM, III, page 62.
3. ACIM, II, page 185.
4. ACIM, II, page 3.
5. ACIM, II, page 4.
6. ACIM, II, page 11.
7. ACIM, I, Introduction.
8. ACIM, II, page 162.

9. ACIM, II, page 62.
10. ACIM, II, page 132.
11. ACIM, III, page 8.
12. ACIM, II, page 374.
13. ACIM, II, page 177.
14. ACIM, II, page 65.
15. ACIM, II, page 376.
16. Refers to Matthew 18:20.
17. ACIM, I, page 24.
18. ACIM, II, page 75.
19. John 5:30.
20. Luke 23:34.
21. ACIM, II, page 213.
22. ACIM, I, page 326.
23. ACIM, II, page 239.
24. Refers to Matthew 13:13-23.

CHAPTER ONE — "FORGIVE US OUR ILLUSIONS"

1. ACIM, II, page 391.
2. Ibid.
3. Luke 23:34.
4. Refers to, *If it helps you, think of me holding your hand and leading you. And I assure you this will be no idle fantasy.* See ACIM, II, page 119.
5. See ACIM, I, pages 426-427; II, page 120 and following.
6. ACIM, I, page 315.
7. ACIM, II, page 48.
8. ACIM, II, page 49.
9. Mr. J. Krishnamurti (1895-1986) was a world renowned teacher and philosopher. (Editor)
10. ACIM, II, page 450.
11. "In God We Trust" appears to have been inspired by a line from the Star Spangled Banner, "In God is our trust," written by Francis Scott Key in 1814. "In God We Trust" first appeared on the coinage of the United States in 1864, during the presidency of Abraham Lincoln. It became the official motto of the United States in 1956. (Editor)

12. The one commandment given by Jesus, ''Love ye one another,'' appears many times in the New Testament. See, for example: John 13:34-35, 15:12, 15:17; Romans 13:8. (Editor)

CHAPTER TWO — APPLICATION HAS NO EFFORT

1. ACIM, I, page 326. This prayer has been referred to as *A Course In Miracles'* version of the Lord's Prayer. See *Journey Without Distance: The Story Behind A Course In Miracles* by Robert Skutch (Celestial Arts, 1984), page 68. (Editor)
2. ACIM, II, page 391.
3. ACIM, II, page 392.
4. ACIM, II, page 391.
5. ACIM, II, page 392.
6. Refers to ACIM, I, page 6.
7. ACIM, II, page 388.
8. Ibid.
9. Ibid.
10. ACIM, I, page 24.

CHAPTER THREE — THE ILLUSION OF THE OPPOSITE

1. ACIM, I, page 326.
2. ACIM, II, page 462.
3. ACIM, II, page 392.
4. ACIM, II, page 388.
5. Ibid.
6. Ibid.
7. Ibid.
8. ACIM, I, Introduction.
9. ACIM, II, page 103.
10. ACIM, II, page 388.
11. ACIM, II, page 392.
12. Refers to *If it helps you, think of me holding your hand and leading you. And I assure you this will be no idle fantasy.* See ACIM, II, page 119.
13. Refers to *I will teach with you and live with you if you will think with me.* See ACIM, I, page 49.

CHAPTER FOUR — ''HELP US TO ACCEPT OUR TRUE RELATIONSHIP WITH YOU''

1. ACIM, I, page 326.
2. ACIM, II, page 392.
3. Ibid.
4. ACIM, II, page 393.

CHAPTER FIVE — WHAT IS ILLUSION?

1. ACIM, I, page 326.
2. ACIM, II, page 392.
3. ACIM, II, page 236.
4. ACIM, II, page 393.
5. ACIM, I, page 6.

CHAPTER SIX — UNWILLINGNESS VERSUS THE CAPACITY TO RECEIVE

1. ACIM, I, page 326.
2. Sri Ramakrishna was a God-lit being who lived in India from 1836 to 1886. He taught that all religions are true, having discovered the truth of each of them himself by practicing them with total devotion. He found that God can be known directly through all forms of spiritual practice. (Editor)
3. ACIM, II, page 462.
4. ACIM, I, page 285.

CHAPTER SEVEN — THE DECISION FOR HOLY RELATIONSHIP

1. ACIM, II, page 376.
2. ACIM, II, page 355.
3. ACIM, II, page 159.
4. See *Journey Without Distance: The Story Behind A Course In Miracles* by Robert Skutch (Celestial Arts, 1984), pages 31-34.
5. ACIM, II, page 355.
6. ACIM, II, page 239.
7. See John 13:34-35, 15:12, 15:17; Romans 13:8.

CHAPTER EIGHT — "TRUTH WILL CORRECT ALL ERRORS IN MY MIND"

1. ACIM, II, page 189.
2. ACIM, II, page 119.
3. ACIM, I, page 24.
4. ACIM, II, page 189.
5. ACIM, II, page 392.
6. ACIM, I, page 24.
7. John 5:30.
8. ACIM, I, Introduction.

CHAPTER NINE — WE MEET TO UNDO

1. ACIM, II, page 306.
2. ACIM, I, page 326.
3. ACIM, II, page 306.
4. ACIM, II, page 277.
5. ACIM, I, Introduction.

CHAPTER TEN — THE BEGINNING OF SELF-KNOWING

1. See the prayer, *Forgive us our illusions, Father,* ACIM, I, page 326.
2. ACIM, II, page 315.
3. Refers to the Lesson, *"I will be still an instant and go home."* See ACIM, II, page 331.
4. Luke 9:60.
5. ACIM, II, page 302.
6. ACIM, I, Introduction.

CHAPTER ELEVEN — IT IS TRUST THAT FREES THE MIND

1. ACIM, II, page 162.
2. ACIM, I, page 24.
3. ACIM, II, page 162.

CHAPTER TWELVE — THE SURVIVAL OF LITTLENESS

1. ACIM, II, page 277.
2. ACIM, II, page 139.

3. ACIM, II, page 315.
4. Ibid.
5. ACIM, II, page 162.
6. ACIM, I, Introduction.
7. ACIM, II, page 315.
8. See ACIM, I, page 6.
9. ACIM, II, page 119.
10. Refers to: *The teachers of God have trust in the world, because they have learned it is not governed by the laws the world made up. It is governed by a Power That is in them but not of them. It is this Power That keeps all things safe.* See ACIM, III, page 8.
11. ACIM, II, page 235.
12. ACIM, II, page 239.

ADDENDA

THE SCHOOL — "HAVING THE EARS TO HEAR"

1. ACIM, II, page 290.
2. ACIM, II, page 394.
3. See: References, Chapter Six — Unwillingness Versus The Capacity To Receive, no. 2.
4. Refers to Matthew 13:13-23.
5. See ACIM, I, pages 426-427; II, page 120 and following.
6. ACIM, I, Introduction.
7. ACIM, II, page 364.
8. Matthew 6:10.
9. ACIM, II, page 277.
10. ACIM, II, page 18.
11. ACIM, II, page 468.
12. ACIM, I, page 444.
13. ACIM, II, page 219.
14. ACIM, II, page 16.
15. ACIM, II, page 18.
16. ACIM, I, page 533.
17. Matthew 5:39.
18. ACIM, I, Introduction.

19. ACIM, I, page 464.
20. Ibid.
21. ACIM.
22. ACIM.
23. Refers to Matthew 18:20.
24. ACIM, III, page 62.
25. ACIM, II, page 132.
26. Acts 3:6.
27. ACIM, II, page 239.
28. See the prayer, *Forgive us our illusions, Father,* ACIM, I, page 326.
29. ACIM, II, page 396.
30. ACIM, II, page 185.
31. ACIM, II, page 376.
32. ACIM, II, page 53.
33. ACIM, I, Introduction.
34. *Journey Without Distance: The Story Behind A Course In Miracles* by Robert Skutch (Celestial Arts, 1984), page 60.
35. Refers to Matthew 18:20.
36. ACIM, I, page 6.
37. ACIM, I, page 326.
38. ACIM, III, page 1.
39. ACIM, III, page 25.
40. ACIM, III, page 4.
41. Ibid.
42. See ACIM, II, page 235.
43. ACIM, III, page 2.
44. See, for example, Matthew 4:19; John 2:43.
45. Refers to John 14:12.
46. ACIM, II, page 302.
47. John 16:33.
48. ACIM, I, page 193-194.
49. ACIM, II, page 235.
50. ACIM, III, page 5.
51. ACIM, III, page 8.
52. ACIM, II, page 53.

PURPOSE OF THE FOUNDATION FOR LIFE ACTION

1. See ACIM, I, pages 426-427; II, page 120 and following.
2. ACIM, II, page 79.
3. ACIM, II, page 107.
4. ACIM, I, Introduction.
5. ACIM, II, page 132.
6. Matthew 6:33.

AUTOBIOGRAPHY OF TARA SINGH

1. ACIM, II, page 239.
2. ACIM, II, page 123.
3. ACIM, II, page 471.
4. Refers to Matthew 18:20.
5. ACIM, I, page 326.
6. ACIM, II, page 79.

OTHER MATERIALS BY TARA SINGH RELATED TO *A COURSE IN MIRACLES*

BOOKS

The Voice That Precedes Thought
Commentaries On A Course In Miracles
"Love Holds No Grievances" — The Ending Of Attack
A Course In Miracles — A Gift For All Mankind
The Future Of Mankind — The Branching Of The Road
How To Learn From A Course In Miracles
How To Raise A Child Of God (forthcoming)

AUDIO CASSETTE TAPES

Discussions On A Course In Miracles
    (three tape album with the book
    "Love Holds No Grievances" —
    The Ending Of Attack)
"What Is The Christ?" (three tape album with the book
    A Course In Miracles — A Gift For All Mankind)
Bringing A Course In Miracles Into Application
    (three tape album with the pamphlet
    The School At "The Branching Of The Road")

A Course In Miracles Explorations, Series One:
     Origin, Purpose And Application
     (three tape album with the book
     How To Learn From A Course In Miracles)
"What Is A Course In Miracles?" (two tape book pac)
The Heart Of Forgiveness (single tape)
Tara Singh Tapes Of The One Year Non-Commer-
     cialized Retreat: A Serious Study
     Of *A Course In Miracles*

VIDEO CASSETTE TAPES

"Nothing Real Can Be Threatened" —
A Workshop On A Course In Miracles
    Part I   — *The Question And The Holy Instant*
    Part II — *The Deception Of Learning*
    Part III — *Transcending The Body Senses*
    Part IV — *Awakening To Self Knowledge*
Finding Your Inner Calling
How To Raise A Child Of God
Exploring A Course in Miracles (series)
     — *What Is A Course In Miracles*
       and *"The Certain Are Perfectly Calm"*
     — *God Does Not Judge* and *Healing Relationships*
     — *Man's Contemporary Issues*
       and *Life Without Consequences*
     — *Principles* and *Gratefulness*
A Call to Wisdom
     and *A Call To Wisdom* — *Exploring*
     A Course In Miracles
Man's Struggle For Freedom From The Past
     and *"Beyond This World There Is A World I Want"*
Life For Life
     and *Moneymaking Is Inconsistent With Life Forces*
The Call To Wisdom: A Discussion On A Course In Miracles
     (Parts I & II)
"Quest Four" with Damien Simpson and Stacie Hunt
"Odyssey" and *"At One With"* with Keith Berwick

Additional copies of *Dialogues On A Course In Miracles* by Tara Singh may be obtained by sending a check, Mastercard or Visa number and expiration date to:

LIFE ACTION PRESS
902 South Burnside Avenue
Los Angeles, CA 90036
213/933-5591
Toll Free 1/800/732-5489
(Calif.)1/800/367-2246

Limited edition, hardbound	$19.95
Softcover	$14.95

(plus $1.75 shipping/handling)

California residents please add 6 1/2% sales tax.

Thank you.

Design: Lucille Frappier and Clio Dixon
Typesetting: Photographics Inc., Los Angeles, California
Printing/binding: McNaughton & Gunn, Inc., Saline, Michigan
Type: Palacio
Paper: 55lb Glatfelter natural (acid free)